MW00795542

Bank Notes

The True Story of the Boonie Hat Bandit

By

Caroline Giammanco

W & B Publishers
USA

Bank Notes: The True Story of the Boonie Hat Bandit © 2015. All rights reserved by Caroline Giammanco.

W & B Publishers

For information:
W & B Publishers
9001 Ridge Hill Street
Kernersville, NC 27284
www.a-argusbooks.com

ISBN: 978-1-6429814-1-1

Book Cover designed by Dubya

Printed in the United States of America

Table of Contents

"We don't find love. It finds us. After that, there is absolutely nothing we can do to stop it."
— Kelsey Grammer as Dr. Frasier Crane, *Frasier*

Acknowledgments

Special thanks go to Lin Waterhouse. Without Lin's encouragement at the right time, this book wouldn't be where it is today. Lin is a great writer, an esteemed colleague, a good friend and a gifted person. Thank you for your supportive words and your willingness to help me get this project off the ground.

Thank you to Christine Oakley and Norma Garrett for smoothing out the edges of the manuscript to get it ready for publishing. You two are my favorite English teachers. Of course, you are two of my dearest friends as well.

Thank you to our children: Elise, Marissa, Rick and Kevin. We know this hasn't been easy for you, but we want you to know we love you and think the world of you. We all learn lessons in life, even when we are adults. Keeping family ties and remembering the joy is important. We are blessed to have you as our children, as different as you each are in your own wonderful ways.

Thanks are due to our many friends who have been there with us through this journey. We appreciate each and every one of you. We also thank the people who have shown us their true colors. Sometimes the lessons we learn best in life are the ones we learn through loss.

Many thanks must be given to my agent, Jeanie Loiacono, and my editor, William Connor, who saw potential in my work, and who ceaselessly encourage and support me.

Note: Names of individuals mentioned in this book have been changed (excepting elected officials) unless explicit written consent was granted by the individual.

Dedication

This book is dedicated to those family members Keith and I lost before we met. Keith's mother, Margie Giammanco, his brother Robert Giammanco, my mother Charlotte Hagaman and my sister Roberta Hagaman are always in our thoughts. We honor them not only with this book but also by loving each other the best that we possibly can. In the end, probably the biggest wish any parent has for a child is that they are truly loved in this world. For that reason, we know our mothers are smiling down from heaven. Our greatest spiritual guidance has come from the Holy Spirit, which is something we never forget.

Preface

Caroline

"We have never been strangers."
— Keith

I met Keith Giammanco for the first time in late March 2012. I was teaching at the South Central Correctional Center in Licking, Missouri where Keith was interviewing for a tutor position at the prison school. Four teachers were looking for new tutors and I was the third to interview Keith that afternoon. The instant we saw each other, and immediately in the next hour, talking during the interview, we knew there was a connection between the two of us. We were like two old friends catching up after a long separation.

By the end of our time, I was certain Keith was the person I wanted to hire. He was bright, thoughtful, genuine and completely honest with me about why he was in prison without me asking. Most inmates do not want to talk about why they are there. Keith believed I had a right to know who was working in my classroom should I hire him. So impressed, I only half-jokingly asked him to do poorly in his remaining interview so I could hire him. He looked at me and said, "I can't do that. It wouldn't be ethical." I could respect that. What I didn't know until later was he left my classroom thinking, *I'm throwing my next interview. There's only one classroom I want to work in.* Keith proceeded to intentionally fail the math quiz portion of his next interview.

One day, a few weeks after he started working for me, a young student was at Keith's desk sounding rather insistent.

He kept making comments like, "Come on! Admit it! You know you are."

Keith responded, "No, I'm not. I'm way too high profile to lie about who I am. Have your family Google me and you will see."

Confused, I asked Keith what the conversation was about and if he was high profile. The young man accused Keith of being a child molester. Why on earth would anyone think he was a child predator? Keith matter-of-factly told me he fit the profile: a middle-aged white guy with no other criminal background. As far as being high profile, he said he was on the front page of *USA Today* and on *Good Morning America*. Keith told me in the interview he was in prison for robbing banks using notes, but I hadn't given much thought to his crimes beyond that.

Then it clicked in my head. Suddenly, I looked at him and said, *"Oh my god!* You're the Boonie Hat Bandit!" He sheepishly admitted he was, adding his daughters, Elise and Marissa, hated the moniker because it offended their fashion sense.

For the next year, Keith and I spent a lot of time talking. Whenever students were working, we discussed any number of topics: religion, current events, literature, the economy, travel, psychology, our children, politics, his crimes and the prison experience. You name it and we had something to talk about. Intelligent, intellectual conversation was hard to come by in a prison. Most inmates were more interested in the latest *Sons of Anarchy* episode or in complaining about the ice machine in their housing unit than they were in discussing anything of substance. Unfortunately, conversation with much of the staff wasn't any more advanced. Having someone who understood and wanted to talk about greater issues was refreshing for both of us.

On April 3, 2013, Keith mustered up the nerve to tell me how he felt about me. We knew it from the first moment we met, but we tried to keep our emotional distance. That spring a number of offenders were transferred, seemingly out of the blue, to other institutions. Keith couldn't bear to think of leaving without me knowing the truth. Later he told me he was more nervous telling me he loved me than he was robbing banks.

A relationship was not easy for either one of us, and neither of us took the idea lightly. I was on the verge of getting out of a dead marriage and I had zero interest in having a relationship with anyone. I had walled myself up with a lot of trust issues. Initially, I was scared to death at the prospect of having a relationship with Keith. My fears were not simply because he was an offender, although that was a consideration. I wasn't trusting enough of anyone to think a relationship was possible. I tried to bury and ignore the feelings I'd had for Keith from the minute we met. The decision of what to do with those feelings took a lot of soul searching. Falling in love with a prisoner was never in my plans.

Greater than the fear, though, was the certainty Keith was the one person I could trust. Our relationship was closer and unlike any either of us ever had. As crazy as it sounded (and it *did* sound crazy), it felt right. We believe we would have ended up together no matter how we met. It could have been at a Starbucks, a baseball game, anywhere—including a maximum security prison. God has a way of making things happen even if it doesn't make sense to us, and *He* is at the heart of our conversations and our convictions. Our reliance on God gave us the faith to continue on our journey together.

Keith had sworn since the day he was arrested he would never have a prison relationship. He received many fan letters from women when he was in the St. Louis County Jail, all of which revolted him more than appealed to him. Keith saw no sense in establishing a relationship with someone he would only know through letters. Some of the scams we have seen perpetrated through prison correspondence are unbelievable. Men writing numerous "one and only" women who put money onto their accounts. Men getting letters from eighty-year-old women portraying themselves as twenty-year-old girls. Men getting letters *from men* portraying themselves as twenty-year-old girls. Men marrying women they knew only through letters. Keith made up his mind he wanted no part of romance while incarcerated…and then we met.

We realize many, including the Missouri Department of Corrections, will assume our relationship was illicit. It was not. We set firm ground rules from the start: no physical contact, no contraband and no favors. Keith never asked me to bring him anything, to do anything for him or to deliver anything for him. Did we want physical contact? Of course, we did. What two people who love each other don't? But we didn't want it in the context of a prison. We stuck by the motto that we were better than that. We realized the value of our relationship and were adamant not to lessen it any. It was worth waiting for. We wasted so many years on bad relationships, waiting for "the right one," even if it meant enduring a prolonged prison sentence, it made sense.

Keith and I shared a unique experience: his as an inmate at a maximum security prison and mine as a staff member at one. Spending ten hours a day for a year and a half side-by-side gave us better understanding of what each of us went through. Not many family members, friends or loved ones get to glimpse into the lives of inmates past the visitor center walls, nor do many inmates get to view prison life through the eyes of staff members. While it is true I am not like most prison employees (a fact for which both the institution and myself are grateful), Keith was able to see situations from an angle other than that of an inmate.

We also know what it is like to be separated the same way most loved ones are. After I left the prison in October 2013, our time apart began. Our perspectives allow us to tell this story in a unique way. This book is about Keith, but it's also about our shared experience in the prison system, of which our love is at the heart. We couldn't tell Keith's story without including the rest.

Some people don't want the public to know what the prison and criminal justice systems are like. The observations we made about them will surprise some and confirm what many may suspect. *Bank Notes* is intended to tell about a high profile criminal's treatment, as well as to give an inside look at Missouri judicial and correctional methods. Most of this story is told from Keith's perspective, but there are times when it is told from mine. Sometimes the same experiences are told from both viewpoints. In a lot of ways, it's impossible to separate the two.

This is the story of the notorious *Boonie Hat Bandit*. Many people are intrigued by crime figures, which entails a certain level of celebrity. Even some of our own family members and friends are captivated by the concept. Keith has been a mystery to many. He, in some respects, is an average guy. That, in itself, makes his crime spree even more interesting. Why would a middle-class father commit twelve bank robberies while living an otherwise normal life? Alas, Keith Giammanco is not an average man. He is remarkable and fascinating and this is his story.

Chapter One

Count All Things Joy

Keith

No one gets up in the morning with the intention of ruining his life. Most of the time we wake up making good, productive decisions; the kinds of decisions we can be proud of. At least we try to. We don't even give it a second thought. There are times when a crisis hits, when our back is pressed against a wall and we don't make good decisions. Out of fear, panic and desperation we start down a path leading us to dark places. I know. I went down that path.

People consider doing things based on the information they have available at that given moment. The catch is, sometimes we only have partial or even faulty, information on which to base those decisions. Pride can cloud sound judgment as well. Life, unfortunately, does not give us crystal balls to see into the future, nor does it give us a rewind button to change past mistakes. Looking back, all of us have decisions we would like to change. Hindsight does us no good in the immediate. The here and now is where life tends to get messy.

First of all, I am not telling my story to garner sympathy. My case was well-publicized and most people who heard about it have already made up their minds one way or another about me. Was I a villain or a desperate Robin Hood? That's for others to decide for themselves. Instead, this is my opportunity to tell what happened. My motivations, my punishment and the lessons I learned are my story. The Boonie Hat Bandit is one part of my story and only a small part of the man I am. *Bank Notes* is not only an attempt to explain how a middle-class, loving father entered into an infamous life of crime, but also to provide a broader picture of the real me. No one should be defined by any one event or period in his life.

That being said, it is wrong to suggest we are not shaped by events. Some, such as a divorce, a death or the loss of employment carry immediate, clearly visible wounds. Others we carry deep within ourselves. Sometimes those wounds are so deep we don't recognize the profound effects they have on our outlooks and daily lives. A crisis, followed by reflection, can allow us to adjust and learn to live life more fully in the future. Nothing can change the past, but the future is always adaptable.

Our experiences, and the effects they have on us as individuals, are not all negative. Events happen and people enter our lives with positive influences. Good experiences can be as transformational as the painful ones. Having people love and understand us for all our strengths and weaknesses creates hope and a new life for each of us. Blessings are everywhere and sometimes we find them at the most unlikely times and in the most unusual places. They all shape who we are. I thank God that healing and regrowth are possible.

Faith is valuable. I learned the hard way the pitfalls of losing faith. The dark path seems the only way when one has no faith to rely upon for guidance. I always loved and believed in God, but for a time, I forgot to have faith. It took a serious jolt to bring me back to it. Throughout my story, I hope the joy I have because of my faith is evident. Without it, all is lost.

I take full responsibility for my crimes. *Bank Notes* is not an attempt to blame anyone for my actions. My fears and motivations were derived from experiences involving others, but my decisions were my own. The wounds, seen and unseen, influence us all. I am telling my story in order to explain what led this devoted father to risk it all in order to lead a double life of crime. I will tell about the people and things influencing me, but everyone is responsible for his or her own actions.

I am not glorifying crime, nor am I intending to provide a how-to book on bank robbery. I will discuss the planning and details of my crimes, but at no time do I encourage anyone to make the same bad decisions I did. Prison is not someplace you want to go. The price your family pays is too high. For that reason, I am not going to go into great detail about each and every one of the crimes. I don't want anyone to think I am gloating or that I am proud of what I did. I have remorse for the mistakes I made, and I don't believe it does anyone, including the tellers or other victims, any good for me to repeat those twelve moments in my life.

I don't want anyone to think I am cavalier about my crimes or the devastation they caused. Many nights I have lain awake, beating myself up for what I've done and for the pain I've inflicted. The two years spent in county jail were constantly filled with those nights. Since I went to prison, there have been many more of those nights. Every time my daughters or Caroline struggle, those angry jabs I take at myself resurface. I am not proud of what I did and I can't apologize enough to the people whose lives I have hurt. My daughters have gone through turmoil, I caused grief and stress to the bank employees and I derailed my own life. I've reached the realization that beating myself up will do no good. If I am to have a life at all, it's time to focus on being a better person today so there is a brighter future ahead. I take responsibility for my actions, but it is time to let go of the self-loathing.

God has forgiven me and nothing good comes of holding onto the cobwebs of the past.

Here is my story. I hope by the end of it everyone can appreciate why my first chapter is called "Count All Things Joy." The concept is the constant thread that now runs through my life and I hope it will in everyone else's as well.

Chapter Two

Looking in the Rearview Mirror

Keith

E verything went according to plan. I casually walked to my car after the twelfth bank robbery just as I had the previous eleven. As I got into the car, I put the envelope with the money and the note used in the robbery on the passenger seat. I took my hat and jacket off, too. Not that any bank robbery is routine, but I had no reason to expect this time would be any different than the others as I made a right hand turn from the bank parking lot. I turned onto a street leading to the state highway which was less than a quarter of a mile away. So far, so good.

As I had in some of the other robberies, I watched as police cars rushed to the crime scene going the opposite direction from me. I had no idea a bank employee went against bank procedures and followed me out of the bank. This time the police had a description of my car.

I watched the police drive by, sirens blaring and lights flashing, when I noticed one car heading toward the bank without its lights on. It made a U-turn as I sat at the stoplight waiting to enter the highway. I saw him in my rearview mirror, a few cars back in the same turn lane. At this point I became unsure. As the light turned green, and I turned left onto the entrance ramp, the police car roof lights began to flash. I knew I was caught.

As other cars between us pulled to their right to let him by, I sped up to highway entrance speed. I thought about running for a split second, then let him pull up directly behind me. I cruised down the highway never going over 60 mph. Later described at trial as a "high speed chase" in order to create drama, I would describe it as faster than O.J. Simpson and much slower than Steve McQueen in *Bullet*.

It might be more dramatic if I said my childhood, my children and my life flashed before my eyes. Maybe it would be more sensational if I became sweaty and nervous or had all the cliché reactions, but that's not what happened. It would not be the truth. The next thoughts I had were very important to the rest of this story and to the way I have chosen to live the rest of my life. With police cars gathering behind me and helicopters flying above, I decided to collect my thoughts for the next few moments. Knowing I was going to jail, I decided to take the time to figure out how to handle this situation. At that point something (God I believe), told me, "Just tell the truth and everything will be okay."

I haven't been truthful at times—not to others and not to myself. Fear of rejection and a desire to please those around me kept me too often from being my true self. Those who knew me before these events know this about me. That's okay, though, because I know I am forgiven. It's what happens in the windshield, not the rearview mirror that counts.

After deciding to tell the truth, I pulled off on the next exit ramp. About halfway up the ramp I saw a blockade of police cars at the intersections, so I figured it was time to stop. I remember a lot of traffic backed up on the ramp which widened into two or three lanes at the top. I pulled over onto the shoulder and gave up.

As I brought the car to a stop, a police officer on foot darted out from between some cars with an automatic pistol drawn and pointed at my face through the windshield. Other police were getting to the site and were yelling for me to get out of the car with my hands in view. Then the door opened.

I was thrown onto the pavement, face first, while one officer put a set of rubber-coated handcuffs tightly on my wrists. As he cuffed me, he held his knee in the middle of my back bearing his full weight. I looked up with my head turned to see another officer with his pistol pointed at the back of my head. I remember thinking, *Boy, you already got me. That's a bit much.* I had no weapons and never used a weapon during any of the robberies. Escape wasn't an option. I realized they were doing their jobs, but a gun to the back of my head after I was already restrained was not necessary. When they pulled me to my feet, I noticed two helicopters and about twenty or so police cars both marked and unmarked and people watching from their cars and gathering from a mall parking lot overlooking the ramp.

For what seemed like hours, but most likely was forty-five minutes, I stood against a police car and watched the events unfold. The officer who pulled me over, Jackson, was heatedly discussing with the officer who aimed his gun through my windshield, Timson, who was going to take me in. A young lady officer, Hoskins, was assigned to make small-talk with me to keep me calm. This wasn't necessary because I was already calm. She asked where I lived, what I did for a living and so forth. I told her I lived in Florissant and that I traded stocks for a living.

My car was in plain sight. I watched as the envelope containing the cash and the note was taken from the passenger seat of my car. The car was searched, presumably to find a gun that did not exist. Eventually it was decided Hoskins and Timson would take me in.

The two officers were young; I'm guessing in their late twenties or early thirties. They put me in the front seat of the squad car. Timson rode in the back and Hoskins drove. As we made a right turn off the ramp for the ten minute ride to the substation, Timson said, "If you would have gone any further I was going to shoot you."

I replied, "And you would have been in more trouble than I am." The conversation lightened up from there.

He then said, "I got as big of a rush arresting you as you got robbing banks." You could tell he was very excited and high on himself.

My reply was, "You don't know anything about me and you obviously know nothing about robbing banks or why someone would do it. It's for the money, not to get high!" This caused Hoskins to laugh. A police van pulled up beside us with two officers giving a thumbs up, showing their excitement for their achievement.

After the stoplight turned green, Hoskins referred back to our conversation on the ramp and asked me, "What do you think the stock market is going to do?" Both officers asked what they should do with their 401ks and their retirement plans with the St. Louis Police Department. Everyone knew at this time, in late 2008, economic conditions were deteriorating rapidly. They were interested in my advice, so I told them what to do when the Dow and S & P reached certain levels, as well as when to pull out of stocks and go into bonds and metals. Ironically, I was doing my best to help some of the very people many in my situation would have viewed as the enemy.

I wore that set of handcuffs for at least an hour until I arrived at the St. Louis County police substation. The cuffs were covered with a sticky rubber coating which caused even the slightest movement of the wrists or the motion of riding in the squad car with hands behind the back, to rub wrists raw. I'm not talking red and irritated rubbing, these cuffs rub to the point of blood running down your hands. Upon arrival, I was put in a cage, my belt and shoes were taken and those God-forsaken cuffs were removed from my wrists. Even the jailer at the substation commented, "These things are ridiculous and unnecessary." I was allowed to use the restroom so I could wash the blood off my hands and wrists.

By now it was past time my twin girls, Elise and Marissa, should be home from school. I asked if I could call them and was told not now, but later. Later turned out to be midnight or so. My daughters were starting their senior year in high school and knew how to fend for themselves. My main concern was letting them know what was going on before the police or media did. Needless to say, the detectives and news reports got to them first.

The girls had no information for the police. To the detectives' and the girls' credit, the situation was handled well without the house being torn to shreds. The initial shock to the girls must have been devastating. My heart hurts to this day when I think about how they must have felt.

There was no evidence at the house and not a soul had any knowledge of any of this but me. I lived for a year with my secret and hadn't told anyone anything about the robberies. It was too risky. I couldn't put my loved ones under the burden of sharing my secret. The only items taken from the house were my notebook and personal computers, which were removed by the F.B.I. The contents were examined and later returned.

After their visit to our home, the St. Louis County detective who was at the arrest scene, Ballwin, along with another detective, picked me up at the South County substation and transported me to Clayton, Missouri where the interrogation and jail facilities are located. It was about a half hour ride from the substation to Clayton. When first put into the car, Ballwin said, "I wouldn't have put cuffs on you, but I have to." I understood.

I definitely understood what was going on. They were both being very nice to me to get what they wanted. One of my best friends, Rob Haley, was in law enforcement for years, so I knew the drill. Little did they know, none of these tactics were necessary. I was going to tell the truth all the way through. The truth was best, regardless of some bumps in the road and second thoughts I might have. It was the right choice.

I had been to Clayton many times, but never in my forty-four years was it to go to jail. This was my first experience with anything like this. We pulled through the gate of the parking garage under the St. Louis County Courthouse and Jail complex, left the car and walked a few feet to a large steel door. Going through the door, we came to a dimly lit, winding hallway leading to an open room area with several wooden doors along the wall. I was led through one of those doors into a small, narrow room with only a very small table and chairs where I was told to have a seat. Detective Ballwin brought in some papers with the Miranda Rights, waiving my right to have an attorney present. I signed them. Some may think it was the wrong thing to do, but if you are look-ing for the truth, having an attorney present may not be best. I have no regrets.

After signing the papers, I told the detectives I wanted to talk to the F.B.I. They assured me I would get to later. The beginning of a power struggle in this case began. They of-fered me the usual items: cigarettes, water, soda, food, etc. I took them up on the food and the soda. The second detective went to order me a turkey and Swiss sub sandwich, a bag of chips and a soda. I never got the chips.

While eating, they began questioning me. I answered most of their questions, but would not initial the photographs of me from the bank cameras. My refusal angered them. I repeated that I wanted to talk to the F.B.I.. Lots of law enforcement wanted to talk to me, they said. That's when I told them, "Look, I am only going through this one time. You need to call them all. Get them down here and then I will talk some more."

Ballwin then left to call law enforcement detectives from local municipalities in St. Louis and St. Charles counties, along with the F.B.I. who had worked to crack this case for a year now. While he was gone, the other detective, O'Neal, felt left out. He played good cop-bad cop. He was the bad cop. I recognized the roles long before this point.

O'Neal said, "You may want an attorney present." He complained that I didn't initial the photos and let me know he wasn't happy. He said, "It wouldn't be a good thing if you swung on me and me on you. I'm sure glad it hasn't come to that."

I stared at him and said, "Look, this is going pretty well for you guys right now. I am cool with it, too. Why would you want that to happen? I will quit talking for sure then. That's a promise. Besides that, do you realize how stupid you sound right now?" He left the room.

It was getting late now, there were no clocks and I was exhausted. This was all part of their plan. That was okay. I knew all along what I was going to do, but they weren't sure. The officers had their own agenda, both personal and collective. Ego, pride, glorification and all that good stuff were in the mix, and there was plenty of all of those to go around. People could make names for themselves with my case. Both detectives came back into the room and, while we were waiting decided to ask me some questions about four of the robberies, Ballwin asked if I was willing for it to be audiotaped.

I thought about it and they started the good cop-bad cop thing again. Finally, I thought, *Why not tell the truth?*

The questions began. Was I here or there? Did I do this or do that? Why did I do it? I remember breaking down into tears a couple of times when they asked me about my girls and my financial situation. One key question Ballwin and O'Neal asked me several times, and my answer was the same every time, was edited from the tape before it was presented at trial: "Why did you have your hand in your jacket at points during these robberies?" It was a crucial piece of evidence. My answer was honest, but it became part of the lies the system would use against me.

As other detectives arrived, I had a brief one-on-one talk with an F.B.I. agent named Tyler. He flat-out told me, "We had no idea who you were or where you were from. We thought maybe you were from out of town. We had not one clue. If you would have stopped after the eleventh one, we would have never caught you. Most of these types of crimes are never cleared by investigators or police work. We either get lucky or the criminal catches himself by making a mistake."

Eight or so detectives and I went into a large conference room after that conversation where I gave details about each robbery. That meeting lasted about an hour. I never did reveal some key details on how I pulled these robberies off, nor how long or how much money I needed before I would have quit. Later I will disclose details that until now only one other person had privilege to.

After the meeting, one detective from a local police department, Stanton, showed up late. I answered a few questions he had about one of the robberies. At the end of our conversation, he asked if I would think about writing a book with him. It was the first time I thought about telling this story and I have thought about it ever since. As far as Stanton or any other law enforcement officer taking part in its writing? Not a chance. Besides, law enforcement played no real role in this. Not a truthful one. Nor did they contribute anything out of their ordinary, run-of-the-mill antics. Agent Tyler said it all about the law enforcement's role in my case.

I asked to use the restroom. I washed my hands and wrists again. Open wounds and dried blood covered them. I washed my face and rinsed most of the black dye out of my hair and the week-long beard I shaved into a goatee. I normally never wear facial hair, but it was an attempt to disguise my appearance.

When I returned from the restroom Stanton said, "Hey, your hair was a different color when you went in there."

I said, "Yes, it was."

By now it was getting close to midnight. Stanton walked me outside on the sidewalk and waited for another officer to drive me the one hundred feet across the street to the eight-story St. Louis County Jail. Little did I know that would be the last time I was outdoors in the fresh air for twenty-four months. Inside the jail walls that I stared at, I would spend the next two years of my life.

After I entered, my property from inside my car (wallet, cell phone, keys) was processed and I signed the claim form so they could be put into evidence. The desk officer had a nurse clean and disinfect my wrists and bandage them. I was put into a very small staging cell for about fifteen minutes. From there, I was released into a huge holding room with both males and females waiting to either post bond or be taken upstairs to the main jail.

In this large room sat a big desk for booking and mug shots. The room was filled with several guards walking patrol. One bank of fifty park-sized steel mesh benches, one bank of four phones, a wall of holding cells (for those who became unruly), a restraint chair for the radical, one uni-sex restroom and four televisions strapped to poles comprised the contents of the room—no windows.

I wanted to talk to my daughters for hours, so the first thing I did was wait to make a call. After about fifteen minutes I got a phone and called home. The land line was busy, so I called Elise's cell. She answered. Everything was okay, she said. Marissa was sleeping and my sister had just left and was coming back early in the morning. We talked for a few more moments. I told her I loved her and would see her soon. After hanging up with Elise, I called my mother who had also been at our house to be with the girls. They were fine, not to worry and for me to take care of what I needed to. She watched the news reports and said she was a bit shocked and puzzled, but she was as comforting, nonjudgmental and loving as always.

I remember a rebroadcast of the 10:00 news coming on. My capture was the lead story. Everyone was aware it was me; some pointed and whispered, others came right up to me wanting to shake my hand or asking for autographs as though I was a celebrity. I, of course, didn't sign any autographs.

At about 3:00 A.M. O'Neal told me my bond was set at $100,000. He failed to tell me it was cash only, which meant the bond was $1,000,000. He said, "It's really not too bad. A judge will most of the time lower it for you at a hearing."

About now, Ballwin walked in saying the judge and prosecutor gave them a search warrant to search the garage at the house. They had failed to do it the first time, so they had to go back. Detective Ballwin said, "I asked if we could take you with us, so you could see your kids. The judge told me no." Who knows why he told me this or if it was even true. At about 4:30 A.M. I was taken to the desk used for fingerprinting and mug shots.

The rest of the night I sat on one of the benches watching all the strangeness at the jail as gross, warm bologna sandwiches in brown paper bags were passed out periodically. People sleeping on the benches used the bologna sandwich bags for pillows. One girl laid down on the bench I was on, put her feet and legs right on me, and complained about her petty drug charge. Her biggest concern was that no one was at her house to watch her primate pets. I thought to myself, *My problems aren't quite as simple as hers.*

The spectacle of humanity I watched that night was my introduction to years of witnessing strange behaviors and odd priorities in action. I'm just glad it's all in the rearview mirror.

At about 6:15 they called me back into a room with five other men. My street clothes were taken while officers searched them and me. Next I was made to shower. County jail clothes were issued and I was taken by elevator to the eighth floor where I was put into a cell. This was the beginning of my two-year stay as a guest of the St. Louis County Jail.

Chapter Three

Open Windows and the Windshield

Keith

The race was on! I was eleven-years-old and flying down the street past my house. I was carefree and in the lead, which surprised me because chasing me were my friends Ron and Robbie, and they were about three-years-older than I was. I must have been given a head start; normally I wasn't allowed to win. As we made our way to the finish at Ron's house, we made the right turn onto Sansu Lane at full speed. I was excited as I went sailing down the hill on my home-modified, root beer brown B.M.X. bike. When I turned my head to see how far ahead of them I was, Wham! I ran into the rear bumper of Robbie's father's pickup truck parked in front of their house. As I hit the truck, without having any chance to brake, the front tire and wheel of my bike wedged under the bumper and the rear wheel came off the ground about two feet or so.

I was thrown into the bed of the truck. Luckily for me, the camper shell window was left open. That open window made the difference between potentially severe injuries and what turned out to be a safe landing. As I emerged from the truck without a scratch or broken bone, I saw looks of concern on my friends' faces. After realizing there was no damage to the truck or myself, we all three fell about the grass and pavement laughing hysterically. We laughed about that wreck for the rest of the night and spoke of it for years after. The lesson learned was to keep my sights on what's ahead, not behind me. The past is the past.

A friend of mine once said we all experience childhood, and then we spend the rest of our adult lives trying to get over it. As I mentioned earlier, the events and people who enter and leave our lives can have profound impacts on us. Knowing what's in the past can sometimes help us realize what our current motivations are. By reaching some sort of peace, it can be a lot easier to focus on the windshield of our lives so we can create a better present and future.

I was born on October 16, 1963 at about 1:00 A.M. at the Old Christian Hospital in St. Louis, Missouri. My parents were Joseph S. and Margie A. Giammanco. My father insisted I was named Donald, which is a name I have never gone by. My family and everyone I know has always called me Keith. My parents took me home to Florissant, Missouri which is a suburb to the north and west of St. Louis where I joined my older siblings: my oldest sister, thirteen, my brother, eleven and my other sister nine-years-old.

Florissant was a wonderful place to grow up. I have so many great childhood memories. Sometimes even nice neighborhoods can't shield you from some cold, hard realities, though. When I was about six-months-old, my parents split up. My father left home, and in late 1964 their divorce was final. I can count on both hands how many times I saw my father before he passed away in December 2008. I was in the St. Louis County Jail at the time. My mother had passed away only a month before that on November 11, 2008. My mother was my constant; my father only marginally involved in my upbringing, but both made a big impact.

I was born at the tail end of the Baby Boom era and had a normal childhood for the most part. Being brought up in a single parent household was rare for those times, but not unheard of. Mine was a typical suburban upbringing, not unlike millions of other people across the country. Children ranging in all ages lived in almost every house in our neighborhood and surrounding subdivisions. Finding friends to play with as a young child was easy.

Mom was a busy mother of four. She supported us by working in restaurants and by eventually running her own. I have to admit, being the youngest had its benefits. By the time I came along, my mom wanted to provide things for me my older siblings hadn't been able to have. Before long, my brother and sisters were either out of the house completely or they were busy with their teenage lives. I reaped the benefits of basically being an only child. Maybe my mom was trying to make up for me not having a father around. I certainly didn't get everything I wanted and I was far from being a spoiled kid. I simply know I had more opportunities and advantages than my mom had been able to afford my older siblings.

All was not perfect, though. Since my mom had to work so many hours and the other kids were gone, I spent a lot of time by myself. I had friends to play with, but there were many times I was by myself at the house. This made me at ease being by myself throughout my entire life. I was comfortable being on my own, but too much solitude wasn't always good for a young boy growing up. Food was plentiful, so I used food to fill in some of the emotional gaps. Childhood isn't always kind to the kid who has put on a few extra pounds. It set the stage for a life of worrying about whether I was accepted by others. I was reluctant to let people close enough to know the real me. I was never one for sharing my thoughts and feelings and it became a pattern until the past few years.

I played with friends outside, so it wasn't like I was completely a loner. I have great memories of playing in their yards and ours. In the summertime, one of my favorite activities was to play with the yard sprinkler or with the garden hose. One hot summer day when I must have been four-years-old, I was messing with the garden hose and decided to play "gas station." My mom was inside getting ready to go to work at the restaurant. I took the garden hose and filled her car up with "gas."

Well, when Mom drove off for work, she only got about a quarter of a mile down the road and the car began to sputter and then stop. She was able to steer it into the parking lot of the nearby Lutheran church. Later that evening, my brother-in-law, Lyle, drained the gas tank, purged the fuel line and refilled the tank with actual gasoline to get the car running again. My family asked if I filled Mom's gas tank with water. I was honest and I told them I thought I was helping. I am sure it was a very stressful problem for my busy mother, but she took it in stride. As the years went by we had many good laughs remembering that eventful day.

Summer visits to see my grandparents in Eminence, Missouri were some of my favorite experiences while growing up. Mom's parents and many of her close relatives lived in that area. For a kid living most of the time near a large metropolitan area, my summer trips to rural Missouri provided me with a love of nature and a break from city living. Great lessons were learned on those trips. My grandfather, my Uncle Willard and Uncle Paul had profound effects on me. They taught me how be a good, kind man; the type of man who shows respect to women and to his family. Whether we were skipping rocks, eating ice cream cones or taking walks down to the river, my visits with Grandpa and Uncle Willard created memories and impressions I will never forget. Those three men were my primary positive male role models.

Because my encounters with my father were so infrequent, I remember them vividly. One of my earliest memories occurred when I was three- or four-years-old. I was playing in the front yard, digging holes as most little boys are known to do, when my father pulled into the driveway for a visit. Not only was *I* excited, but I knew this was a special occasion for my brother and sisters. I can still picture him getting out of his car and walking over to me in the driveway. Instead of an embrace or a hello, he spanked me and chastised me for digging holes in the yard. He never even went into the house to see the rest of the children. He turned, got into his car and drove away. I was devastated. Not only had I angered and disappointed my father, but I felt guilty because I ruined the visit for my brother and sisters. As an adult I can't understand what he was thinking, but as a child I *certainly* couldn't. All I knew was it was my fault Dad had gone away.

The next few times I saw him were at my Aunt Ruth's home on Minnesota Street in St. Louis. Mom took us to Aunt Ruth's to visit. Sometimes my father was there, sometimes not. We mostly went to see Aunt Ruth. She was my father's younger sister; always fun, kind and loving to us kids. We had a good time visiting her. Her great sense of humor is what I remember best about Aunt Ruth. Children appreciate lighthearted, happy people. Going to Aunt Ruth's house was always enjoyable.

As an adult, I once saw my father at my sister's home. Looking back, it was a much more heartbreaking experience than I thought at the time, and it may have even had some lasting effects on my young family and me. It was a wedding reception held for my niece, Summer, and her new husband, Steve. Everyone in the family attended, including my father and Aunt Ruth. My wife at the time and I had recently been blessed with our twins, Elise and Marissa. My beautiful stepdaughter was about ten and Marissa and Elise were about a year old. My wife was excited to meet my father for the first time. I remember telling her not to expect much. Well, he delivered on that. He paid plenty of attention to my older siblings and their families, but he did not even acknowledge me or any of my family.

That day he was loud and obnoxious. My mother took him outside for a talk. No telling what she said, but he was very quiet for the rest of the evening. He still didn't say a word to anyone in my immediate family, which upset my wife. In hindsight, maybe I should have started the conversation. If I had it to do over again, I would. Who knows how he felt? Maybe he did not know how to start a relationship with me.

The last time I saw my father was in 2001 at my brother's funeral. The twins were eleven and I remember being determined for them to meet their grandfather. I had tears in my eyes when I approached him as he sat on a bench inside the parlor.

I said, "Hi, Dad. These are your granddaughters, Marissa and Elise." He and the girls exchanged hugs.

He apologized to them and said, "I know I haven't been much of a grandpa, but I am happy to meet you two beautiful girls." This was the last time any of my immediate family ever saw him.

I wonder what made my father tick, what was really in his heart, what kind of experiences he had, who he really was in this life and why he was the way he was. There are a lot of unanswered questions. I wonder if I should have done things differently. Should I have stepped up to the plate myself? Am I the little boy in the front yard still wondering what I did to alienate my father? I am quite confident that I will see him again in the next life and these questions will be answered.

For most of my life, I believed you can't miss what you never knew. I'm not sure that is entirely true, though. Even if I didn't want to think about it or admit it while growing up, it was impossible to avoid that other children had fathers in their lives. I tried to shrug it off, but who can ignore the emptiness you feel when you realize your friends have fathers who play catch with them, who take them to hockey practice and who spend lazy afternoons fishing with them? I saw my friends' fathers giving them the type of advice fathers do when raising children and I knew I didn't have that.

I don't know what kind of psychological effects these experiences may have had on who I was and my actions. People react differently to growing up without a father, but I'm not blaming my father for my mistakes. I do know I always felt compelled to be a better, more involved father than mine had been...no matter what. It was the no matter what part that got me into trouble in the future. In my quest to make sure I never let my children down, I took a path eventually leading to prison. Like that kid racing down the hill on the B.M.X. bike, just when I thought I was ahead, I came to an abrupt stop.

Chapter Four

How I Got into This

Keith

The idea of robbing banks as a solution to my problems came from a most unlikely source. It was my mother who unknowingly planted the thought into my head. Visiting her one afternoon at her home, we had a conversation about my current financial woes. Although I was not entirely truthful about the severity of the situation, she jokingly made the comment, "I hope you are not thinking of going out and robbing a bank or something." I laughed, but this comment made me start to think.

In no way do I place any blame on my dear mother for these crimes, nor is she responsible in any way for my actions. I am the only one who is accountable for my own mistakes. No one else is to blame but me and me alone.

Seeing bank robberies reported in the news or playing out in movies, left me wondering why anyone would try it or how they had the guts to do it. What would it accomplish and why would they think they could get away with it? Suddenly, I understood the answers to those questions.

That night, after visiting with my mother in the late summer of 2007, I waited for the girls to go to bed and began researching how to rob a bank. I went to today's source of all sources: the Internet. A bank would be the best place to obtain large amounts of untraceable currency. I ran across a short article about a bank robber who was asked why he robbed banks. His answer was simple and straight to the point. He said, "Because that's where the money's at." My thoughts exactly.

My research began two months or so before the first robbery in November 2007. Looking into alarm and security safe systems, I quickly realized bypassing a bank's alarm system and then getting into a safe to get to the money would be next to impossible.

I thought about using this method to break into other businesses, but I did not go that route for a couple of reasons. For one, I did not want to invade some entrepreneur's place of business and steal his hard-earned cash. Small businesses may be uninsured. I worried robbing a private business could take food directly out of some family's mouth. While trying to keep my own family from going through that, I didn't want to do it to someone else.

I also worried a robbery could give the owner a bad taste about doing business in our community. Economic times were bad enough, and as a businessman myself, I didn't want to make things worse for anyone already struggling to keep their doors open.

My final reason for not robbing a business was simply one of risk versus reward. Why risk going to prison for a robbery that may result in very little cash? If I was going to put my future on the line, it needed to be for something that would pay the bills. With those factors weighed, I turned my thoughts entirely to bank robbery.

I considered what it would take to rob a bank. My approach was different than most bank robbers have taken. Instead of thinking first about how to rob a bank, I studied what was done by the people who had been caught. If I understood what didn't work, I could make a plan that would work. This backwards thinking was very successful.

I quickly realized it was not necessary to use a weapon. Since I have never been an owner of firearms or a proponent of violence, this was a huge plus. Employees of banks are under strict rules and undergo training to do what they are asked or told during a robbery. Policy dictates they give up the money. Unlike most other establishments, bank policies and protocols took out the likelihood of danger. The chance of harm coming to employees, customers or myself was reduced.

Robbing banks was a safer option due to a number of factors. Most other businesses do not have the advanced training and planning for a robbery banks do. People who own and operate their own businesses are much more likely to defend their goods, money and property with violence. They are also more likely to keep and use weapons. Not so with banks. If I was going to do this, it was going to be without a weapon, real or fake. Should I be caught, my research showed people who used guns were sentenced to much more prison time. A weapon wasn't necessary and it wasn't worth getting more time.

I began to study only those bank robberies where the robbers used no weapon. Of those, some would give their demands verbally and others would use notes given directly to the teller. My research became much more in-depth. At first I looked at archives of news reports from television and newspapers about bank robberies. Those came up by typing in key words and phrases on a search engine. I would scroll further down the page to find other sites with more detailed information.

The most informative site was the F.B.I.'s Most Wanted site. Tabs took me to unsolved crimes by category. I hit the tab for unsolved bank robberies, which soon became my largest source of information. The site had great detail about the unsolved cases and I absorbed every bit of information about those crimes possible. The FBI site, in addition, showed bank robbery cases they had cleared, including information about how the robbers were captured and what mistakes led to their capture. This was perfect. I now knew how and why people got away with it and how suspects were caught.

I was later asked by F.B.I. Agent Tyler, "How did you find out how to do this?"

I simply replied, "You showed me."

"How's that? What do you mean?"

I explained to him about their website.

Stunned, Tyler replied, "We may have to look into some changes to that site."

I said, "You might want to do that."

Using a note was the way to go. It posed less risk for everyone involved, was quiet and didn't draw attention. Only once did an employee other than the teller serving me notice a robbery was taking place, and that was during the last robbery. I knew the method of demanding money and I began to focus on when to commit the crimes.

According to my research, most bank robberies occur on Fridays and in the mornings. Most robbers think tellers have the most money behind the counter at those times. Published amounts taken from banks in solved cases revealed there was no truth to the myth. No pattern existed as far as when the most money was available from tellers. Authorities don't publish the amount stolen until after the robber has been captured. In unsolved cases, the only information given is "an undisclosed amount." For the ones that had been solved, I was able to see there was no advantage to robbing a bank on a Friday morning.

I pulled off some robberies on Fridays, but not because of how much money was available. Times when banks were busy with high traffic were ideal to commit a robbery. Fridays are busy at banks. Around lunch time or late afternoon is prime time. Many people do their banking business on their lunch hour or on their way home from work. Around noon, staff is usually short due to lunch breaks. After lunch people tend to be less alert after eating. The later in the workday it is, the more sluggish people become. Finally, high traffic inside the bank and in the parking lot made it easier to blend into the crowd to make escape easier. After research and careful thought, I had decided on two critical factors: the timing of the robberies and the method of demand.

I considered every detail when planning the robberies. The location of banks was an important element. Having a viable entrance and exit strategy would be of the utmost importance. The most logical targets were bank branches in stand-alone buildings sharing parking lots with large department stores or strip malls. A high traffic business location would make my movements less noticeable and it would be easier to blend in with other customers. The parking lots are designed with many entrances and exits. Those exits spilled onto a main thoroughfare close to the entrance of an interstate highway. Locations such as these are not hard to find. The same factors making it convenient for customers made getting away with bank robbery much easier.

As most real estate agents will tout: location, location, location. Banks in the outlying, upscale-to-middle-class areas least expect a robbery and have little-to-no security measures. Banks in more affluent areas like to make their customers feel comfortable and safe while doing business and heavily-armed guards make people nervous. The customers were safe during my robberies and I felt confident I would be, too, by choosing banks without heavy security. I never harmed anyone and never had any intention of harming anyone. Robbing a bank with an armed security presence increased the odds that someone (not me) would use a weapon. I wanted to completely avoid that possibility.

The robberies themselves were simple. I handed the note to the tellers and let them read it. I used the same note for several robberies. The notes always asked for all of the money in both the top and bottom drawers. No alarms and no dye packs. No personal threats or to harm anyone were made. I gave the teller a large manila envelope or a United States Postal Service envelope to put the cash into. During the last few robberies, I began to carry an extra envelope in my jacket. During a previous robbery, the envelope was filled to overflowing and I dropped banded bundles of ten dollar bills in the bank lobby while leaving. I calmly picked them up, put them back in the envelope and walked out. I didn't want to risk ever drawing attention to myself again, though, so I brought an extra envelope.

I walked in and out of the bank casually and I never spoke loudly, if at all. At no time did any customer or other bank employee know the bank was being robbed. I made sure everything stayed low-key so no attention was drawn to myself or to the situation. I didn't want anyone to play "hero," causing harm to anyone or myself. An off-duty or undercover cop spraying bullets around was the last thing I wanted.

I carefully chose parking spots. I parked within 100 yards of the bank and between two larger vehicles, such as pickup trucks and vans. I could duck out of sight and into my car with no one really knowing where I had gone in the bustle of the parking lot. On one occasion, I parked behind a huge snow pile left by the plow that had cleared the nearby mall parking lot. On that day, my escape was otherwise typical. I was able to pull out from behind the snow pile directly into the traffic of the busy mall parking lot. From there, I exited onto the south outer road to Interstate 70, then onto a nearby entrance ramp to the highway running right in front of the mall. Once on the highway, I headed east to St. Louis County and home. Parking and routes of escape were methods I had to come up with on my own without any kind of template or reference material. I couldn't find much material on escape. It worked out well eleven times.

Once in the car, I immediately stripped off my outer layer of clothing, beginning with the hat. Sometimes the hat came off before I even got to the car, exposing my dyed black hair, which was part of a not-so-elaborate disguise that proved highly effective. Any eyeglasses I may have used were removed. I did not wear eyeglasses during all of the robberies and I only used them in regular life for reading. After removing my jacket and one shirt, my clothing was totally different than what was seen in the bank. As far as pants and shoes went, I almost always wore jeans to give a common look. Shoes were black or white athletic shoes for the same reason. A couple of times I wore business-type attire. When I did, I stripped down to a t-shirt and shorts after entering the car. Next, I shaved off the facial hair I had grown and dyed to match my hair. I would shave in the car. Shaving, coupled with the change in clothes, completely changed my appearance in less than ten minutes.

After changing my looks, I peeked into the envelope containing the take from the robbery to see if it was sufficient to keep the family afloat for the immediate future. One day, it wasn't. On that day, I felt an urgent need to commit another robbery, so I did.

Getting home undetected was another worry of mine. I was concerned a neighbor might see me returning home. I knew my black hair would arouse curiosity or suspicion and we all know how nosy neighbors can be. Because of this, I used the garage door opener, pulled the car in, closed the door and then entered the house through the garage so I wasn't exposed. After we relocated to a house without a garage, I parked the car on the side of the house and went in through the back door to avoid being seen.

Once home, I walked into my bedroom or office area and locked the envelope inside my brown leather attaché case, then headed for the shower to wash the dye from my hair. Afterwards, I put the events out of my mind. I had to.

I had to move on with the rest of the day and the days to come in as normal a manner as possible, both mentally and emotionally. I picked up my children from school, mowed the lawn, shoveled snow, made dinner, did market research and spent time with my family and friends. I carried on while keeping my crimes to myself. Regardless of the emotional strain going on inside of me, it had to be this way. Oh, there was some stress, too. With the immediate financial stress gone, we lived for another day, but the other life I was living was constantly eating away at my conscience. I was never free from it. My own behavior haunted me and I couldn't tell anyone.

What did I do with all of the cash? The urgency of bills needing paid (or checks written), would determine how quickly I deposited the cash into my personal checking account. Many times it needed to be the same day.

I developed a process for depositing the cash from the robberies careful to avoid being tracked. First, I took the time to sort and count the money, mixing in any bait money (new bills banded together with the serial numbers in order) used for tracking currency with older bills already in circulation. I then deposited the cash into my personal checking accounts in small bites, using different branches by rotation to avoid suspicion. I never deposited more than four thousand dollars at a time. Sometimes I made two deposits in one day at different branches. One time I robbed a branch of the bank I used for my own accounts. I took some of the money and made a deposit the same afternoon in a different branch to cover my account. In other words, I deposited stolen money into an account at the very bank it was stolen from. Many times I transferred a small portion of the money to active trading accounts electronically. I wrote checks out of my account or used cash, money orders or electronic methods to pay bills and take care of family expenses.

On one occasion, when making a deposit, I had a few tense moments. I went into a branch of my bank to get a cashier's check. Three months of back due mortgage and late fee payments on our home needed to be covered. This was urgent. The home was going to be auctioned off on the courthouse steps the next day. This happened early in the string of robberies and it was a couple of days after I robbed two banks on the same day in order to cover the mortgage and other overdue bills. I was trying to save our home.

When I went to the teller's window, I had less than an hour and a half to deliver payment to save our home from auction. I told the young teller which two transactions I needed to make. First, I had to make a cash deposit into my account. Then, I needed a bank draft for the mortgage company.

Apparently, she was new on the job and had a problem with the bank draft portion of the transaction. She called the bank manager over to help her. When the manager looked at the screen showing my account information, she said, "My, you have been making a lot of deposits lately."

My only reply was, "Yes, I have. I've needed to get this together to save my home from foreclosure."

I thought to myself (after my heart skipped a beat), *I hope she doesn't investigate further and report any suspicions she has to law enforcement.*

The manager proceeded to instruct the teller how to construct the draft and print it out. My thoughts were racing and my heart was pounding. As the cashier's check printed, the manager left the teller's area. The teller and I completed the transaction. I left the bank feeling a sense of relief knowing the manager had not taken the time to write down any information when looking at my account. I hoped she would not look any further into it. I went about my business and was able to save my home, at least for the moment, from foreclosure. That experience was one of only two close calls I know of during the course of the robberies.

This quiet, subtle approach worked until robbery twelve. Finally, in spite of careful planning, a bank employee broke protocol and followed me out to the parking lot, giving a description to the police. The house of cards collapsed.

<hr/>

Chapter Five

What led up to It

Keith

What events or circumstances could trigger a crime spree of robbing twelve banks? Financial problems played a major part in me turning to crime, but there was more to it than that.

Personal finances are something many of us have problems with at some point in our lives. Some people go through life with no monetary concerns. Most people have at least a few low points when they scramble for money to cover basics. My experience has been no different than the majority of Americans. However, my methods of rectifying the financial woes in my life were unorthodox at times and no more so than from July of 2007 through September of 2008.

Many people work hard to gain everything they have and it is difficult to grasp the thought of robbing banks to solve financial distress. Some may understand or have thought about doing it and a few have followed through on those thoughts as I did. I worked hard to make a living, but lacked the discipline needed to live within my current income. I learned financial restraint and the importance of faith the hard way. When I began robbing banks I moved away from trusting in

God. Leading up to this string of robberies, I was a complete financial, spiritual and emotional train wreck.

We may learn our financial habits from our parents. Some see their parents save, so they save. Some see their parents spend money carelessly, so they repeat the same habits. In my case, my financial blueprint was self-drawn. My mother provided a great example of living within her means. She worked hard and was well-aware of what she could and could not afford. There are three types of financial personalities: spenders, savers and those who have found the perfect balance between spending and saving.

I will strive for that perfect balance in the future since I'm a spender and have to be more disciplined. I know what it takes to work with the talents I have in order to earn enough money to be comfortable.

My financial problems began following a divorce in 2003. Divorce isn't pleasant, but I was happy being a single dad, and my children were able to stay put in their home. They continued to keep their friends and they went to the same school. Their stability was important to me. From the time they were born, I was an involved father, and as things deteriorated further and further with their mother, they needed me to provide stability. The court agreed and decided I could best provide a home free of conflict and strife. Some believe children should always be with their mother. I will only say it is not true.

At that time, I was employed in the printing industry. Advancements in digital technology made it clear printing was a dying business. Long hours and little opportunity for long-term employment convinced me I needed to make a change. I was interested in the equity (stock) markets and, while working a forty-hour-a-week job, I became infatuated with making investment changes in my retirement plan from a previous job. When I divorced, the money in my account was split between my ex-wife and me. I took my share to a large brokerage firm and opened a personal account. I began making traditional investment choices in stocks through a broker. A passion for trading stocks was ignited in me.

I wanted a career trading the markets independently, so I began to educate myself. My financial goals and my family life fit perfectly with a trading career. I could make a good living from home while having quality time to care for my children. I could give them stability, see them off to school every morning and be there when they returned home. Extra-curricular activities for the girls would be no problem. My schedule was flexible. Our home and all of the chores that came along with it were taken care of. Meals were prepared and eaten together. It was the perfect situation for a single parent and two children who needed stability. Shortly after the divorce was filed in the early summer of 2003, I quit working in the printing industry and lived off of the investment profits.

Our financial condition was good. All bills were paid, the mortgage on our home was current, I paid off all credit card debt and we owned a three-year-old vehicle with no payment due. During this time, the autumn of 2003 through the spring of 2006, the girls attended the local public middle school. It was the same one I attended many years before. Elise and Marissa were doing well there and they are to be commended for keeping their grades up and excelling even though there had been upheaval in the household.

In September of 2003, before the divorce was finalized, I became involved in a rebound romantic relationship. It was the result of the blindness caused by loneliness. This lasted about a year. Regretfully, I admit I neglected the girls during a time they needed me. The woman I was involved with moved into our home for several months. It turned into an emotional disaster and ended up with me taking a large financial hit. I still spent time with my daughters, but in hindsight I know I paid attention to the wrong people. Even though my intent was to devote my time and life to my daughters, loneliness and the desire to please others interfered. I lost sight of what was important. I was conflicted between being the dad they needed and providing everything to everyone else around me, too. My insecurities caused me to seek approval instead of focusing on my children. This became an unfortunate pattern in the years to come. Even today I can't give my daughters the time they deserve. Now it is due to my incarceration.

The financial hit I took during that relationship, however large it may have been, was not a crushing blow. I maintained discipline in my trading and investments and was able to get back on track once the relationship ended, but my spending control was lacking.

While working from home, I continued to educate myself about the financial markets. I soaked up all the information I could on websites and I watched CNBC throughout the day. I was picking up bits and pieces of knowledge about the options market. Trading options on stocks instead of owning them outright seemed to be what many successful business people did.

Then in May of 2005, I met someone who was also interested in trading the markets. This romantic relationship was off and on for over two years. We had a shared interest in trading the markets and this was appealing. She was in the beginning stages of an options trading educational program. We traveled and shared expenses together while attending classes for a year and a half or so. I began trading options as I learned more advanced methods along the way. Life was going pretty well at the point we met. Once again, I fell into the trap of trying to impress someone else instead of dedicating my time to my daughters. I feel guilty about that.

I made the decision to enroll Elise and Marissa in an all-girls private high school. It was one choice I made during this time period I do not regret, even if it was made through the persuasion of the woman I was involved with. Her two sons were going to comparable all-boys schools. I wanted my daughters to be on the same par socially. She was a successful professional and I wanted our family to appear "good enough." The school was over twenty miles from my house, but it was a good investment in my daughters and it provided them with an excellent education. Marissa and Elise graduated from that private school in 2009. It was an expense, in reality, I couldn't afford, so my financial situation deteriorated as I struggled to keep up the façade of wealth.

My relationship went the same path as my finances: everything spiraled out of control. It was a rollercoaster; just as things seemed to get brighter, it would plummet again. As bad relationships tend to do to a person, I was drained. Drained emotionally. Drained financially. Drained spiritually. Anyone who has been in a similar relationship can understand. I developed a conditioned sense of distrust of the world. I felt isolated and I didn't feel as though I could reach out to others. My defense mechanism I had grown to shield myself from emotional hurts also caused me to shy away from confiding in others. By the end, I felt I had no one I could trust or turn to.

Desperation, loneliness and distrust pushed me further down the road to commit crimes I never would have considered in the past. It's not her fault. She didn't tell me to rob banks. I take responsibility for my crimes. I will only say I reached a low point in life that clouded my judgment. During this time, the rollercoaster was in full swing.

The school expense was only one factor in my financial downfall, but it's a good example of the greater problem. Besides the school, I tried to keep up with my girlfriend's spending and lifestyle in every way. I ran up some debt and I eventually became less disciplined and attentive to my income versus spending. I made more risky trades than I would advise anyone making. I was looking for the big trade. I realized I was making mistakes, but I had a reputation to uphold now. I had to support the lifestyle I built for the kids and myself. With every emotional up and down, my finances were in tow. The harder I tried to make the relationship work and the more I tried to prove myself as worthy, the worse my financial situation became.

During the years 2005 to 2007, I ran up debt by spending more than I was making. I tried to solve my financial crisis. In the late summer of 2006, I filed for personal bankruptcy. Its advantages were limited, but it stopped the constant calls from credit card collections agencies.

I put our home up for sale in the spring of 2007 in what rapidly became the worst housing market in history. I had already refinanced the mortgage for a lower interest rate, so that was no longer an option. The home value quickly fell below the amount owed. There were so many homes on the market at the time I was unable to sell ours, so I decided to let the mortgage lapse and turn the home over to the lender. Even when robbing banks, the late fees and penalties plus the principal payments became too much to continue to keep it out of foreclosure. The lender offered me a cash sum of three thousand dollars to have our things out and the interior swept clean. I had a rental home set up for us, so I took their offer.

By mid-summer of 2007, the relationship came to an end for a number of reasons. In the spring of 2008, my daughters and I moved into a smaller home. Oh, by the way, I told everyone our home had finally sold. I had to keep up appearances.

It may sound as though things were getting better once I was out from under the mortgage and the relationship, but there were still very large debts and obligations to be met. Some people asked me why didn't I go out and get a job. Well, during those times, good jobs were hard to find.

The state prosecution at my trial asked me on the stand if I applied at McDonalds. My answer was a simple, "No, counselor, I did not."

It was a matter of pride. Keeping an image and lifestyle were important to me and I thought to the girls as well. I was wrong. On a more practical point, with the remaining large debt and obligations I had, a job at McDonalds would be little help at all. Working a forty-hour week without the ability to pay the majority of my bills didn't solve anything.

The largest debt remaining, by far, was to the I.R.S. I delayed filing a return for 2005 even though I had been paying quarterly as a business from 2005-2007. I owed the government and could not make the payment. I continued paying quarterly through the third quarter of 2007, working with the I.R.S. on a payment plan. The payments were beyond my means. Anyone who has worked with the I.R.S. knows they are demanding, and interest and penalties add up rapidly. I went to prison with this debt not completely satisfied. The debt to the I.R.S. was one of my biggest considerations when I decided to rob banks.

Of course, there were everyday bills to be paid. Some were necessary and some were to maintain the lifestyle. Rent, utilities, health insurance, car insurance, gasoline, telephone and the other daily expenses of life required money. I was taking my daughters to family counseling to help them deal with the divorce. It wasn't cheap, but I was trying to help them through a painful situation. I owed my mother. I used her credit cards, with her permission, on occasion. I borrowed small amounts of money from friends at times and I felt the need to pay those debts back promptly. At times there were bounced checks I had written for household expenses that had to be covered. Lifestyle expenses such as cell phones, cable television and internet service added up. Yet through it all, I continued to lend money to people when they were in need. This was important to keep up the appearance that everything was okay.

When I could no longer afford health insurance for the girls, I applied for state aid. We received assistance and a small amount of food stamps. I hadn't planned on getting food stamps, but the agent insisted we get them because on paper we qualified.

Applying for state aid was another blow to my ego and sense of pride. I went from capably supporting my family to being on public assistance. It was a train wreck. I had exhausted myself, my finances and my options. I was alone, broke and desperate. The stage was set for me to take my mother's joke and turn it into an unfortunate reality.

Chapter Six

County Jail: Heartache and Hostility

Keith

The St. Louis County Jail is the only jail I have ever been in. It is described by most inmates as being more comfortable than many jails. The building is decent and the upkeep is adequate. I was told they keep the place clean because of an earlier outbreak of a deadly staph infection. The deaths, coupled with the obsessive-compulsiveness of most inmates for cleanliness, kept the place sanitary. Prison, as I would later find out, is much the same way. Cleanliness aside, after spending twenty-three months of my life there, I can tell you the county jail is a dangerous place. In many ways, it is more dangerous than prison.

After I was given a shower and a change of standard county brown clothes, I took the elevator ride to the eighth floor. I was placed in a cell with a man awaiting transfer to different county jail. The cell had only one bunk, but there was a plastic stretcher with a worn, thin, green mattress known as a "boat." Those are used in jails and prisons where overcrowding is problematic, which is a common occurrence in American jails and prisons. I spent my first night in jail in the boat.

I spent the morning talking to my cellmate, Mark, sharing stories of how we had gotten where we were. We talked about where in St. Louis County we were each from and we exchanged simple small talk about our families. Mark knew about the Boonie Hat Bandit and was surprised to hear I was the one who committed the robberies. Most of the men at the jail were surprised until my story unfolded in the media over the next few days.

This cell was a holding place I stayed for two days until they placed me in a wing on a different floor. Each floor in the jail placed suspects based on the severity of the crimes they were accused of or they had been found guilty of, committing.

I had barely eaten since the morning of the last robbery the day before. Upon arrival to the eighth floor, they served breakfast shortly after I got there. I don't recall what it was, but I remember eating very little of it. I had little-to-no appetite. I skipped lunch altogether and had just a few bites for dinner. I wasn't fond of the meals at the jail and I disliked them even more as time passed.

My main focus at this point was to figure out a way to make bail so I could get back to my children. This would be my focus for months to come.

At dinner, I talked more with my cellmate about what jail would be like. Mark gave me some of the ins and outs, telling me the way they did things around there and what to expect. His advice turned out to be accurate. Getting solid advice is not always the case in that environment and I appreciated his honesty. I then went to sleep very early. The physical and mental exhaustion finally caught up with me and I was no longer able to keep my eyes open.

The next morning I was awakened by an officer banging on the steel door of the cell. He let Mark know to prepare to leave in fifteen minutes. Since that morning, I have seen hundreds of people come and go throughout the years.

After breakfast that day, I experienced my first recreation time in the county jail. Everyone was let out into the day-room of the wing. Some called it "the pod." About a dozen small, round tables with four chairs at each of them were assembled in the dayroom. The tables had board games (chess, checkers and backgammon) printed right on the table tops. Playing cards, dominoes and other games were available to play.

Meals were served in the dayroom, brought up on rolling carts from the kitchen located on the ground floor of the jail. The dayroom had a carpeted area for watching television. There were two televisions on small stands and seating was made up of plastic lounge chairs connected in groups of two, three or four and were placed in rows in front of the televisions. All of the chairs in the jail were made of plastic.

That morning, a group of men older than me asked if I would be their fourth player in a game of dominoes. The men seemed very relaxed, as though they had been in jail many times. I had not played dominoes since I was a kid with my grandfather. I said, "Sure, why not?" I figured anything that would help me take my mind off the horrible situation I was in couldn't hurt.

The other men in the group were no strangers to jail life. Cass, an older gentlemen, offered many comforting words for me. "Gentleman" is not a word I use to describe the vast majority of the men I have met and lived with throughout my incarceration. Yet, there have been a few. Cass was one of them.

Of course the men knew what was reported about my crimes and were interested in hearing the story from me. I did not tell them everything for several reasons, but I did have a conversation with them about it. My domino game was a little bit rusty, to say the least. They were understanding, just passing the time. I later found out competition is taken more seriously in jail and prison. There is usually some sort of gambling involved no matter what the game is. In the months and years to come, I saw this turn into some dangerous and volatile situations. As far as our game on that day, it was a friendly one.

The rest of the day was uneventful. I played several more games of dominoes in the afternoon and evening with Cass and the other men. Many of the inmates looked at me while I was talking to the men at the table, discussing me as they watched. At this point, I felt defensive and was not ready to open up and talk about my crimes. Some would approach me to talk about it and I would kindly tell them I didn't want to talk about it. It took me a long time to want to open up.

I did not have a cellmate that night, so I put both of the thin mattresses on the wall-mounted steel bunk. I was mentally and physically exhausted, so I fell to sleep quickly.

The next morning I moved to the seventh floor. I spent the next twenty-three months of my life on that floor. I didn't realize it would be for that long. The seventh floor would be where things became tense and much more interesting.

The sixth and seventh floors of the St. Louis County Jail housed only those who accused of committing A and B Class felonies, repeat offenders of lesser felonies and parole violators. Most were awaiting trial or a plea agreement for A and B Class felonies. In Missouri, A and B felonies are crimes such as murder, assault, manslaughter, robbery and severe cases of child molestation. Some might say, "The worst of the worst."

Once I moved down to the seventh floor of the jail, I began to settle in. The wings or pods, have an upper and lower tier. At the St. Louis County Jail, the lower tier is made up of two-person cells and the upper tier consists of single-person cells. An inmate must put his name on a waiting list for the single-person cells. I put my name on waiting list the day after I was placed on the seventh floor and I was thankful it only took a few days to be assigned a single cell. Some people do not like being alone in a cell. I prefer it. I have no problem being a loner in that environment. The majority of time, while I waited twenty-three months for both the federal and state prosecutions, was spent in that cell.

About a month after my arrest, I was called in for questioning by a Webster Groves detective. He had an unsolved bank robbery on his hands, and he wanted me to admit to committing it. I hadn't robbed that bank, and I wasn't going to say that I had. The detective was irritated and insistent, but I wouldn't budge. The whole conversation bothered me. First of all, why would I be stupid enough to admit to a crime I did not commit? Secondly, this detective was more interested in clearing the case off of his desk by pinning it on an innocent person than in finding the perpetrator. Unfortunately, this happens more than we as a society would like to believe. He left unsatisfied that day, and I went back to my cell shaking my head at the unwillingness of the system to carry out actual justice.

So many things happened during my stay in the county jail and there were so many characters (both inmate and staff), it would be impossible to explain and describe all of them. For now, I will give a general idea of life within.

Sometimes I had visits from my attorney, my family and my friends. Occasional trips were made to medical and dental appointments. The vast majority of my time was spent in my cell reading, writing letters and eating food from the canteen.

A few days after I was placed on the seventh floor, I began receiving mail and making telephone calls. Phone calls were sometimes difficult to make because only eight phones served fifty-four people at one time. Calls could only be made during the three recreation periods. Inmates were given one free thirty-minute phone call per week. All other calls were collect and were charged at a flat thirty-minute rate. They were less expensive than some calling plans out there, but calls were still quite expensive.

Phones were a constant problem and source of disturbance. Many fist fights and instances of bullying concerned the phones. I never had much of a problem, but there were many "phone hogs." Weak or unpopular inmates had a difficult time getting access to phones. Tensions were high. The staff ended up giving everyone one thirty-minute phone call per day at an assigned time to keep the violence down. It worked out pretty well. I, of course, spent most of my phone time keeping in touch with my daughters.

When I started receiving mail, most of it was from reporters connected with television, both national and local. They all wanted interviews. It wouldn't be until much later that I took them up on their requests. Fan mail streamed in. Some was in good taste with empathy. Some was a bit on the groupie side. I never expected, nor did I want it. Maybe people craved attention or wanted to be part of my newly-found infamy. I couldn't believe I was propositioned by strangers who saw the news stories about me. I also got much-appreciated mail from Elise and Marissa, from extended family members and from a few friends. My cousin was kind enough to have a monthly spiritual magazine sent to me. She renews the subscription each year for me.

Visiting time was one of the most prized events for inmates. The visiting area for each wing consisted of three booths with a telephone on each side of a glass divider, with two more booths used for attorney visits. Family and friends were not allowed contact visits and all communication was done over the monitored phones in the booths. With limited space available, an inmate had to put in a visiting request slip. Slips were completed by filling in who was coming, on what date and what time slot of the six available requested. The visits were one hour in duration.

Elise and Marissa visited me often when I was in the county jail. There was a lot of emotional trauma to get through during some of those visits. My daughters were dealing with the unknowns of living on their own and they were trying to adapt to the new realities thrown their way. They looked to me for guidance.

Parenting from inside a cell is not easy. I struggled with everything myself and I needed Elise and Marissa to handle some necessities for me. Since they were children, this was difficult. Needless to say, some visits were very emotional, although most were spent talking about normal life—school, their boyfriends, what activities they were taking part in and all of the other normal conversations parents have with their children. The girls were great about coming; sometimes even bringing their boyfriends or other friends of ours.

Friends visited from time to time, but those visits waned as the weeks and months passed. Finally, they stopped altogether. Since I have been in prison, not a single friend has come to see me except one, and he didn't visit until I was incarcerated for six and a half years. My oldest sister stopped by the jail to see me fairly often. The jail in Clayton was on her way to work and it was nice to get to see her. She didn't stop contacting me until I had been away for five years. My other sister never came to see me, nor has she ever written to me or sent a card of any type since the day of my arrest.

A set procedure was in place for visiting and for dealing with scheduling problems. When I turned a visiting slip in, the officers would call me up to the desk if the time slot I requested was filled, allowing me to choose an alternative available time or day. If I heard nothing, I knew the visit was on schedule.

On November 6th I put a slip in for November 8, 2008 at 1:00 P.M. to have a visit with my mother. She was eighty-one-years-old and no longer able to drive herself. We made arrangements for a friend of mine to bring her to visit me. I had only talked to Mom by telephone from the jail and we were excited to see each other. The date of her visit drew near and since I heard nothing about the need to reschedule, I thought everything was a go.

The next morning I went into the dayroom, and as I was walking by the guard desk I spotted my request slip sitting on the counter. The visit was denied because the time slot was full. Unlike other officers, this particular staff member did not let me know ahead of time so I could make other arrangements. Prior to this I hadn't had any problems with her, but I witnessed her using her position of power to punish people. She operated on her own biases and prejudices, playing favorites. Racism, in all forms, is an ugly thing.

I tried to get a different time slot for that day to no avail. We were going to reset our visit for another day, but we had to work around the schedule of the person giving her a ride. Before that could happen, three days later, my mother died of a sudden cardiac arrest. I felt and still feel, I was cheated out of seeing my mother alive for the last time because of personal grudges held by a staff member. This same guard was fired several weeks later for bringing contraband into inmates.

A request to attend my mother's funeral the next week was denied. The prosecutor and judge said I was allowed to go to the funeral home, in handcuffs, escorted by detectives, to view my mother's body after hours, but I wasn't allowed to take part in the funeral or to help my children through this terrible time of loss. I hadn't asked for anything out of the ordinary. Others were granted weekend furloughs to attend family funerals, even those of aunts and uncles. I saw it happen. I was not even allowed to give my final respects to the one person who was always my rock.

Less than a month later, my father died. Although I was not close to my father, it was a hard blow to take. It was a tough one-two punch after my mother's death. The way I found out about my father's death still stings. My last name isn't a common one, so one day another inmate asked me if I knew a Joseph Giammanco. I said, "Yeah, that's my father."

He then said, "Is he the same Joseph Giammanco whose obituary was in today's paper?" He had been considerate, saved the paper and brought it to me to look for myself. It was my father.

When I was able to call Marissa and Elise, I let them know about their grandfather's passing. Neither of my sisters said a word to me about his death then and they have never mentioned it since. If it wasn't for another inmate, I'm not sure when or how I would have found out. I would have much rather not heard it from a stranger, though. Being in jail is a difficult and isolating experience. Sometimes death reminds us how costly it is to be incarcerated and teaches us how quickly we are left out, forgotten.

Everyday life inside the jail is no walk in the park. It can be an intense, volatile and dangerous environment. The slightest spark can set off an altercation between two or more inmates. This is true inside prisons, too. County jails have a different element involved—fear of the unknown. In a county jail, most inmates have the anxiety of not knowing what is going to happen in their court cases. Others know exactly what is going to happen or they have a good idea about it and are angry at the world. They know they are going to go to prison, but for many of them, they don't know exactly what will happen to them once they are there. In a jail, the whole place is constantly on edge, ready to erupt into a frenzy.

During my twenty-three month stay, I saw countless heated arguments, well over a dozen all-out fights and one instance I would call a brawl between several inmates. Most of these altercations were over trivial matters. While I have never considered myself a violent person and I normally consider violence a senseless way to solve disputes, there are certain survival skills needed when incarcerated. Being able and willing to defend yourself and what little property you are allowed to possess is crucial. Keeping to yourself and minding your own business is also helpful in avoiding physical violence in jail or prison.

Some may remember the days before every kid in the house had his own cell phone; times when we all relied on one family land line phone to communicate with our friends and more than one of us wanted to use the phone. Well, telephones in a jail are like that; a point of contention; a major reason for the outbreak of many fights. When a person is in jail, contact with family and friends on the outside is very important. Some are willing to fight for it, risking harm to themselves or even potential prison time by assaulting another inmate in an effort to get telephone time.

Theft is another. I saw people beaten badly over stealing a seventy-five cent honey bun or even something as small as a postage stamp. A related cause for violence are debts from gambling or owing another inmate for canteen items, stamps or phone time. Some inmates believe having people owe them is a symbol of status and power. The same goes for having money on their canteen accounts to buy products to lend and consume. Of course, when they lend out those products, they expect more in return as interest. This can add up quickly at a rate of 50-100%.

Unlike prison, I neither witnessed nor heard of knives being used in county jail fights. One person was punished for having a small piece of metal that could have been converted into a shank (a homemade knife used by prisoners for cutting or stabbing). I did witness plastic chairs being hurled at others in the jail; sometimes thrown as weapons and others as a means of defense.

The most effective weapon used in the county jail was simple to make and easy to use. This was an ordinary tube sock with a few bars of bath soap inside. The sock was swung at victims, striking them multiple times in the head. It inflicted very serious damage and caused long-lasting injuries. In prison and the county jail, items other than soap are placed inside the sock. Master and combination locks inside a tube sock have been known to cause death. It is a simple but effective weapon.

It doesn't take much for violence to erupt. A particular seat at a table during mealtime or a disagreement in a conversation can lead to physical violence. The worst physical damage I have seen inflicted on someone occurred at the county jail when a simple conversation escalated into a first degree criminal assault.

I was out in the recreation yard, which was inside and consisted of a few basketball hoops, a concrete floor, a twenty-foot ceiling and large windows with a thick steel mesh covering them. The streets of Clayton, Missouri, seven stories below can be viewed through some of those windows. A small amount of air comes in from the outdoors and there is no heating or air conditioning, so the jail can claim it is "outside." Believe me, it's not.

As I was walking laps around the "yard," I could hear a commotion going on inside the wing. As I looked into the wing through the large window, an inmate named Mitchell threw a plastic chair at Lytle, another inmate. Lytle brushed it aside and proceeded with his counter-assault. He beat Mitchell in the head multiple times until he fell to the floor and was up against a wall. Then Lytle jumped on top of Mitchell and continued to mercilessly beat him. While falling on top of him, he inflicted a compound fracture to Mitchell's right leg just below the knee on the shin bone. He also caused numerous abrasions to his face before guards came in several minutes later to stop the onslaught using pepper spray.

As I walked past the injured Mitchell lying on the floor, his right leg was in an awkward position underneath his body and I could see the blood coming out from his pant leg. He was bleeding profusely from the head. Blood was puddled and splattered throughout the entire area where the beating had taken place. Mitchell's face and head were swollen and bloody, completely unrecognizable. He almost did not look human anymore. It was a sickening sight.

As it turned out, I was acquainted with both men. Mitchell was about sixty-years-of-age and was in jail for bank robbery like myself. It was not his first time in for it. In fact, he was released from a prison term three weeks prior. I spoke to him several times about our crimes. Mitchell was a very confused man who'd been groomed to a life of incarceration. It seemed like he wanted to go back to prison. It was familiar. It was what he knew.

Lytle was thirty years younger. I helped him understand some legal terms a couple of days before. He was uneducated and mentally unstable. Lytle took medication for his medical condition; had freely discussed this with me in the days leading up to the fight. Others had also warned me Lytle was unstable. I had agreed after a little interaction with him. He was very tense, volatile, like a time bomb. Well, the bomb finally went off with catastrophic results.

Lytle ended up with a first degree assault charge which added ten-to-thirty years on top of whatever time he was already facing. Mitchell was badly injured and was hospitalized. I never saw either man again.

The fight started because Mitchell was talking "too loudly" during a heated conversation and he had "disrespected" Lytle. Who knows? All that damage was done to two lives over a useless discussion.

Holidays happen when you are incarcerated. Deaths also happen. The two, a holiday and a death, coincided to create a memory that has stuck with me over time. Some deaths are of a violent nature and some occur because people simply stop willing themselves to live.

Porter was a middle-aged African-American man. I had several brief conversations with him in the months prior to his death. He was at the county jail before I arrived. Other than that, I did not know much about him except he was serving a long sentence at the federal prison in Terre Haute, Indiana. Porter was in the jail on what is called a writ of transfer from federal prison to face a separate pending state charge in St. Louis County.

One day I didn't see him anymore. Then, several months later, Porter returned to the wing and said hello to me. I did not recognize him. He was a small man to begin with, but he must have lost somewhere between fifty and seventy-five pounds. I was shocked, but I didn't mention it to him. Someone later told me he had given all of his meals away for months. Porter was trying to starve himself to death. During the months he was out of the wing, they had been force feeding him in the infirmary. They finally released him into the general population, into a two-man cell, in the same wing where I was.

Once back in the wing, he picked up where he left off and began giving his meals away. I don't know if the medical services were monitoring his situation or not. I also don't know how they determined Porter was not endangered any longer by his own self-destructive behavior.

A month or so after he returned to the wing, on Easter Sunday 2010, he was found dead in his bunk by his cellmate. The cellmate said Porter was "sleeping" in his bunk for a couple of days. Well, he finally succeeded in suicide by starving. I spent the entire morning and most of the afternoon of that holy holiday locked in my cell, along with the entire floor, with the dead body of a man in full view laying in the middle of the floor below. The jail staff left his body lying there, for everyone in the wing to see, until the coroner finally had the body removed late that afternoon.

When asked, his cellmate said Porter did nothing but sleep. Early Easter morning, when the guard needed to get a message to him, the cellmate tried to wake him. He was stiff. He had been dead for twenty-four to forty-eight hours. No one noticed. Not the man living in the same cell. Not the guards. No one.

A lot of questions were raised by Porter's death. Shouldn't someone on the staff have noticed this? From that day forward, the staff changed the way they accounted for inmates. Standing counts were conducted several times a day. Had standing counts been a policy in the past? Had the policy been ignored? If not, should this have always been the practice? Could this death have been prevented with proper care and monitoring of the situation? If they knew Porter was prone to self-destruction, should medical have taken more interest in his well-being after his release from the infirmary? None of those questions were answered, at least not with answers made public. County jail was filled with turmoil, heartache and hostility. Flaring tempers, fear and apathy combined for a dangerous situation.

Chapter Seven

Under the Big Top

Keith

After spending two nights in county jail, I realized how confusing and complicated it was to be arrested for a high profile crime. My daughters found this out as well. Our names and faces were suddenly all over the news. Everyone thought they knew about our lives. I was used to living a private life. That disappeared. Now we were in the spotlight.

I understood the reporters had their job to do. The media didn't shock me the most. The lawyers did. Some appeared out of the woodwork. Lawyers watch the news for possible clients because not long after my arrest, lawyers were contacting me. Others were talked about or recommended by people I knew. Some were recommended by other inmates at the county jail. I hadn't anticipated finding a lawyer would be such a circus. Choosing one when there is a media frenzy going on, is truly a nightmare, especially if you have no money.

Other than in a corporate setting or while filing for divorce, I had no experience with attorneys. I found out criminal law was a totally different world. Crime shows on television make it look cut and dry. The attorneys work hard to either defend or prosecute the defendant and in the end justice prevails. In reality, it can be a world of deception, backstabbing, half-truths and flat-out lies. Money, greed and publicity are important, not justice.

Over the next few months, finding an attorney would become an absolute quagmire. It was confusing and frustrating for myself and for the friends and family who were trying to help. So many things played out. In the early stages of this long process, my instinct was to not trust anyone I didn't know (and also some people I did know). My instincts were correct.

It wasn't until I was in prison for a number of *years* that I would find an attorney whom I believed was up front and honest with me. Too many played games behind the scenes, closed doors *and* my back.

The court had twenty hours to conduct an arraignment on the crimes. It would be months before I was formally charged with four counts of robbery in the first degree by the State of Missouri via a grand jury indictment. To this day, I have never seen a copy of the transcript of that indictment. Transparency is not a strong trait in the Missouri court system.

On December 31, 2008, the federal government handed down an indictment via grand jury charging me with twelve counts of robbery of a financial institution. This indictment contained the four counts (which would later become seven) I was charged with by the State of Missouri. Those counts were for the crimes committed in St. Louis County. The indictment also included the five other counts committed in St. Charles County, Missouri. I would face no other charges in Missouri for those robberies. St. Charles County referred their charges to the federal government, meaning St. Charles County chose not to prosecute me after I was charged by the federal government.

The federal court system was far more professional and transparent compared to the system operating in the State of Missouri. I received a transcribed copy of every court proceeding by the federal court. I was physically present for every hearing and happening throughout the entire process, including the formal charges, bond hearings, pleas, conviction and sentencing. Not so in Missouri's assembly-line-to-conviction court system.

Part of the difficulty in choosing an attorney was not knowing who had jurisdiction to prosecute me for these crimes. Some attorneys are qualified to defend both federal cases and state cases. Others are not. I needed representation in both jurisdictions.

Attorneys (including one I eventually hired) told me from the beginning the feds would pick up these crimes. I was told when they did, the state would drop their charges. I heard this all the way up until the day after my federal sentencing. Little did I know or expect I would be convicted and sentenced by both the federal government and the State of Missouri for the exact same crimes.

For me, this is the most interesting and controversial aspect of this entire story as far as the crimes and court system go. As Americans, we grow up believing we have protection from double jeopardy. Constitutionally, we can't be convicted of the same crime twice. We think we have protections under the law. We don't. If it can happen to me, it can happen to any other American. Being prosecuted twice is a sham and a miscarriage of justice.

From the very beginning, I researched the precedent law and theories on double jeopardy. I needed to know how the laws are implemented and commonly practiced. The St. Louis County Jail had a mobile law library that moved from wing-to-wing and I studied the federal and state law books it provided. My daughter, Elise, sent me what information she could find on the internet.

Attorneys will say they like an informed, educated and proactive client. From my experience the vast majority of them don't. They prefer clients who know nothing about the law. They are in total control of your life. They are 'the experts.' They are free to tell you what they believe is best for them and the system, even if it isn't what is best for you. Some practice deception. They twist the finer points of law so clients believe attorneys have their best interests in mind. When the rubber meets the road, they like a dumb client so that their actions aren't questioned. They know the clients are the boss, but they don't want them to act like one.

Attorneys don't want to "rock the boat" of the judicial system. It's rare to find an attorney willing to break out and do something bold because it is the right thing to do. The judicial system is a country club of sorts. Attorneys get to know the judges and how they run their courtrooms. They get to know the prosecutors, the defense attorneys, socialize, go to the same legal conferences and are on the same team, but simply get their paychecks from different sides of the field. Judges are former attorneys and attorneys are jockeying for their position in private practice. You scratch my back, I'll scratch yours.

Judges, prosecutors and defense attorneys want a client who is anxious and scared. This gives them the ability to persuade the client to willingly give up his rights to do what is best for them and the system. This is not necessarily what is best for the client. It's all in the name of truth and justice supposedly, but many people are given bad legal advice limiting their rights instead of upholding them.

Except for hardened criminals, most of us don't have much experience with the legal system. We believe lawyers are there to fight for us. We listen to the ads on television telling us we need an attorney who is "on our side." Nevertheless, many people have been convinced to give up their rights or to make bad plea deals. If arrested, rightly or wrongly, a person needs to remember lawyers and judges are acting as officers of the court. Plain and simple.

My first experience with an attorney took place on the Sunday morning after my arrest. His name was Peter Atwell. He said he and his wife read about the case in the local St. Louis paper. He worked as an associate with a well-known criminal law firm in St. Louis. His wife felt sorry for me and had told him he had to represent me. I was not ready to commit to hiring anyone yet, but said I would keep him in mind. Later I found out he entered as my attorney of record the next morning without my permission. While reviewing court records months later I discovered that detail.

Why would he do that? What advantage would that give him? It's simple: he was eliminating the competition. Other lawyers who might have been interested in taking the case would see I retained an attorney already. They would move on. Immediately my pool of potential attorneys was limited. If the media decided to get in touch with my lawyer to do a story, they would contact him and he would have his name advertised.

Peter Atwell didn't do this on his own, and it sure wasn't because his wife felt sorry for me. The firm he worked for put him up to it in order to gain publicity. Another young attorney was brought in by them for the same purpose. Remember how I said it was very confusing and overwhelming to be at the center of a high profile case? I quickly found out the world didn't operate the way I'd always thought it did. I was a quiet, non-assuming, middle-class dad. I wasn't prepared for the spotlight nor for the propensity of some people to grab onto my celebrity for their own gain. I would learn.

Chapter Eight

Divisional Court

Keith

A defendant is taken before a judge for the first time in the lower divisional court, the charges against him are read and the defendant states who represents him (if they are not there to do so). If he doesn't have an attorney, a public defender is appointed, then a plea is officially entered into court.

The Monday after my arrest I was taken before the divisional judge. Judge Rankin asked if I had an attorney. I said, "No, I am still working on retaining one." I waived the public reading of the charges against me (count-by-count) and told her I understood them. Judge Rankin entered a not guilty plea on my behalf and set another court date about two weeks out, pending my ability to retain an attorney.

During the next two weeks, several area attorneys visited me. Scrambling for the funds to hire an attorney was underway and I wanted to find the right one. It took several months to finally retain an attorney for the state charges of first degree robbery. I had no money. That's why I robbed banks. My life hung in the balance and it was beyond stressful trying to hire an attorney with no money.

In the two weeks leading up to the next court date, I had several visits and telephone calls with my daughters. I trusted my children and I sought their help in finding an attorney. We tried to figure out how to raise funds to hire one. They were only seventeen (a month away from turning eighteen), but they were bright, intelligent girls who were wise beyond their years and they wanted to help in whatever way they could.

I was desperate and anxious. I wasn't accustomed to being in jail and my daughters wanted to help get me out of there. Elise and Marissa were going through the most trying time in their short lives and all three of us were unsure and emotional. I was desperate for someone, anyone, to get me out of that county jail. The girls had their own emotions and they did not know what to do. It was stressful for our small, but loving, family. I gave my daughters suggestions and the names of people to contact and we did the best we could.

Elise and Marissa contacted people with nothing but the best intentions. They asked people they knew for advice and they turned to their school and to the church for guidance. Little did we know this would cause others to stick their noses into our family business. Their prying, they said, was "for the good of the girls." Because of this, I had an unexpected encounter with an attorney named Susan Cliff. She was someone connected to both the school and the church, I would find out later.

At the next appearance in divisional court, when I was called in front of Judge Rankin, a middle-aged woman I didn't know appeared from the gallery and approached the bench along with me. The judge knew her. Judge Rankin asked if she was representing me. I was shocked when she said she was entering in the interest of the girls. Susan Cliff was going to represent them, and apparently Judge Rankin knew about this beforehand.

I stood there, unrepresented, while Judge Rankin chastised me for soliciting help from my children to raise funds for an attorney. The court frowned upon that and "would not have it," she said. My daughters were minors and I was out of line for seeking their help. I was shocked and angry.

Keep in mind, the girls were going to be legal adults in three weeks. Had they been standing in front of the judge facing criminal charges, the court would gladly consider them adults. Perspectives can change based on the motivations. I stood in court, unrepresented and my daughters were not present to speak for themselves.

After chewing me up and down for a few more minutes, the judge ordered Susan Cliff be present for all visits and phone calls between my children and me until they were eighteen (or as long as the girls wanted after that). Judge Rankin finally got around to asking me if I had an attorney. I told her I didn't, so she set one more court date for two weeks later. She stated how serious the charges against me were, "You had better find an attorney or I am going to appoint one for you."

She dismissed the newly-appointed guardian 'ad litem' for the girls. While still in front of the bench, Judge Rankin realized I had gotten my ass chewed out by the court with no representation. She decided to appoint me a public defender then and there.

I was led into a back room and interviewed by a nineteen-year-old sympathetic young pre-law intern for the public defender in St. Louis County. She interviewed me to see if I qualified for a public defender. Was I broke? Did I own any property? I was and I didn't. I qualified and was sent a note from the public defender the next day. I never met the public defender I was assigned.

A few days later, Elise and Marissa came to see me. Susan Cliff was present. I had a short, pleasant conversation with Marissa and Elise while Cliff sat outside the booth close by the girls. Cliff asked my daughters if she could speak with me for a moment, so they switched places with her.

We formally introduced ourselves to each other. Cliff worked as an attorney for the social services department of the Catholic Church. Her daughter attended the same high school as my children. At this point, I started to put it all together. Apparently, the girls talked to her daughter or someone who worked at the school. No matter how it transpired, she was notified our family was having a crisis. She volunteered or was asked to put herself in the middle of our situation.

We had a cordial conversation. Susan told me she knew the public defender assigned to my case; that he was a great lawyer. She assured me the feds would pick up the case and I would no longer have to worry about the state charges. It was the first of many times I would hear that. She vowed to help the girls in any way she could. After talking for about ten minutes, Susan Cliff said she did not think it was necessary for her to be present at the girls' visits or during our phone calls. She had a stereotypical impression of me without meeting me and realized she stuck her nose where it was not needed.

Susan helped the girls out on several occasions in the year or so to come. She assisted getting some bills paid, provided gas money and even arranged some spending money for them through Catholic Charities. She had the girls' best interest in mind and was a good-hearted person. Nevertheless, her methods were typical of a lawyer. She made knee-jerk assumptions I was a terrible father before getting to know me or our family. This resulted in her rash actions to become involved where it wasn't necessary.

The court, the prosecutor and others went out of their way to involve themselves in a high profile case under the guise of being "do-gooders." Regardless of what consequences, inconveniences or outcomes it caused my girls or me, they planted themselves in our lives. The incident with the guardian ad litem created one more emotional blow our family had to withstand during an already difficult time. My daughters were looking for help in finding an attorney. They didn't anticipate creating another barrier between us (as if the jail bars weren't already painfully sufficient). I appreciated Susan's decision to back away from our visits.

Word had it the public defender assigned to my case was the best one of the bunch in St. Louis County, but here, once a defendant is indicted or his case is bound over to the circuit court for trial, he is assigned a different public defender from the pool. I never met with the top-notch defender. I was passed on to someone else. This is counter-productive and a disadvantage to the accused. It creates confusion and unfamiliarity. It wastes effort and resources on the part of the public defender bureaucracy.

The search was still ongoing for a private attorney to handle what, at this point, were only state charges. Every attorney I spoke with was certain federal charges would be handed down for these robberies.

Many of the attorneys I interviewed wanted anywhere from $10,000 to $25,000 to retain them for the state charges. Those who were qualified to deal with both the feds and the state would cost even more. Some younger attorneys were willing to take the case for as little as $2,500 or pro-bono (for free), but they had little experience. Only one young attorney was licensed for federal cases. Keep in mind, those interested at this point wanted the publicity the case brought. Even the best and most well-known criminal defense attorney in the region was willing to take the case for $15,000. Considering he was going to work the case himself and not an associate, that was a bargain. He usually started cases at $25,000. Publicity was the pay-off for these attorneys.

My best friend, Roger Pettinelli, was willing to take out loans against his properties to fund my defense, but given the economic climate in 2008-2009, he was unable to secure a loan. Lenders were tight. In spite of Roger's efforts, it was back to square one.

Meanwhile, my choice of private attorneys narrowed. All of the attorneys I interviewed visited me periodically to check on my status. Even the best ones in the area wanted my case at this early point. The problem was money. I was desperate for money when I robbed banks and I was desperate for money now. Behind jail bars, I didn't have any options for improving my finances.

A grand jury indicted me on four counts of robbery in the first degree. The state officially bound the four counts to circuit court, pending trial. While the public defender system was informed my case was set to go before a grand jury, I was not for several weeks.

One day I received a surprise visit from the chief public defender in St. Louis County, Jacob Tomkins. I would be assigned a new public defender once an indictment was handed down by the grand jury. Clearly, Tomkins watched the news and read the papers about my case. He was sure I would be indicted and face charges in Missouri. This was the extent of the defense I got from a public "defender." He fancied taking on this case himself, with visions of the chief public defender versus the county prosecutor in a high profile case.

My first priority was to get a bond reduction hearing so I could get back home to care for my children. My goal was to have the $100,000 cash only bond reduced to a reasonable amount. According to the Constitution, we are entitled to a reasonable bond. I asked if it could be converted to a property title bond. Roger was willing to put up his properties to secure my release pending trial.

The conversation turned sour. Tomkins showed his ego and true colors. He screamed at me (through the glass and speaker) that *he* would set the goals and priorities in this case and *he* would call the shots. Tomkins said I wasn't the first celebrity criminal who tried to tell an experienced public defender what they were going to do. Celebrity was not my motivation. I was a concerned father wanting to get home to my children. Since celebrity was in the forefront of his mind, Tomkins made it clear things would be done the way he wanted them done.

He calmed down, somewhat, after a heated exchange and said, "First we are going to wait for a decision from the grand jury. Then we will see about a bond reduction."

Well, I did not believe him. I was told by several well-known attorneys my best chance of getting out on bond was when the case was still in divisional court. I quit trying and the bond reduction saga continued.

Tomkins made a belated attempt to be compassionate, saying he knew I was concerned about my children, but most likely I would not be with them until I got out of prison. He didn't seriously consider bond as an option for me. I couldn't help but think, *How nice. The public defender system does not like their clients to be out on bond. They have easy access to them in the jail.* Tomkins had no incentive to get me out on bond. Maybe he was right and I would be denied a bond reduction, but to not even try for one guaranteed it. Telling me I wouldn't see my children until I was out of prison was an added twist of the knife. This was the first of many disappointments in the impotent Missouri Public Defender System.

Chapter Nine

Circuit Court

Keith

I was brought before the circuit court for my arraignment. A second arraignment later added three more counts via suppressed indictment. The intent was to bully or scare me into making an open (or blind) plea so the case would not go to trial.

Supposedly, I was represented by the public defender system. While sitting in the courtroom with about a dozen other defendants, one young public defender intern brought paperwork by to each defendant without private representation. Each of them was asked to sign the paperwork which said we were brought before the court and the attorney was entering a not guilty plea on our behalf. I never saw or spoke to my so-called lawyer.

During the twenty minutes to half an hour we were in the courtroom, a judge never appeared. We marched in, signed the papers and then marched out. This process is part of what I call the "assembly line to conviction."

Before the public defender intern got me to sign the paperwork, a young man I had spoken to during my arraignment in divisional court approached me and asked if I remembered him. He was Scott Wilkerson, a young attorney and partner of Peter Atwell, the attorney who came to see me at the county jail the Sunday after my arrest. Both were working out of the office of a well-known St. Louis criminal defense attorney, Joseph Myers. These two young men were soliciting (also known as "ambulance chasing") to sign on to my case from the beginning. I was sure it was to gain public notoriety, but at this point I had to weigh my options. They boasted of resources and of being connected to Joseph Myers in order to make their services sound more appealing.

When Scott approached me at the circuit arraignment he said, "You don't have a lawyer yet."

I said, "No, I have a public defender."

He smirked and said, "You need proper representation in this case."

I told him I had not been able to raise the money to do so.

"We aren't worried about getting any money," Scott said.

He later admitted he was in it for the publicity and for the experience, in that order. At the time I was told he and Mr. Atwell and Atwell's wife felt sorry for me and wanted to help. Out of the kindness of their hearts they wanted to represent me. I was desperate for my cause to get some attention. I was inexperienced and vulnerable. I was somewhat skeptical, but I believed him since he seemed so genuine.

Scott Wilkerson asked if he and his partner could represent me. I thought, *What the hell?* I agreed to it and I thanked him. He said he had to go call his partner, Atwell, and check with him. He returned from the lobby a few minutes later telling me they agreed to take on my case. Little did I know then, Atwell had already declared himself my attorney.

Scott had me sign the not guilty plea, then he signed it as representing me. He went to the clerk and entered Peter Atwell as the attorney of record in my case. I would not know Scott Wilkerson's name was not listed in the court docket for many months. This played an enormous role as the trial date approached.

Leaving the courtroom that day, I felt some (okay, a lot) of relief thinking two hungry, aggressive, young attorneys backed by a well-known firm represented me. "Hungry" was the word Scott Wilkerson used.

***

The Christmas season of 2008 fast approached and I had been under a lot of stress for weeks. The heartache of being away from my children at Christmastime was immense. I wanted to believe I'd found real help. I trusted and leaned on God, but my faith in the justice system rapidly decreased in the weeks and months ahead.

On December 31, 2008, the federal government indicted me on twelve counts of robbery of a financial institution (bank robbery). Scott Wilkerson informed me of this on January 2, 2009. This was by no means a shock. I knew it was coming eventually. During our conversation, Scott said he would not be able to represent me in federal court because he was not licensed to practice in federal cases. Peter was, but he was newly certified, so I was advised to seek someone with more experience in federal court; Peter had virtually none. Scott agreed to make some calls.

After interviewing several qualified lawyers, Roger called back an attorney who agreed to take the case pro-bono. My relationship with Jerry Nance began. While Scott and Peter were afraid of the federal system, Jerry was not. He was an old war horse of the federal system, a former federal assistant district attorney (a federal prosecutor). Later this became a subject of conflict between us.

I asked Jerry during our first conversation about federal public defenders. According to Jerry, they were very good and were much better than the state public defender system. He said hiring a private attorney would still be better than having a public defender. I agreed to let him represent me in federal court. Looking back, I'm not sure it was better than having a public defender.

If you plead guilty in federal court, the system is very streamlined. I saw any fears Peter had to be unfounded. The federal system is much less cumbersome and less corrupt than the state system. It is more transparent; not as much of a good old boys network as state court is.

Jerry and Scott considered themselves a team. Scott handled the state case and Jerry the federal. Scott came to see me one day in February. The state prosecutors put the state charges on hold "pending the outcome of the federal case." The court docket sheets reflected the continuance of court dates seven times by the state prosecution.

Scott told me if I pled guilty in federal court, the state would have no reason to prosecute me. I would already be sentenced to federal prison time. The state would then refer or drop, their charges against me. Jerry agreed with this prognosis strongly and said we shouldn't worry about the state charges. So, I concentrated my options in federal court and awaited arraignment and a bond hearing.

While waiting for my cases to unfold, I intensely studied state and federal law. I learned about the sentencing guidelines for federal cases, the various sentencing matrices and the jury vs. judge options in state court, using the mobile law library.

In some smaller legal matters in life, I understand having complete trust in your retained attorney. When your life (or many years of it) are on the line, I recommend defendants play an active role in their own defense. We have heard lawyers are untrustworthy. From my own experience, some are and some aren't.

When I became a "jailhouse lawyer" (as the professionals would call it), it created an intense conflict with my attorneys. Looking back, this hurt me in some ways with the state court judge, but overall it was (and still is) an advantage for me. It saved me many years of freedom (and maybe even more to come).

My mother gave me some good advice while growing up that applied to my current situation. During my teen years, I was not doing well in one of my math classes. Mom questioned me about my poor grade and I said to her, "What do I need all that math for? I won't use it. I am going to be wealthy and have an accountant watch over all that."

Her very witty and wise reply was, "Who is going to watch the accountant?" I retained her sage advice and recognized the need to keep an eye on my attorneys.

Chapter Ten

Federal Court

Keith

After I was indicted in federal court in the Eastern District of Missouri, Jerry informed me things would move along swiftly in the federal system; that I was going to plead guilty in the federal proceedings. Jerry had vast experience and a pretty good knowledge of the federal sentencing guidelines. I studied them and was prepared for whatever was to come.

The federal court consisted of three court appearances where I would be handcuffed, shackled and transported from the St. Louis County Jail in Clayton, Missouri, which also serves as a federal holdover facility, to the Eastern District of Missouri Federal Courts are located in the Federal Building in down-town St. Louis.

Court appearances were via custody writ with the United States Marshal Service, lasting the entire day. The time spent in federal custody has some bright spots. Being transported was a chance to get out of the jail for a van ride. Although I never got to set foot on "outside" ground (the vans were parked in secured, sealed sally ports at each location), it was nice to ride the familiar streets. The van windows were cracked to let in much welcomed fresh air. The lunch served at the federal building in the holding tank was much better food than in the jail. Boxed lunches prepared by an outside vendor or a cafeteria were a welcome change from jail food. Finally, I relaxed, somewhat, since the federal system was spelled out clearly with no surprises. No doubts about what was going to happen clouded my fears.

The professionalism of the federal courts was refreshing. Between my conversations with Jerry and talking with other inmates who had been through the system and the knowledge I gained through self-education, I knew exactly how things were going to proceed, what was likely and what the worst case scenario results were.

The process had a few negatives, though. Spending the entire day in a holding tank and van was not enjoyable. I was with five to ten other inmates from various counties from 6:00 A.M. until 5:00 P.M. I understood what would happen at the proceedings, but there was still lots of anxiety. It is impossible to be stress-free in court.

The entire process in federal court lasted only seven and a half months, including three trips to federal court. One continuance was agreed upon by both parties. The process would not have been much longer even if there had been a trial. The federal system moves quickly.

The first proceeding in federal court was two-fold in purpose. The first plea (not guilty) was entered and a bond hearing was held. This appearance took place before a federal magistrate. My handcuffs were removed when Jerry and I went before the judge.

Present at the first federal hearing were Roger, Elise and Marissa. Someone else was present in the courtroom that day and at every other proceeding to come. Mystery Lady. She was not one of the tellers, but she may have been an employee of one of the banks. Maybe she was a victim of a bank robbery herself in the past. I am not sure who she was or what exactly her role was, but I assume she was some type of advocate for the tellers. No one knew who Mystery Lady was. She always sat with the tellers, but she was neither a reporter nor a lawyer. She would sit and stare at the proceedings and at me. Whoever she was, Mystery Lady made it clear she had a hatred of me.

Jerry and I approached the podium in the courtroom. The magistrate, Judge Stewart, entered through a door in the rear of the courtroom and sat at the bench. She read the charges against me in their entirety to us and the Assistant United States District Attorney, Montgomery, who was present. She asked if I had an attorney present and Jerry introduced himself. When asked how I was going to plead I said, "Not guilty, Your Honor."

We moved to the bond hearing. If charged with a crime, as Americans we are innocent until proven guilty and we have a right to a reasonable bond. That's what the Constitution says. Well, those rights are not in practice. In many ways, the Constitution of the United States of America has lived and breathed itself to death.

The morning of the plea and bond hearing in federal court I was interviewed without counsel. Jerry did not feel it necessary to be there. The interview was conducted by a federal probation and parole officer to see if I was fit to be granted a bond. I thought the interview went well.

That afternoon, the bond hearing commenced. The magistrate read the charges against me and I entered a plea of not guilty. Jerry argued the reasons I should be granted bond. The only two reasons a defendant can be denied bond are if he is a threat to the community or a flight risk. I had no prior record and no violence was committed during the robberies, proving I was no threat to the community. Jerry argued I was not a flight risk because I had ties to the community (close family members, children to provide for and a home to live in) and had no history of jumping bail in the past.

The 6th Amendment of the Constitution says a man's bond is his word he will show to answer charges. I had no history of breaking my word. Roger was there to provide titles to real estate he would use to secure my presence and Elise was there with my passport to surrender to the court so I could not leave the country. I was willing to wear a G.P.S. ankle bracelet so I could only leave my home during hours I worked. To disobey would mean bond revocation.

The parole officer recommended I be held without bond. Suddenly, it would have been a good idea to have my attorney at the interview. The magistrate asked the U.S. Attorney, John Clarkson, for his argument against my release on bond. Clarkson's argument was based entirely on me being a flight risk. He argued that I was a "master of disguise" and since they had no idea of my financial situation at this point, I was a high risk for flight. He brought up that the State of Missouri was holding me pending the posting of a $100,000 cash only bond. Clarkson said even if Judge Stewart granted the bond, the state would continue to hold me anyway.

Judge Stewart's decision was quite surprising to all the parties. In light of the U.S. Attorney's comments, if I was able to post bond pending trial by the state, she would hold another hearing and strongly consider honoring the state bond. If that happened, she would release me until the federal case was resolved.

In a sense, she had hammered the ball into the state court. A U.S. Marshal put me back into handcuffs as Judge Stewart was closing the hearing. Jerry spoke briefly to me saying, "I have a plan. Now we go to the state." He would inform my girls and Roger of his plan and be in contact with me. Jerry was off to the St. Louis County Courthouse where he and Scott would set up a bond hearing. Jerry acted as though the situation was promising. He sure made me feel that way. I was very hopeful.

Scott Wilkerson and Jerry Nance set up an in-chambers conference with the judge presiding over the state charges early the next week. Armed with what the federal magistrate said, Jerry thought it was advantageous to us. If the federal court was willing to allow my release, maybe the state would choose to not get in the way.

We sought the state court to grant a lien of property bond. In lieu of the $100,000 cash only bond, we hoped they would accept $100,000 of appraised property that was free and clear and within St. Louis County. Roger owned three homes in the county. Their value combined was well over the $100,000 requirement. The practice is common and this type of bond reduction is used in St. Louis County and in courts throughout the country.

On the scheduled date of the hearing, I was very anxious, as were Roger and the girls. Roger was all set to bring deeds to the courthouse to post the bond. All day, time seemed to stand still.

I talked to a couple of inmates at the jail who had been to court, asking if they saw my attorneys anywhere. One of them said they saw a younger guy and an older man running around from room to room in the courthouse. These men looked like they were on a mission. He described them in more detail and I knew he was talking about Scott and Jerry.

At this point, Jerry and Scott were working hard for me to be released on bond. It was not so I could make arrangements before I went to prison. It was not so I could spend some time with my girls before I had to leave. More importantly to them, when I was released they could pose in front of cameras and news reporters as my attorneys telling of their great accomplishment. I would be good for future business. Whom they were working so hard for was questionable, as became apparent in future court proceedings.

The prospect of my release on bond, parading in front of cameras, was also a concern of the court and of the St. Louis County Prosecuting Attorney's Office. They did not want to see me out. They wanted me behind bars. If I was in jail, it made them look better and it made me look even guiltier. The state prosecution would object and put up a defense against this proposal.

When Jerry and Scott came to see me later that afternoon, I could tell they had bad news. When they explained what happened and how close we came, it made the news even harder to take. The judge presiding over the case in Division 10 was out due to illness, so Jerry and Scott ran from judge to judge trying to get one to hear our case for release. One very liberal judge, McElroy, was set to sign the order. He believed the federal magistrate's position sounded reasonable and I could be released as long as I wore a G.P.S., but the prosecutor's office had gotten wind of what was happening and called the Chief Judge in the county. While Jerry and Scott were still in chambers, Judge McElroy received a call from Chief Judge Harrison. He overruled McElroy and squashed the bond reduction. That's the story I got from Jerry and Scott.

It was back to square one. We would try again. We had one more chance. The sitting judge in my case would be back from leave. We would try again a couple of weeks later.

Bond needed to happen quickly. Time with Marissa and Elise was at a premium since the federal case against me would move rapidly. We were looking at six months at the most before I was sentenced to a term in federal prison. I was eventually going to plead guilty, pending a plea agreement. Too much evidence was against me to fight the case and risk a stiff sentence in federal court. If getting a bond reduction in state court dragged on too long, it would be worthless to be granted bond in the state court. Soon I would be going to federal prison.

While there are set sentencing guidelines, federal judges have the right to depart upwardly from those guidelines if a case goes to trial and the defendant loses. They can also run sentences consecutively. In my twelve cases, by statute, a federal judge could have sentenced me to 240 years in prison. Twenty years for each count, run consecutively, if I was unreasonable and lost at trial. It was highly unlikely a sentence that long would be handed down, but it was possible. I would have lost in a trial. I was guilty, so I planned on a plea agreement.

Jerry thought the judge in Division 10 of the circuit court, Judge Davis, was "a reasonable person." He was not, to put it nicely. When Jerry made a last attempt to convince him to reduce the bond and let me out pending trial, it was a slim chance…but still a chance. In early 2009, Jerry decided to make this last ditch effort.

In the early evening, after this meeting with Judge Davis, Scott came to see me. I wasn't at the meeting. I was hopeful. I am a positive thinker. Those hopes were dashed by the news. Jerry and Scott made the same case for my release as they did to Judge McElroy. We were turned down this time. The judge said, "Hell, if I were facing thirty years or life in prison, I would run." He said this while leaning back in his chair, laughing.

Judge Davis wasn't me. I *was not* going to run and I was angry he made that assumption about me. His assumption cost me dearly. This was my life, not some hypothetical situation. Davis considered me a flight risk, even though I had no history of being one. He simply didn't want to be the judge facing the cameras, admitting he let me out on bond. He would have angered the prosecuting attorney's office.

Davis might have faced criticism from his peers. He wouldn't gain anything by letting me have bond.

I expressed my thanks to Scott. "Thank Jerry. He did all the work in there. He fought like a bear for you. He was a beast," Scott said. I wasn't present, so I could only hope what he said was true.

I was devastated. I would get no time with Elise and Marissa before going to prison. Defendants are often released on bond if they are not a threat to the public or an obvious flight risk. In some counties, states and federal courts, even if everyone knows guilt is apparent, bond is granted. It is our right as citizens.

Chapter Eleven

Let's Make a Deal

Keith

After realizing a fair and affordable bond from the state was out of the question, it was time to concentrate on a plea agreement with the Federal District Attorney. Jerry was in contact with the Federal Assistant District Attorney assigned to the case, Charles Montgomery. Those negotiations moved forward at a faster pace during the winter months of early 2009.

The federal guidelines for sentencing in my case called for seventy to eight-one months of imprisonment. Guidelines were based upon several factors. One was criminal history. I was on the very lowest end of the scale since I had no previous history of convictions. Being a first-time offender was a huge plus when dealing with the federal guidelines. The months of imprisonment accelerated rapidly with each prior conviction. On the other side of the matrix, the severity of the crime is taken into consideration.

Guidelines are based on a point value system. Points are added to the base points of the crime. The point base for robbery of a financial institution is eighteen. Points can be added for brandishing a firearm or other weapon and more are added for discharging the weapon. Those issues were of no concern in my case, other things were. Points can be added based on how many robberies occurred and if there was more than ten thousand dollars taken in any of the robberies. There were several in my case in which over ten thousand dollars had been taken. If there was evidence that any teller felt threatened there were points added, which became the only sticking point in the bargaining of a plea. Montgomery wanted a total of twenty-three points: the eighteen base points, two points for multiple occurrences, two points for bank employees feeling threatened and one point for over ten thousand dollars being taken in any single robbery.

Taking one finger from the top (the criminal history side) and one from the left side of the matrix (the severity of crime side), one's finger would meet at seventy to eighty-one months. That is the range in which the judge could sentence me upon agreement. It's fairly cut and dry. If the scenario was different, (say if I robbed one bank and took less than ten thousand dollars as a first-time offender) the sentencing guidelines would have been twenty-four to thirty-six months.

Actually, there were two sticking points to the plea agreement. One was the two points assigned for fear of harm to the tellers. The second was, upon reading the draft of the agreement, I noticed the language stated I committed the robberies using violence, intimidation and fear. I had problems with the wording.

While all of this was being negotiated, I continued to study how the state charges could unfold. My attorneys kept telling me they weren't concerned about the state charges. Scott and Jerry had differences of opinion on this, but Scott was kind of on the sidelines at this point. Off and on throughout the next year and a half I got mixed signals and messages on this subject. Meanwhile, the state kept continuing court dates "pending outcome of federal case." I had to cover all bases. I felt the need to protect myself. Those feelings were well-founded.

When covering my bases, my concern was the language in the federal plea. It included the words "fear" and "violence." Knowing the state could use my federal plea against me in a trial if they proceeded to prosecute me, I did not want those words used. I wasn't concerned with the added six to eight months those words would give me in federal prison. If I agreed to those terms, robbery in the first degree would be a slam dunk for the state prosecutor in front of a jury. I was told it was boilerplate language in bank robbery pleas. Maybe it was, but I was not going to admit to committing violence. There was no violence involved in these robberies. Everyone knew it. I would stick to my guns, so to speak.

During a meeting with Jerry on this subject, he became angry with my persistence. If I planned on taking this case to trial, I would have to find a new attorney, he said. He would withdraw. I had no plans of going to trial with the feds on this. My concerns were pleading to something I didn't do. Jerry agreed talk to the District Attorney, Matthew Reich and see what he might do about the language in the plea. I asked Jerry if we could use the state case as a bargaining tool. I requested that the D.A. convince St. Louis County to drop the charges against me and I would agree to the language as is. Jerry said it was a good idea. He would try.

Reich made a compromise. After Jerry presented this idea to him, Reich said he talked with the state prosecutor, Charles Montgomery. They were not going to drop the charges. He could not make them do so. What Reich would agree to was something he had never done before. He was willing to leave the word "violence" out of the agreement. As far as the word "fear" went, Reich would have the tellers come to the hearing and testify as to whether they were in fear or not at sentencing. That is, if Judge Stewart would agree to it. The judge could decide if the other two points should be added and whether the word "fear" would stay in or not. Judge Stewart agreed to this. We were set to reach an agreement I thought was reasonable. The word "violence" was gone.

While Jerry's defense of me had many shortcomings, in this one instance in the federal case, he did a good job. I think he surprised himself. In reality, though, I had to push him to ask for something completely logical to me. If I hadn't stood my ground, he wouldn't have asked for it. Jerry didn't think D.A. Reich would agree to it. He would not have done it when he was a federal prosecutor, he said. I started to get the feeling he was sorry he wasn't a prosecutor any longer. I also began to get the feeling he didn't mind seeing me get time in prison for these crimes.

Jerry often talked about his days as a prosecutor, as well as of me going to prison. In fact, I had to ask him one time to quit talking about me being in prison. I also asked him why he never even mentioned probation for me. Probation was a long shot in the federal case, but he never even proposed it and it made me angry. He accepted a lengthy prison sentence was in my future and he'd forgotten he wasn't hired to accept that. He was hired to fight for me in every way he could.

I flat out asked him, "You still wish you were a prosecutor, don't you?"

He said, "Yes, I do!"

I had him hooked into the conversation and I wanted to see how much of his personal feelings he would be willing to divulge. During our talk, he made it clear what his true feelings were.

Jerry said, "I loved prosecuting them to the fullest!" So, there it was out in the open. My "defender" really viewed the world as a "prosecutor."

I became alarmed. I said, "I feel like you want me prosecuted for these crimes."

He said, "Well, you are guilty, but I promise you I will do everything I can for you." His mind was in it and the need to do so was there, but I could tell his heart was not.

I became skeptical. Rightfully so. I later learned Jerry told Roger Pettinelli in a phone conversation he didn't like bank robbers. Jerry had left the prosecutor's office, but the prosecutor had never left Jerry.

When I asked Jerry how he parted with the federal government as his employer, to his credit he was honest with me. He was let go and lost his right to practice law for a period of time. He could never practice as a prosecutor again. It was an old wound opened up, but he felt the need to tell me.

Jerry became romantically and physically involved with one of the defendants in a case he was prosecuting, and it cost him dearly. At that moment, I didn't stop to think of the *personal* toll it took on him, although now I realize it must have been very difficult. My immediate concern was the *professional* toll it took on him. I had to keep my ongoing interest in mind and consider how this could affect my case. How did Jerry's past influence his willingness and ability to give me a proper defense?

I previously thought Jerry had connections and was well-respected within the system. That had just gone out the window. Most likely people in the federal system had sympathy for Jerry and wanted him to continue to practice law. I was just not sure that sympathy was going to help my cause. I had to weigh everything at this point. He offered to withdraw from the case.

Chapter Twelve

Fear versus Character

Keith

The next visit to the Federal Court Building was for a change of plea hearing. My plea changed from not guilty to guilty. We informed Judge Stewart the prosecution and defense had reached an agreement on the terms of sentencing, if it was agreeable to the court.

This appearance went quickly. The charges were read to me in open court once again by Judge Stewart. Afterward, she asked how I pled to the charges. I entered a plea of guilty, on the record, before the court. The judge set a sentencing date of August 13, 2009 and court was adjourned.

Judge Stewart was aware of the sticking point of the agreement, the violence and fear phrase. The prosecution agreed no violence had taken place in these crimes. The fear of the tellers was still at issue. Reich had no problem bringing the tellers in at sentencing to testify to their fear. I agreed to that.

We would have to use their original statements given to police immediately following the robberies. Those statements were somewhat mixed and sketchy. Most of the tellers in the outset of their statements said they were not in fear; said I was calm and polite during the robberies. Then, late in their statements, some of the tellers said they were somewhat fearful. It appeared as though they were coached through the interview until the police detectives got what they wanted.

In preparation for the sentencing hearing, some questions need to be decided. Did we want the tellers on the stand verbally stating their fear? Was Jerry willing to drill them about their original statements? Was it worth six to eight fewer months or possibly six to eight more months in prison? How would their testimony sway the judge? If at all? These were things we needed to think about in the next couple of months. Jerry was willing to question them about their statements.

We needed to put together a list of character witnesses to testify on my behalf. Character witnesses showed I had family and friends in my corner. It may not reduce the sentence since pre-determined guidelines were followed, but it would prevent the prosecution from getting a sentence on the upper end of the guideline range. It prevented, perhaps, an upward departure from the guidelines that Reich could ask for. It was better to have allies in court to speak to my good character.

Jerry voiced it was best to call no more than three character witnesses. As it turned out, three were available and perfect for the task: Roger Pettinelli, my lifelong friend, my daughter, Marissa and my high school hockey coach, Jeff Parker, whom I had stayed in contact with until the present time. I had a solid team of witnesses. The plea agreement was worked out and the witnesses had been chosen. Everything was set on our end for my defense.

Judge Stewart had three things to determine of her own accord. First, if the tellers were in fear or not and whether or not the word "fear" should be included in the agreement and final judgment. Second, how much time would I serve for supervised release, the federal equivalent of parole. Unlike state courts in which parole is the remainder of the total sentence, in federal court it is a one-to five-year term determined by the judge upon sentencing. Thirdly, restitution would be considered. Would I have to pay the banks back the money taken during the robberies?

My last trip to the federal courthouse was to be sentenced for twelve bank robberies. Even though an agreement was made, I have to admit, I was nervous. Anyone would be.

The first step was an interview with another probation and parole officer at about 8:00 A.M. The interview was a formality since an agreement was already made. The lady interviewing me was kind and professional. Again, Jerry saw no need to be there. He believed I would do well on my own. If I was the attorney, I would be there to support my client. An attorney should want to make sure nothing caused an upward departure in the sentencing agreement. I had already been burned in the bond hearing by his absence. Jerry chose not to be there.

The probation and parole officer gives a recommendation to the judge before sentencing, but in most cases they are not compelled to depart from the guidelines in their recommendation. Normally, sentences aren't lengthened; only if something found in the interview warrants a deviation from the agreement will they suggest either an upward or downward adjustment.

The interview consisted of questions about my past: childhood, education, family members, marriage, children, job history and what kind of support I had from family and friends. Questions about hobbies, sports I liked to play and possible career plans I had were asked. I had to answer some questions on a scale of one to five, telling whether I liked, disliked, felt strongly or not so strongly, about a series of items. The interview was over an hour long and was recorded on the probation and parole officer's laptop.

Afterward, I went back into the holding tank with the other prisoners. Since my sentencing was in the early afternoon, it was going to be a long day. The other prisoners held with me were in various stages of proceedings in their cases; some were about to be sentenced or arraigned, others were pleading and some were in court on parole violations.

Of all of the people sentenced that morning, I don't remember any of them getting any more or any less time than their guidelines called for in their plea agreement. Although, I vividly remember one man who was sentenced that morning by the same judge I was going before. He was sentenced to life (360 months) in federal prison. For a time, I had been in the same wing of the St. Louis County Jail as he was housed. His name was Clarence Woods. He took the case to trial and was found guilty by a jury of conspiracy to distribute rather large amounts of cocaine.

Upon returning to the holding tank, Woods remembered me and my case. He encouraged and reassured me, saying Judge Stewart would certainly stay within the guidelines spelled out in the agreement because of my lack of criminal history. Woods was also realistic. He believed a downward departure from the guidelines would never happen. Woods was not fond of Judge Stewart because of his dealings with her. Of course, our cases were completely different. I took responsibility for my actions by pleading guilty. Taking that responsibility weighs heavily with the federal court. Whether this man was guilty or not, I don't know. I only heard his side of the story and hadn't seen any of the evidence. Maybe he felt he had to fight for his innocence.

I will say this for Woods, he did have a fairly light criminal history. He knew the ropes of the judicial system and took his harsh sentence like a man. He had a wife named Doreen and two young children who strongly stood by him. He admitted, in spite of his outward reaction, he was torn up and crushed on the inside. Woods and Doreen had a nice home, she had a good job in the medical field and they had their children. It was hard not to feel for someone whose mistakes would keep them in prison for life. His devoted wife and children must go on with their lives without him. I couldn't help but think of Elise and Marissa and the length of time we would be apart.

I am an optimist and a positive thinker. I clung to the possibility of a downward departure in sentencing. I realized if the judge did so, the prosecutor would balk and appeal the sentence. Reality told me the chances were slim. Even though a lesser sentence or probation wasn't realistic, I believed my attorneys should have fought for it.

Elise was not going to be present at the federal sentencing. She was leaving for college in Wisconsin that week and needed to set up for her freshman classes which began the following Monday. I understood and I was completely supportive of her. It was not comforting that my sister whom she was living with had made the decision for Elise. Supposedly the only two days my sister and brother-in-law could drive Elise to Wisconsin were the same days my sentencing happened. They had a convenient excuse to not be with me themselves. Blood is not always thicker than water.

Elise did write a letter to Judge Stewart explaining why she could not be there, what her circumstances were and how I was a kind and gentle father who provided a good, loving home for her and her sister. She described to Judge Stewart how I provided for their needs, supported them in their activities, was always there for them and that I was the only functioning parent they had. I never saw a copy of the letter and I don't know precisely what it said, but Elise told me a rundown of her letter. I am sure it was well-articulated and compelling.

A friend of mine, Tom Sappington, wrote the judge in support of me as a person, friend and parent. Two more letters were submitted by others. I asked my sisters and one or two other friends to do so. A letter from my sister was nice to have, although going to the courtroom in person to support me would have carried more weight with Judge Stewart than a letter did. Had my sister needed my support, I would have made sure I was there.

After lunch in the holding tank, I was escorted by two federal marshals onto the elevator for the ride up the ten-plus stories to the courtroom. Upon arrival in the hallway leading to the courtroom, I was put into a small holding cage with two other prisoners awaiting hearings in the same courtroom. One went into court before me and one after me. I sat and waited for about a half an hour praying for an outcome we could all live with.

After everyone involved with the case was assembled, I was brought into the courtroom and the handcuffs were removed. Jerry and I sat at a long table on the left side of the courtroom, then Judge Stewart entered and sat at the bench.

She stated the case and case number before her and that we were assembled for sentencing in the case. Judge Stewart asked, on the record, whether or not a plea agreement was reached. Jerry and D.A. Reich said there had been. Judge Stewart stated she was aware of the "fear" issue which held up the agreement.

We were there before the court to render sentence in United States v. D.K. Giammanco. Judge Stewart had read the agreement and the letters she received in support of me, which she added would be taken into account in her decision.

We presented our case first. The first witness to testify on my behalf was my high school hockey coach. Coach Parker was asked by Jerry what kind of a person I was. In his testimony, he said he knew me since I was fourteen- or fifteen-years-old. I had been polite and law-abiding. We played hockey together on a weekly basis during the winter months until I was arrested, showing we had a long-standing relationship. When asked if he knew me to be a violent person, he assured them I wasn't. Even when I played hockey, he referred to me as a "flashy" player and not a violent one. He was stunned by my arrest; that no one on our hockey team could believe I robbed banks. Coach Parker reiterated how my daughters were my world and how I never stopped talking about how wonderful they were.

Roger was next to testify. We had been friends since before I went to high school and grew up in the same neighborhood. We saw each other on nearly a daily basis. Roger mentioned the toll my destructive marriage had on me. He testified to what a non-violent, caring person I am. Like Coach, Roger explained my focus was on caring for my daughters. Furthermore, he made it clear I did a good job raising them.

Marissa was the last to testify. She told what an important part I played in her life. I was the person she went to no matter what her problem was. She discussed the abandonment she and her sister had gone through by their mother and how they saw the divorce as a relief even if they did still wish for the return of their traditional family. Her reconnection with her mother after my arrest was one of the most difficult parts of her testimony to listen to. Marissa told of her own addiction to heroin that resulted from that contact. She was brave to talk about her weaknesses in public and I was proud of her.

I was, of course, very emotional when I heard what Coach, Roger and Marissa said on the stand. Especially Marissa. Even though Coach Parker and Roger told how good of a person I had always been and still was, it was difficult to hear Marissa speak about the hardships of her current life and the difficulties she was having without me at home. Knowing I was the only one she had and now was gone was painful and it's something that tears at my heart to this day.

Chapter Thirteen

Federal Sentencing

Keith

After the testimony, a snap decision was made. Before the prosecution presented their case for a stiffer sentence, when the judge asked if there were any more witnesses, Jerry responded by saying, "No, Your Honor. We rest." Jerry decided not to have the tellers testify. I knew what his reasoning was and I was in agreement with it.

Our character witness testimony was compelling and Jerry and I agreed the testimony of the tellers could possibly do more harm than good. Our contention the tellers were not in fear was dropped right then and there. If an atmosphere of sympathy for me had been created for the judge, we did not want to turn the tide. The chances of a lighter sentence than the guidelines called for was slim, so there was little to gain from the tellers' testimony. We could have lost anything we gained from the testimonies of Coach Parker, Roger and Marissa. All in all, it was a good move for Jerry to not have the tellers take the stand. D.A. Reich had no reason to call the tellers to testify since their statements were on record. They were robbed and in fear, according to the agreement.

My quarrel with Jerry's snap decision was the lack of discussion or input from me. While I agreed with this particular decision, it was a major one and should have been discussed with me beforehand. This shoot-from-the-hip style of Jerry's would continue in the state case against me, with more damaging results.

The prosecution's cross-examination of Coach Parker, Roger and Marissa was short and simple. First, Reich tried to demean my "good guy" character their testimonies had painted. His argument was simple: good guys don't rob banks. Some may agree with that. Some may not. My character witnesses were compelling and they saw me as the good guy I always was. I made mistakes, but by nature, I was a good human being.

Next, Reich questioned my honesty. He claimed I was a liar since I hadn't told anyone else about the robberies. By not telling my loved ones about my crimes, I had lied by omission. This was a weak argument. Obviously, I could not disclose what I was doing to anyone for their own protection. I didn't want them punished for any perceived involvement, so I kept them in the dark. By keeping them unaware of my crimes, it protected them from being guilty of withholding information from law enforcement. When asked, they could honestly say they knew nothing about my crimes. They couldn't be charged with obstruction of justice, nor could they be implicated as an accomplice.

I could not, nor would not, put my family and friends on the spot like that. Nor could I provoke them into making a personal choice of right and wrong. These were my crimes and no one else needed to face punishment for what I was doing. I knew from the start this had to be a solo venture. That didn't make me a liar. That made me a caring father and friend.

My other motivation for not telling anyone about my crimes was purely one of self-preservation. I had to protect myself from arrest. Obviously, I could not risk having anyone turn me in for any reason, especially since there was a reward for information leading to my capture. I couldn't risk being turned in by someone who wasn't as discreet as I had hoped. A slipped remark to someone who wasn't emotionally tied to me could have left me vulnerable. That left me with one option: don't tell anyone. That didn't make me a liar. That made me a realist.

After the prosecution rested, Judge Stewart asked Reich, "What is going on with the state?"

During his final argument, D.A. Reich expressed his personal views on the federal guidelines. The guidelines were way too lenient, too soft on bank robbery. His comments caused Judge Stewart to inquire about the state prosecution. Reich responded he was in constant contact with the state prosecutors in St. Louis County and to his knowledge they had every intention of prosecuting me for these same crimes. She angered at his reply.

The federal and state prosecutors were in collusion to have me serve more prison time. Why else would the Federal Assistant D.A. be in constant contact with the state prosecutors? How would he know what the state's prosecution plans were? By having the state delay proceedings against me until after a federal prosecution, they would accomplish their goal. I was indicted by the state first, so the state prosecution should have been first.

The state planned on prosecuting me using the "dual sovereignty" doctrine, which most of citizens would claim as a double jeopardy violation. Missouri delayed its proceedings time after time so the state trial would be last. By doing so, state prosecutors knew my federal conviction could be used against me. Had I gone to state trial first, the federal government would drop its case against me. The federal government, unlike the State of Missouri, does not convict people a second time. The state and federal prosecutors were well aware of this. An orchestrated plan to prosecute me twice was in the works and the federal prosecutor admitted in court he was aware of their plans. Not only that, he was in favor of them.

All states don't practice dual sovereignty after a federal conviction. Missouri and in particular, the St. Louis County District Attorney, Bob McCulloch, do. Mr. McCulloch made a name for himself in front of the cameras during several high profile cases. Mine, of course, was one. Many people across the country heard of the racially charged shooting in Ferguson, Missouri in 2014. McCulloch was reluctant to prosecute a white police officer who shot an unarmed black youth. High profile cases bring lots of press and attention. Egos and authority can be powerful influences and the St. Louis County District Attorney's Office isn't immune to them. I have no doubt in my mind Bob McCulloch saw the opportunity to bring attention to himself and his office by taking me to trial.

Another piece to their plot was, since I was already in state custody, the Federal Bureau of Prisons could make me serve my federal sentence consecutive to any state sentence handed down. My prison time would be significantly lengthened. Missouri wasn't looking for a conviction. The prosecutor's office was looking for vengeance.

After a lengthy side bar between the judge, Jerry and the prosecutor (during which I assume they discussed the state prosecution), Judge Stewart imposed sentence. She asked if the defense wanted to say anything before she did so. Jerry asked the court to give the lightest sentence she could considering the circumstances and the agreement.

But first I had an apology to make. The remarks that follow come directly out of the court transcript: "Your Honor, first I would like to thank all of those who have offered their support, those who are here in the courtroom today and those who are unable to be here. Next, I would like to offer my most sincere, heartfelt apologies to those whom I have victimized and/or put in fear by my actions: my beautiful daughters, my beautiful mother in her passing, who I have shamed, my two sisters and sister-in-law, all of my remaining family members and all of my friends both past and present. A special apology to the twelve tellers, their co-workers and shareholders of the banks, for I know I have victimized them and put them in great fear that I didn't realize. To the people of St. Louis and St. Charles County, to the people of the State of Missouri and to the people of the United States of America.

"I would also like to thank and apologize to the following for offering or having to take their valuable time to bring this matter to a close: Her Honor, the Court, counsel for the Government, my counsel, Jerry Nance and all the others who do their honorable jobs for the courts. Thank you, Your Honor."

When handing down the sentence, Judge Stewart said she considered all of the letters, testimony and facts. Since she had no idea how the Federal Bureau of Prisons would look at my jail time and since she had no state sentence to run it concurrent to, she guaranteed my sentence would start "today" at the very least. Considering the amount of cash taken and how many robberies there were, she also had to consider the prosecution's case. Her decision split the seventy to eighty-one month guidelines in half. I was sentenced to seventy-six months (six years and four months) in prison with three years of supervised release (parole). I was ordered to pay restitution for all money not recovered from the first eleven robberies, totaling around $105,000.00. All in all, it was a fair sentence for everyone involved.

Transcripts from the proceedings provide these comments from Judge Stewart: "...I have considered the history and characteristics of the defendant, including the fact that he has been a law-abiding citizen his whole life, he has had a difficult personal life, given his ex-wife's addiction and being a single father to his twin daughters, who he apparently was doing a very good job of raising, except for the fact that he was out robbing banks, which of course is not a very good parental behavior, of course, as you recognize. It's a family tragedy for your family.

"I will say, Mr. Giammanco, one of the things, when you made your statement, I have to tell you that I think the things you said in your apology to the people that you have harmed was one of the most appropriate statements I have ever heard a defendant make. You apologized to the right people. You recognized who you hurt, including the bank tellers and their families, the bank owners, the people you put in fear for their lives, as well as your own family and everything else and I think you have truly shown acceptance of responsibility, so I think this sentence is sufficient when you consider all of the factors, including the large number of bank robberies and the large amount, because it's just a lot of bank robberies and a lot of money, so I'm going to impose a sentence of seventy-six months."

Judge Stewart was as kind under the circumstances as her position allowed. After the sentence was handed down, she asked, "Do you wish me to make any recommendations to the Bureau of Prisons about where the defendant might be housed?"

I replied, "Just as close to home as possible and the lowest security possible."

Her humanity was obvious. Judge Stewart said, "What I will recommend is that the Bureau of Prisons house the defendant as close to the St. Louis area as possible within their regulations and that would include they will do the security classification and so within the regulations, obviously I don't know what their security classification is on a case like this and so that would be up to them. In my opinion, you should be eligible for--in my opinion, if I were doing the designation, I would think you would be in the lowest possible security clearance, but the Bureau of Prisons has a system for doing that and it involves a lot of points and different things and they may consider twelve bank robberies to put you in a higher security classification than those of us who actually know all about you and have heard about this would think what you deserve."

The federal court felt the sentence I was given was sufficient for my crimes. Once again Jerry told my daughters and other family members and friends, "I am not worried about the state."

In Jerry's opinion, after the way the federal sentencing went, surely the state would drop its charges against me. I received a pretty stiff federal sentence, was given supervised release and was ordered to pay full restitution to the banks involved. Jerry said it was doubtful Missouri would continue its proceedings, even though Reich said in court he believed the state would continue its case against me. As the days went on, Jerry's confidence was in question. The state was not backing down.

Chapter Fourteen

Pro Bono: You Get What You Pay For

Keith

Following the closure of the federal case, trust in my attorneys quickly deteriorated. Our relationship took a sharp turn for the worse as we prepared for the state proceedings. For all practical purposes, those proceedings came to a standstill for nearly a year while I sat in the St. Louis County Jail. In the twelve months following the federal sentencing, I was called to appear only twice before the state judge prior to the actual trial. What happened between my attorneys and myself, as well as the actions of the court, in the year leading up to the trial were controversial.

It became increasingly clear to me the St. Louis County Prosecuting Attorney was hell-bent on getting second convictions on the seven counts of robbery I committed in that county. I asked my attorneys to take some action. Since Jerry was convinced the case would never go before a state judge and Scott was so inexperienced, neither had taken the proper measures to prepare for a state trial. This was a serious problem.

Several days after the federal sentencing, Jerry visited me at the jail. First he talked about how well the federal process went. Discussion moved to the state case. Jerry would talk to the prosecutor and ask what they planned on doing. He would try to persuade the state to drop the charges in consideration of the federal conviction. I asked him to start filing some pretrial motions, but Jerry said it was a bad idea at the time.

Jerry said, "We don't want to piss them off."

I told him I wanted to do it anyway.

He said, "Okay, I will file any motion you want." He clearly wasn't happy about it. In reality, he never filed any motions on my behalf.

Scott Wilkerson never believed the state would drop the charges. Scott and Jerry had met with the state prosecutor. Scott became much more apprehensive about the case the more apparent it was the state was continuing its prosecution using the dual sovereignty doctrine. Scott feared his own inexperience. It was evident. The state prosecutor, Montgomery, was not even offering a plea agreement.

This was a far cry from Mr. Wilkerson once telling me, "After looking at the case, I might be able to get you probation."

Since it was the first time I had been in trouble, I was a family man, I had no weapon and no one was hurt, Scott was optimistic in the beginning. Now it was late in 2009 and his tune was changing rapidly. Scott's new focus was to make me accept an open (or blind) plea in front of the judge.

A blind plea meant throwing myself on the mercy of the court, pleading guilty and then letting the judge sentence me within the guidelines of the crime. First degree robbery carried a possible sentence of ten-to-thirty years with an 85% mandatory minimum requirement or life with the possibility of parole after twenty-five and a half years. The judge alone would be in control of my sentence. I could be signing my life away with no chance to appeal afterwards. While Scott claimed Judge Perkins, the state judge, had told him this case was a misuse of the Dual Sovereignty Doctrine, I believed I stood a better chance going before a jury. I trusted my peers more than I did a judge who may have an axe to grind.

Jerry tried to get me to go along with a blind plea when the case was in front of Judge Kincaid (who retired before the case was settled). After witnessing strange and erratic sentencing practices in Judge Kincaid's court, I said, "Absolutely not!"

I wasn't going to risk opening the door to a harsher sentence than I could receive with a jury trial. Jerry later agreed with me after witnessing some surprising sentences in Judge Kincaid's court himself. This transpired after the federal proceedings and at that point, Scott was going with the flow. He listened to whatever Jerry thought was best.

Between Thanksgiving and Christmas I talked with Jerry Nance at the jail who agreed to work with Scott on the state case. I think Scott was relieved. Jerry officially entered in the state case in June 2009 to help correlate the bond hearings in state and federal court, at my request. However, Jerry did nothing in regards to fighting or preparing for the state case—no one had.

I only had one more meeting with Jerry until a few weeks before the trial date. It did not go well. When he visited me, he tried to convince me to accept Scott's renewed quest to get me to take a blind plea. Following Judge Kincaid's retirement, the case was transferred to Judge Perkins's court. Things had changed. Now both Jerry and Scott talked about how "fair" the new judge was and how I should go ahead and accept a blind plea offer.

In the coming months, I was hauled into the newly-assigned judge's courtroom several times. Once I saw Judge Perkins appear on the bench. In the courtroom, he was as unpredictable as Judge Kincaid had been, both in mood and sentencing. My own observations (coupled with what other inmates had told me) made a blind plea with Perkins no different than one with Judge Kincaid: a crap shoot.

That late November 2009 meeting with Jerry was the last time I saw him outside the courtroom until two days before the trial. During our meeting, he brought in a laptop with a short piece of video from one of the robberies showing me with my hand in my jacket pocket. He said, "The jury is going to think you have a gun." The truth was, I did not have a gun. I never said I had a gun. I never threatened to use a gun. The jury was going to convict me of first degree robbery, he said.

If there was no plea agreement offered comparable to my federal sentence, I told Jerry, we were going to trial. Furthermore, I would never take a blind plea, ever. I was against pleading twice to the same crimes. Pleading subjected me to double jeopardy and anyone who passed ninth grade civics class knows we are constitutionally protected.

When I told him this, Jerry became angry and said, "I never wanted any part in this state case!"

He continued yelling, raising his voice louder and louder. I remained calm. He kept telling me to think about my kids, saying I did not know what I was doing. He was the one who went to law school, he said. His anger was boiling and he wanted to bully me into accepting a blind plea. It was an easy way for him to wash his hands of it all.

If Jerry did not want to defend me vigorously at the state trial, I told him we had a conflict. I was sure I would do better with a jury than with a blind plea, especially having seen for myself what had happened to other people who entered blind pleas. The jury might choose the lesser charge of second degree robbery. After all, I never had a weapon and I hadn't threatened to use a weapon. I researched these crimes before I committed them. I intentionally made sure I had no element of first degree robbery in my crimes so I would not face a longer prison sentence if caught. The state didn't care what the facts were. The prosecution was going for the highest level of prosecution possible. I needed my lawyers to fight for me.

As I watched his temper flare, and as I considered how Jerry never filed any motions for me, I came to a strong conclusion. I fired him. He agreed to withdraw from the case, leaving me with an inexperienced Scott Wilkerson and an absent Peter Atwell.

Roger contacted Peter Atwell and Scott Wilkerson. Atwell never responded. Scott came to see me a few days later. During his conversation with Roger, Scott said, "You need to tell him to stay out of the law books and to think about his kids. Tell him to plea." Roger told me about this. It was very upsetting. Using my friends and children as tools to force me to make a decision they wanted was downright unprofessional. No, it was sick.

When Scott came to see me, we talked. He had no problem going to trial, but we would lose. Well, I knew that. It was a matter of first or second degree. Since the state could enter my plea of guilty in federal court as evidence to the jury, a guilty verdict was inevitable. My case was poisoned anyway by all of the publicity. The trial would be a sham.

The necessity of filing pretrial motions was pressing for several reasons. One motion asked for dismissal of the case. The second requested withheld evidence. The third kept all appeals (post-trial) intact. Scott agreed to file those motions as instructed. Finally, I wanted all of the state's witnesses deposed. This was standard pre-trial procedure. Scott agreed in the December 2009 meeting.

Scott was going to talk to some of his friends with more experience for advice on how to do this. His fear and inexperience was showing. I was in even more trouble. Time was ticking and my attorneys were either unable or unwilling to present a strong defense for me.

Soon I received letters from Scott. The first few were on the letterhead of the firm he had been associated with throughout, which stated Joseph and Caryn Myers (the firm's senior partners) agreed with Scott. In no uncertain terms, I should *not* take this case to trial. Attorneys around the area told him the motions I requested would do no good. I began to see the firm's best interest was being taken into account, not mine. They took my case pro-bono and while the publicity was good for them, they didn't want to expend the effort nor cost of pursuing a vigorous trial strategy. Knowing this, I filed motions in the court *pro se* (myself) in January 2010.

During a pre-trial conference, a trial date was set for later in January 2010. I was present in the courtroom, but the conference took place in the judge's chambers where I was not able to take part. This non-transparent way of practicing law is commonplace in St. Louis County and across the state of Missouri, allowing for good old boy bargains to be reached without the defendant's input. This conference came about after I started filing motions myself in the court. One of those motions was a request for a speedy trial. I requested Scott and Jerry to file that motion months earlier. My constitutional rights were being violated by the delay and if they wouldn't do anything about it, I had to.

Jerry filed a motion to withdraw from the case which eventually was denied. During the conference, I never saw Jerry other than a glimpse through a doorway into the courtroom. Scott ran back and forth from the judge's chambers to the courtroom to speak with me. He told me things like, "The prosecutor is not going to budge. They won't agree to second degree robbery. I think the judge will go easy on you if you plea. You need to think about what you are doing."

He was still bullying me into taking a blind plea. His letters claimed Judge Perkins promised no more than ten years. A later letter changed it to twenty years. I didn't trust any arrangements he was making with the judge. When asked if he had it in writing, the answer was always "no."

After the third time he came into the courtroom, I told him, "I have told you I am not going to plead guilty twice to the same crime and I will never take a blind plea. I am not scared to invoke my rights, so man-up and go in there and get me a trial date." In order to get my point across, I said this at a volume everyone in the courtroom could hear. I made sure Scott's peers were included in the audience, including both prosecutors and defense counsel for other cases. Heads turned when I spoke.

Scott was angry. He mumbled something to the effect of "Man-up, huh?"

It wasn't my style nor what I wanted to do, but it was quite effective. He finally did one thing I asked him to do that had substance. He came out of the judge's chambers with a trial date of August 13, 2010, a date nearly two years after I was arrested.

Over the next couple of months I received several more letters from Scott in response to letters I wrote requesting the filing of motions and deposition of witnesses. His responses were unprofessional. One, written after midnight, was laced with profanity and scare tactics. It read more like a drunken rant than a professional letter from attorney to client, all in order to get me to plea. I had to ask him officially, on paper, to preserve my rights to appeal in the future based on ineffective assistance of counsel. My so-called counsel had no intention of doing any footwork. They did not prepare a defense nor did any research for my case. Jerry and Scott were convinced I would eventually break and accept a plea.

Scott's response to my request to file motions for the violation of double jeopardy protection, selective prosecution and the violation of my right to a speedy trial were brushed aside. He talked to his buddies and they said my claims were frivolous. Scott asserted he was not required to do what I asked. Furthermore, he said not only would he refuse to file those motions but he would not file any motions on my behalf. I proceeded to file them myself in order to preserve my right to appeal. It was good I did it myself. Doing so made my later appeals possible. If it had been up to Scott, I would have been procedurally barred from appeals in the future. Becoming a "jailhouse lawyer" was all I had going for me.

As far as the depositions, he said it cost money to take them and to file them. If I wanted the depositions, I would have to pay for them. He and Jerry were willing to take the case on for publicity, but they were not interested in actually defending me. In Missouri, the law states a public defender or pro bono defense attorney, must take on all expenses to give a proper defense of their client. Scott volunteered to take my case pro bono and knew I had no resources from the beginning. So much for what he told me at the start, "I'm not worried about money. I just want to give you a proper defense." Apparently, that was a lie.

I noticed the letterhead on Scott's letters changed to Wilkerson Law. He was no longer associated with the larger firm of Myers and Associates, the firm he had boasted of in the beginning. Myers firm had plenty of resources to provide me a vigorous pro bono defense, Scott had bragged. The terms the attorneys parted under were unclear, but I soon found out evidence they were not good.

I had Roger telephone Caryn Myers and ask her to come see me. She did. I was encouraged by our visit. In fact, it gave me hope. First off, she told me Scott Wilkerson "has no idea what he is doing." She was somewhat familiar with my case; was sure it was a second degree robbery. I asked if she was willing to take the case. She then agreed to sign on as my attorney. I thanked her and God. Finally, someone agreed with me and was willing to give me a real defense. Caryn would talk to the judge the next morning or as soon as possible. I was excited. That was the last time I ever heard from Caryn Myers or anyone from that firm.

Scott came and saw me once more prior to the weekend before the trial. It was his last ditch effort to get me to plea. In his letters, he said Judge Perkins promised he would not give me any more than twenty years. I needed to think about my kids, Scott said. He wanted to repeat that to me in person. I told him, once again, we were going to trial; that he needed to prepare. The conversation became heated. When I asked what happened to Caryn, he said this was his case and no one was cutting in.

I then asked him, if the judge was willing to make a commitment of no more than twenty years, why wouldn't he put that on paper? "He's not going to do that!" was his response.

I knew he was lying to me. I could sense it. Judge Perkins never made any promises. When I told him there was no way I was going to enter a blind plea, he said, "You are going to prison for the rest of your life and I will make sure of it!" I calmly told him he was fired and he stormed off.

Chapter Fifteen

The Assembly Line to Conviction

Keith

I could not take Scott's word about Caryn Myers, so I had Roger try to reach her. There was a conference in a couple of days. I was sure my own attorneys were working with the machine to convict me. They even said they would make sure I received a long prison sentence. All because I wanted to invoke my rights and wasn't willing to put my fate in the hands of a judge who gave me no tangible assurances.

The next court appearance took place in the early spring of 2010. The subject addressed was my representation. In reality, it addressed my unwillingness to plead guilty or to let the court have carte blanche in sentencing me.

First, Judge Perkins dealt with Jerry's withdrawal from the case and with Scott's firing. The judge's viewpoints of me, the case and his intentions began to surface publicly at this meeting. He was offended by anyone invoking his or her rights in his courtroom. No matter if those rights were constitutional or legal, he wasn't happy with me insisting I maintain mine. When the issue of Dual Sovereignty came up, he practically spat at me while saying, "You may not think it's fair, but it's the law!" This was a far cry from what Scott had told me after the pre-trial meeting he had with Judge Perkins.

At that time he claimed Perkins believed this case was unconstitutional. Judge Perkins gave no indication of having any sympathy for me or my constitutional rights. I had been smart to go for a jury trial instead of putting my life in the hands of this judge who clearly had it out for me.

As dismal as things looked, there was an element of joy in this court appearance. It was my first chance to speak in open court and on the record. Most of the pre-trial proceedings in this case were behind closed doors between my attorneys, the prosecutors and the judge. For once, I had the chance to have some input.

Judge Perkins asked why I wanted to let my attorneys go. I explained there was a conflict of interest and they weren't doing what I had asked of them. He asked if I had arranged for new counsel. I told him about the interest Caryn Myers took in my case and how she vowed to sign on as my representation.

Judge Perkins asked if Caryn Myers was whom I wanted as my counsel. I said, "Yes, Your Honor, it is."

He wouldn't let Jerry nor Scott be withdrawn until he knew I had representation. He saw no need to appoint me a public defender since I had two "perfectly qualified" attorneys representing me at this time.

I thought, *Qualified was one thing, but willing to give me a vigorous defense and not leave me to the wolves was another.*

I did not protest because I believed Caryn would keep her word, sign onto the case and aggressively defend me. History showed she never did.

Even though Scott was an associate of the Myers law firm, Judge Perkins would not hold the firm responsible for my representation. I believed at the time and still do, they were responsible for representing me. If not technically by law, they had a moral or ethical obligation to do so. They were the source of Wilkerson and Atwell's ambulance chasing. The two boasted of the firm and its resources when pursuing my case and they used the firm's letterhead during correspondence with me. Scott and Peter gave the appearance it was the Myers law firm backing their representation of me.

I held my tongue and didn't immediately attack the judge's decision. Missouri law plainly states a client can release his attorney at any time without having to specify a reason. I didn't need to provide any reason for firing my attorneys, so I was able to accept or deny legal representation from whomever I chose, regardless of what any judge decided. In the months to come, a scramble to find new representation ensued. Meanwhile, I had no contact with Jerry, Scott or Peter. I saw this as a non-issue in the process.

With only a few months left before the trial, I was back to square one searching for an attorney. The first step was for Roger to get in touch with Caryn. When he finally did, she had cooled off. She said after looking at the case closer, she decided to decline. We knew it had something to do with her relationship with Scott. She pledged her support of me and then she dropped me without letting me have forewarning. Had she chosen to change her mind, she could have at the very least let me know. She knew the clock was ticking as my trial approached.

As the search continued, we ran into one roadblock after another. Many lawyers who were so eager to take on the case earlier were disinterested now. We heard many excuses. Some now wanted money (which they were aware I did not have). Others said it was unfair to charge one client and not another. Word had spread through the good ol' boys (and girls) network of attorneys that the judge and the prosecutor had it in for me. It was in everyone's best interest to stay away. It wouldn't look good for anyone who defended me.

Yet another reason was they thought some of the media attention had worn off. Because of this, I decided to do some interviews. I had not spoken to anyone in the media up to this point. By conducting some interviews, I might renew some of the interest attorneys previously had in my case. Sadly, the interviews may have had the opposite effect. In my interviews I was truthful and some attorneys may not have wanted a client who was willing to openly express his opinion about their quality of work.

Some attorneys may not have liked that I was a client actively involved in my case. Scott and Jerry were resistant to this and most likely attorneys didn't want a hands-on approach from the client. It wasn't them facing decades in prison, though, and I wanted input into what was going to happen to me.

Finally, attorneys may have seen it as a lost cause. I already given a guilty plea and was sentenced in federal court. For whatever reason, lawyers were reluctant to take the state case on. We reached stonewall after stonewall and the situation was looking dire.

To this day, I am so thankful to Roger for the hours of footwork he put in trying to get adequate counsel for me. He spent hours and hours on the telephone calling countless attorneys for me.

One young attorney, Steve Lawson, offered to take the case on for $2,500 to cover his expenses. He was recommended to me and I wanted to meet with him. He came to see me at the jail where we had an honest discussion. It was obvious Steve was eager for the exposure, which was perfectly fine with me, and was also willing to take the case to trial. As the interview with him continued, Steve said he had limited trial experience, but he would work hard in preparation. In the state arena, his experience was more than Scott's but less than Jerry's.

This twenty-seven-year-old attorney worked out of office space with a well-known St. Louis area defense attorney. That being said, Steve was candid in telling me he would have no assistance in trying this case nor in his preparation for it. I appreciated his honesty throughout the interview. He was better than what I had and he was eager to please. He also had no loyalty to the system.

I thought the $2,500 was do-able. I told Steve I would get back with him if I was able to pay him. Well, when discussing the prospect with my sister, she said she hated giving attorneys any money. She said that before and never offered any financial assistance for my defense. She, like everyone else, expected to be compensated for her work, but she wasn't willing to pay an attorney for the work he did. She claimed a paid attorney would not be any better than a public defender; that my attorneys didn't seem that bad and would do as good a job as any other. Where on earth had she been? Besides, she said the judge would have to appoint me a public defender and a public defender would do "just fine." Anyone who has ever been represented by the Missouri Public Defender System knows this is not true.

Some of you may be thinking, *What do you expect for free?*

Well, in Missouri defendants are required to sign a contract to pay the system at a later time, subject to wage garnishment and confiscation of Missouri state tax returns. Public defense is not free and it's not effective counsel.

After speaking with my sister, I realized I was unable to raise the relatively small sum of $2,500 to hire Steve or any other attorney for that matter. But, I had a plan. I was sure in light of how things were playing out (and because of the conflict of interest between my attorneys and me), Judge Perkins would not force me to go to trial with my current representation.

Since all prospects were failing in retaining another attorney on my own, I put Roger on an aggressive effort to contact Peter Atwell. Peter was now working in the Kansas City area according to Scott who told us he had no contact information for Peter, which I found hard to believe.

Scott's story became harder to believe when he said Peter was now representing low-income people in federal court in Missouri's Western District after moving there with his girl-friend. Hadn't he told me it was at the pleading of his wife Peter first wanted to take my case? Had he ever been married? Was that a story he told me to get my case? If Scott had no contact with Peter, how did he know so many details?

Over the next two-plus months we had no luck in contacting Atwell. It appeared he had abandoned the case which is un-lawful. He, after all, had placed himself as my attorney of record after the first time I spoke to him; made himself my attorney of record without my consent a few years before, but now he walked away without a trace.

For the better part of three months I sat in the county jail awaiting trial without contact from any of the three lawyers so eager to represent me in the beginning. Late in the at-tempts to contact Peter, Scott said Peter was withdrawing from the case. I knew under Missouri law an attorney could not withdraw from a case without contacting the client first. I figured the judge would follow the law. Besides, he did not let Jerry withdraw even with my knowledge and consent. Remember, Judge Perkins did not follow the law in my at-tempts to fire Scott, so who knew?

As the trial date approached, I planned on going into the courtroom with no representation. With no counsel, there would be no trial on that date...or so I thought. The judge would continue the case and appoint me new counsel, right?

On the day before the trial, the jailer said I had an attorney visit. Scott and Jerry had shown up. I asked what they were doing there and they said they were there to prepare for trial (after twenty-three months). Jerry was dressed in golf attire and Scott looked like he was dressed to go hiking in the mountains. Neither had even a note pad or laptop. They had never read the complete discovery of my case, so I asked why they had the sudden urge to prepare for trial now. I told them there would be no trial tomorrow, they were not my attorneys and I had nothing more to say to them.

They gave one last ditch effort to get me to enter a blind plea before I told them, "There is no fucking way; I want nothing to do with you!"

At that point, they told me the judge was not going to let them withdraw nor let me fire them. They stormed out of the visiting room. The entire exchange lasted five or ten minutes at most.

They had smirks on their faces from the moment they had arrived in the visiting booth. They had met with Judge Perkins and knew I was getting railroaded into a trial the next day. They, along with the judge, were going to be major players. Everything about it was sinister. I hoped and prayed the judge would do the right thing and follow the law, but they had a plan already in the works.

Chapter Sixteen

The State of Missouri versus Giammanco

Keith

Why I would take this case to trial? Well, I felt I had to. For one, I did not believe I committed first degree robbery. Those charges were for people using or threatening a weapon. I did neither. Robbery without a weapon constituted second degree robbery and that crime carried a much smaller sentence.

Secondly, the jury had the right to nullify. If any juror believed the trial was conducted in error (for example, it violated someone's right to freedom from double jeopardy), he or she had the right to nullify it. Most people don't know jury nullification is an option and the State of Missouri definitely doesn't include it in the jury instructions.

Thirdly, I had the right to a trial by a jury of my peers and there shouldn't be any ramifications for doing so. From what I saw of the state judges I dealt with, I didn't trust my life to one of them. I would rather take my chances with a jury of my peers. There were no guarantees, but at least I had a fighting chance.

I had to go to trial to preserve my appellate rights. If I pled guilty in state court, I could not appeal my case later. I would be stuck with whatever the judge gave me in a blind plea. That didn't sound like a good idea to me.

Finally, there was one more, altruistic, reason. I took this case to trial for all Americans and Missourians, not just for me. The trial that followed was an injustice for all of us. I was prosecuted for the same crimes twice, which is a clear violation of our Constitutional rights as intended by the founders of this country. It doesn't matter what doctrine Missouri wants to use as its hatchet. The fact is, the Constitution says we are free from double jeopardy.

I was almost certain to lose in court. I already pled guilty in federal court and it would be a slam dunk for the St. Louis County Prosecutor. I was facing more prison time in Missouri whether I took a blind plea or whether I went to trial. Someone had to stand up for Constitutional rights. I knew it was a risk. A jury could sentence me to life, but I believed, rightfully, my peers would not be as vindictive as the judge was. I was willing to take the chance. I would do it again. I'm even more determined now after what came to be in the trial.

Surprisingly, I slept well the night before the trial. I wasn't nervous that morning as I awoke. Maybe I had been through so much and had felt anxiousness for so long I was numb to it. Plus, I still did not believe there would be a trial that day. I had no willing or reliable counsel.

I was allowed to shave the night before which is customary for most county jails ahead of a court appearance. I wore my hair in a ponytail, not because it was my usual style, but because I saw too many men come out of the jail barbershop bleeding. I refused to get my hair cut the entire time I was in jail for that reason. I was not overly concerned about my appearance since a trial was unlikely.

At about 7:00 A.M., I was taken to the holding tank on the ground floor of the jail. I was with other inmates who had court appearances that morning. Some in the group were experienced in the court system. Given the ongoing conflict with my counsel, everyone agreed the court would have to continue my case.

As we settled into the courtroom, Scott sat at the counsel table with an angry look about him. I was seated next to him wearing my county jail brown uniform. I also wore leg shackles and handcuffs. Scott told me Jerry was on the way to the courthouse. The prosecution team was stirring about.

Scott told me, once again, I should plead guilty in this case.

I said, "You are not my attorney any longer."

He said, "I talked with the judge this morning and tried to withdraw from the case. Judge Perkins will be out to address us shortly." I assumed it would be on the record which was a rarity.

Judge Perkins came into the courtroom just as Jerry did through the same back entrance. Jerry walked in just before the judge. As the court recorder took his seat, Judge Perkins stepped to the bench and sat once the standard "all rise" had taken place.

I asked the judge, "May I address the court?" He said I may. I explained I was not properly prepared for trial. My attorneys were unprepared. When asked if I had obtained new counsel, I had to tell him that I hadn't. I explained about Scott's threat to make sure I spent the rest of my life in prison. The judge flatly denied a continuation.

What happened next was a railroad. I moved the court let me release my attorneys and asked Judge Perkins continue the case until he either appointed or I obtained new counsel. He denied my motion saying it was untimely, citing the State

v. Black as precedent. I told him the trial was an unfair sham. He wouldn't let me fire my attorneys, even at their request, and he *wouldn't* postpone the trial. His demeanor showed he already knew what would to happen to me.

When I asked about Peter Atwell's absence, given he was the attorney of record in my case, Judge Perkins said he received a request to withdraw from Peter Atwell a few days prior. Jerry and Scott would not be removed, but since Atwell had little-to-no involvement in the case he was granting his withdrawal. In no uncertain terms, there would be a trial that day whether we were prepared or not. Judge Perkins was determined to ramrod me through a sham trial without proper defense.

This so-called 'fair judge' was working along with my own attorneys to make sure I received a hefty state prison sentence. I bucked the system by invoking my rights. I expected a proper and vigorous defense. What I was getting was anything but that. No impartial justice was found in that court.

Even before the case was reassigned to Judge Perkins's courtroom, I asked Scott and Jerry to file for a change of venue. At first, this was because of the extensive local media coverage my case received. A change of venue meant more travel and expense for them, so they failed to request one. I later asked for a change of venue out of Judge Perkins's courtroom. They failed to do as I asked once again. Scott told me Perkins wasn't happy with me because I refused the blind plea. Based on that, I thought a change of venue to a neutral court seemed like a good idea.

When I studied change of venue law, I discovered a defendant only had ten days to file a request whether to a different county or to a different courtroom. Of course, Scott and Jerry knew this and knowingly let that time lapse. When I began filing motions myself, I didn't even bother filing one for a change of venue. I knew it would be untimely. Unless the judge removed himself, I was stuck. In court, I asked Judge Perkins to remove himself from the case because he was personally biased against me. He denied it, seething and angry.

Next, was the issue of my apparel. The judge asked why I was not in street clothes. Jerry and I discussed this a few moments before. I asked Jerry (if there a trial took place) could I get some clothes from home. Jerry said it looked better for me to be in my jail uniform since it showed I was already serving time for these crimes. Judge Perkins demanded I was taken downstairs and put in street clothes. A family member couldn't bring my own clothes, Jerry said, because there wasn't enough time. Instead, I was taken down to the dressing area where donated clothes were stored. The only ones I could find were ill-fitting. I did not look presentable for trial.

Maybe by now I should have been getting nervous. I may have been except I was so angry. All I could think of was how I could defend myself. I was going to get very little defense from anyone else. My attorney vowed to send me away to prison for a long time and I was sure the judge had it out for me. It was important I keep my wits about me.

In the dressing room, a locking leg brace was put on my right leg under my pants. Defendants don't wear cuffs or shackles at trial. The brace is designed to lock at the knee in the event a defendant makes a break for it. A button on the outside could be pushed in case it locked on me, which it did several times during the proceedings. It was awkward to walk in and it was obvious to everyone I was not walking correctly.

The change of clothes and the leg brace were not an asset for me in my defense. If the jury saw me in visible restraints or in my brown uniform, they might realize my double jeopardy rights were violated. One of the first things the prosecutor, Charles Montgomery, asked me when I was on the stand was if I had any physical disabilities because everyone in the courtroom could tell I couldn't walk normally. The hidden leg brace gave the impression I received a fair bail and was not jailed.

One unexpected sentimental encounter occurred in the dressing area. The clerk distributing the clothes asked me if I used to work at a particular company. I had. He asked me if I knew Georgie. He then told me Georgie was his brother-in-law. I then knew who the clerk was and let him know Georgie spoke highly of him. I remembered his name was Lou. I asked him to tell Georgie hello for me, and he said he would. Lou then wished me luck.

He was sincere. I could tell. I knew from past conversations with Georgie that his brother-in-law worked at the jail, but over the years I had forgotten it. Once we got to talking, I couldn't believe I spent nearly two years at the jail without it ever crossing my mind.

This exchange brought back good memories for me. Georgie and I worked together in the printing industry. He became a good friend. We even worked together on the same press for a while. One time, I attended a NASCAR race with Georgie who was a big fan, and then another different race in Indianapolis. Used tires from cars were selling for twenty dollars. I bought a couple, including one off Dale Earnhardt Sr.'s car. Georgie had to have it when I told him. I offered it to him for free. He took it, but insisted on paying the twenty dollars. He then gave it to Lou, an Earnhardt fan. At this time of high stress, it was helpful to have warm memories to think about.

As I was escorted to the courtroom, I thought about strategy. After taking the elevator ride upstairs with the guards, I walked into the courtroom. I spoke with Roger the evening before and asked if he could be there in case he needed to testify. I needed his support. He assured me he would be there for me. When I entered the courtroom, a smattering of people sat or stood around the room. I spotted Roger and signaled to him, asking him to call the media and inform them the trial was taking place. I also asked him to call my girls and my sister. Otherwise, I was going to be all on my own in the courtroom.

Judge Perkins hadn't come back into the courtroom yet. I noticed the prosecuting attorneys were sitting at the same long, narrow table directly across from me and my counsel. It was odd both sides sat together and worked from the same table.

When Judge Perkins entered the courtroom and called it to order, I saw no one I knew, not even Roger. No media had arrived yet, either. A day or two before the trial, I called Elise and asked her if she could please make it down to support me in case there was a trial. I wanted to have her with me and for her to testify as a character witness. Elise was a sophomore in college at the time. She did not hesitate for one moment and said she would get there. She booked a flight out of Milwaukee for the early morning of the day of the trial. She was a rock during the two years since my arrest. She along with her twin sister, Marissa, would be there. Both of my daughters put their lives on the public stage to help defend their dad. At that moment, no one who was in my corner sat in the courtroom.

Judge Perkins asked if there were any pre-trial motions. The prosecution spoke up and said they had one. Since they knew I would use the federal case and plea as evidence my double jeopardy rights were violated, they moved to have the federal case stricken from this trial, knowing the judge would deny it, which he did. He cited I had the right to testify about the federal conviction if I liked. It was a window dressing motion they made. The prosecution knew Judge Perkins would strike down their motion and they knew they would use the federal case against me. In fact, the prosecution was the first to bring it up to prospective jurors during jury selection.

Judge Perkins asked if the defense had any motions. Well, he and my counsel were aware I filed several pre-trial motions pro se. Since I was represented by counsel, I wasn't allowed to argue them myself. Scott and Jerry filed no pre-trial motions on my behalf (not even the most standard ones) even though they promised to early on. Later, Jerry didn't keep his word and Scott refused to do so in writing. Hell, they didn't even want to be there and it showed.

My attorneys answered the judge's question by stating, "The defense has no pre-trial motions."

Chapter Seventeen

Jury Selection

Keith

Judge Perkins ordered the bailiff to send in the pool of forty citizens from which a jury would be chosen. Jury selection began just before lunch time. I had some decisions to make both before and during jury selection. It all seemed surreal. I had to suck it up, curb the anger and do the best I could on my own. I began to figure out how to participate.

Jury selection was an interesting process. The prosecution went first. The judge put on a fake smile and thanked the jury pool for coming in to do their public service. Montgomery explained how the process would work. He told what the jury's obligation to the law was and then gave some background to the case.

The dual sovereignty elements, the media coverage and the fact that a person could be convicted of first degree robbery, even without a weapon, in Missouri were points Montgomery made. He explained that someone only had to think there might be a weapon in order for the state to pursue a first degree conviction. Montgomery approached these items like a classroom teacher instructs his students. He asked the prospective jurors to raise their hands if they were aware of certain facts. I must admit, it was effective. He asked questions then answered them himself in a very slanted manner. He was doing his job. Would it be countered?

Montgomery introduced himself as an assistant to the St. Louis County Prosecuting Attorney who was elected by the people. He was concerned about the publicity in the case, asking if anyone followed the story in the media. Nearly everyone raised his or her hand. Judge Perkins then asked if this element would have any effect on their ability to serve on this jury. Following the story would not necessarily disqualify them from serving on the panel, he said. I could see wonder on a few of their faces. Montgomery asked if anyone had heard of the Boonie Hat Bandit. Again, many raised their hands. He asked if any had questions about the media coverage and how it might affect their ability to serve on the panel.

A few had questions and Montgomery picked a few other people out and asked what they knew about the federal plea and other aspects of my case. Anyone who has ever served on a jury knows how this goes, with the only exception being the level of publicity the case had gotten. The judge explained they would not be excused from the panel of prospects unless they were unable to listen to the evidence and make an unbiased decision based on the facts of the case.

Scott introduced the defense to the prospective jurors. It was his first experience at trial. He began by introducing himself and then asked if anyone had ever heard of him. No one raised a hand. He made a poor attempt at a self-serving joke saying, "Well, I guess my flyers and postings in local stores are doing a lot of good."

This was completely in bad taste and was irrelevant to the case. He introduced Jerry and then thanked them for their commitment to serving on the jury and for doing their civic duty. The only thing Scott mentioned about the case itself was that we were even there. "Why are we here?" he asked, referring to the issue of double jeopardy and the preceding federal conviction. It was a poor attempt at a theme I suggested for the trial long ago.

When Scott was finished, Judge Perkins asked if anyone thought they should be disqualified from the panel based on what they heard or for any other reason. He already explained to them that missing work was not a reason to be excused.

One man raised his hand and said, "Yes." Judge Perkins asked him why. The man said, "I don't agree with the prosecution." The judge excused him immediately without asking any further questions. Most likely, the young man disagreed on the grounds of double jeopardy. Judge Perkins did not inquire further because he knew the response could poison the jury by exposing the trial as an unconstitutional sham.

Another panel member, a lady this time, raised her hand. She was reluctant to give her reason, so the judge asked her to approach the bench. The prosecutor and Jerry approached the bench along with her. She gave her explanation to the judge and he dismissed her from the panel. When Jerry returned to the table, I asked him what her reasoning was. She had some unfavorable experiences with law enforcement in the past, one of them recently. She disliked law enforcement and wasn't sure she could keep that bias out of her decision.

When this part of the process was over, probably thirty-four to thirty-six prospective jurors remained to choose from for a jury of twelve citizens and two alternates. I participated in the selection. Each side could strike three from the list. We used general personal information to make our choices. Age, gender and profession were considered.

Jerry was the only one of the three of us who had any experience in the jury selection process, so we paid attention to his advice. Defense attorneys generally liked housewives, younger people, minorities and professionals such as teachers and tradesmen. We were looking for professionals in nurturing and caring fields. We also were looking for people who would not nitpick details of the law but instead would make decisions based on emotions and common sense. These traits were exactly the opposite of what he was looking for when he was a prosecutor. Fortunately, some prospective jurors matched what we were looking for as we began going through the information.

Choosing prospective candidates for the jury is an educational process and it was the only part I was allowed to participate in. If I hadn't, I could have complained about Scott and Jerry's choices. I would already have plenty of issues to cry foul about and they didn't want to give me one more.

Jury selection turned out well after each side made its preferences and exclusions. The panel was diverse and balanced in almost every way. As the trial went on, jurors were purposely misinformed or uninformed by officers of the court, but the initial candidates were a fair group for both sides.

Once the jury was selected, the jury pool was called back in. The numbers of those chosen were called out, Judge Perkins told them to remain in the courtroom. The others were released to go home and thanked for their services. It was getting late in the day, so the presentation of evidence was held off until the next morning.

By this time, Elise arrived in town from Wisconsin. Jerry kept the girls informed and Roger was in the loop. Interested family members were kept abreast of the proceedings to this point. Elise, Marissa and Roger knew it wasn't necessary for them to be there until the next morning.

Before the jury was dismissed, members were given instructions as to when to arrive the next day. They were also told not to discuss the case with anyone. Honorable Judge Perkins failed to instruct them on one very important issue and wouldn't until the next day after the damage was already done. He failed to inform the jurors they should not listen to or access any media coverage of the case during their service. Those are standard instructions. It wasn't until the first break in the trial the next morning that Judge Perkins tried redeeming himself by telling jurors to avoid media coverage.

Many of the fourteen jurors were already familiar with the case. In all of the excitement of being chosen to serve in such a high profile case and because the judge neglected to give them instructions about the media, some of them unintentionally broke the rules. When Judge Perkins finally got around to giving them media instructions, he said it had come to his attention some members were using electronic devices in the jury room during breaks. Cell phones and laptops were accessed. He advised them that behavior was against the rules.

No indication of whom they were calling or texting or of what information they were accessing was apparent. We will never know for sure, but my attorneys should have called for an immediate mistrial because irrevocable damage was done. When I asked them to object, as would be the case many more times during the trial, they blew both me and the issue off as if it was no big deal.

After jury selection was completed and court was adjourned for the day, I was taken back to the jail in handcuffs and shackles by two St. Louis County transport guards. One of the guards, Curtis, had recently been promoted to the transport division. He previously worked a regular shift in the wing where I was housed. The other guard was a younger man, Sanders, who sported quite a smart mouth, a know-it-all type. Sanders asked too many questions that were none of his business and unprofessional. These same two guards would transport me to the courtroom from the jail holding cell every day. They must have been assigned to the Division 18 Courtroom regularly.

Earlier that morning, when I was still dressed in the county brown uniform, Sanders asked if I was going to trial today and why I wasn't wearing street clothes. He told me about his court experiences, complete with a smartass attitude I found annoying. He belabored how he had seen judges refuse to let people fire their attorneys and how the judge made them go to trial anyway. Sanders already knew what was going to happen. It was the way he wanted it to happen. Curtis saw I was rattled; tried to smooth things over by telling me Sanders sometimes talked too much and to not let it bother me.

That night I made it back to my cell at the county jail with a lot to think about. I talked to my girls, my sister and a couple of friends on the telephone. The most important of those conversations was with Elise. She was helpful in so many ways. First of all, she got together some decent clothes in case I needed them. My own clothes were not going to fit. I gained a lot of weight in the twenty-three months I had been in jail eating food from the canteen. Elise and my sister bought a new shirt, pants and a nice purple tie for me to wear. They also brought me a pair of my own shoes. All of these items were dropped off at 7:00 A.M. the next morning at the courthouse. I wore my new clothes with the same donated blue blazer I wore the day before.

Chapter Eighteen

And So It Began

Keith

The next morning, I awoke from a hard, deep sleep eager to get started. I was taken downstairs to get ready for trial. It felt good to have on regular street clothes and shoes that fit. With the exception of the hand-me-downs the court gave me the day before, I had worn nothing but jail browns for twenty-three months. I felt normal again for the first time in ages.

The courtroom was upstairs, and when we walked in I was seated at the long table. Opposite the jury box sat Jerry and Scott. I was seated to their left, closest to the judge's bench and facing the jury. Two pitchers of water, Styrofoam cups, a note pad and a pen were provided for me. Montgomery sat directly across from me and his assistant prosecutor sat opposite of Scott and Jerry.

This set up had several problems and I still don't understand it. The prosecution heard every single conversation I had with my counsel. Privileged or not, those conversations shouldn't have been within earshot of the opposition. Montgomery could clearly look at any notes taken by myself or my counsel. He and his assistant were less than two feet away. Any strategic conversations (even at a whisper) were overheard and any notes or papers were easily viewable. Neither in real life nor on television, had I ever seen the prosecution and the defense at the same table during a trial.

I asked Scott and Jerry to object or to request another table be brought in. They said, "It doesn't matter and we don't want to piss the judge off."

I didn't think the judge could be any less in my favor. Several times I asked them to object to irregularities. They refused every single time.

The assistant prosecutor combined with the seating arrangement was problematic. She was a young, attractive, blonde woman who wore short skirts and tight clothing each day of the trial. I have nothing against attractive blonde women, but Jerry and Scott paid more attention to her than they did to the case. Scott was gawking and drooling and Jerry was flirting. At one point, he even moved closer to her, making small talk about personal things. She never once presented anything at trial or even spoke a word on the record. Could this have been a strategy of distraction to keep my counsel preoccupied? If so, it was effective.

The real trial was about to begin. The jury entered and took their seats to hear the opening statements. Questioning was immediately combative toward me, both from the prosecution and Judge Perkins. The transcript is public record, so I won't go over every exchange, but I will relay my emotions and thoughts during the trial.

Many people came to watch and I scanned the courtroom to see any familiar faces. I recognized several local media personalities. My sister dropped Elise off, gave me a wave and went on to work. Marissa made her own way to the courtroom shortly thereafter. I needed friends and family there and Elise and Marissa were the only ones who came through when the chips were down. They stayed through the entire trial and played a key role. The girls sat in the front row, as close to me as they could get. It gave me a sense of home and comfort I had not felt in what seemed like forever. I let Marissa and Elise know I was thankful to have them with me. They smiled and gave me two thumbs up which made me feel confident and supported.

It was a decent distance from the public seating in the courtroom gallery to where I was. I saw a couple of the reporters with whom I had done interviews and others who covered the story from the start. I relayed to them my thanks for being there. The reporters understood what I was saying and gave me nods and smiles.

Roger was in the courtroom for a short time before the girls arrived, but like my sister, left for work. As it had been so many times in life before, it was just us three: the girls and I. I know my mother would have been there had she still been alive, but it was heartbreaking to know the family and friends of the past were nowhere to be found. I made mistakes, but I didn't know those mistakes would cost me nearly every connection I had with the people who mattered to me.

By almost anyone's standards, the attorneys on both sides did a very poor job of presenting the case. From opening statements to closing arguments, I was amazed by the lack of quality practice and by the poor choices of subject matter argued. To say I was left high and dry without adequate representation is an understatement. When I tried to defend myself, the prosecution badgered me.

The list of state's witnesses consisted of all seven of the bank tellers, one detective, a bank vice president and one uniformed police officer. The witnesses were not the problem. It was the way my attorneys handled these witnesses that was the problem. Months before the trial began, I requested Scott and Jerry investigate and depose each of the witnesses. The defense can get an idea of what these witnesses are going to say on the stand. Therefore, a strategy based on that insight can be formulated. Scott and Jerry had refused due to cost, so that valuable information was lost. We were going into the trial blind.

The lack of background information about the tellers came into play immediately. While they were not wholly untrue, their testimonies differed from, and were much more dramatic and embellished than, the original police reports were. Tellers who initially told the police they were never in fear now testified to terrifying ordeals during the robberies. This, of course, after intense persuasion and coaching from prosecutors over the course of two years.

The testimony of the tellers, going from one robbery to another, took a while. The questioning was similar and all of the tellers had experiences that were pretty much the same. Apparently, the prosecution wasn't holding the jury's attention because two members fell asleep right in the middle of testimony. One was an alternate juror, but the other was a full-fledged juror.

When I brought this to Scott's attention, he told me they most likely were "resting their eyes." How gullible did he think I was? The assistant prosecutor tapped Montgomery on the shoulder, pointing out the sleeping jurors. Both looked worried because this irregularity could have put the trial in jeopardy. Looking back, I should have objected myself. If I had it to do over again, I would. That would have required me to jolt the judge back into consciousness as well. He was "resting his eyes," too.

The testimony of Officer Timson, would be a source of controversy. At issue was whether these were second or first degree robberies and the questioning of this officer was critical. I did a taped interview with the police after my capture and it was clear I never had a weapon and never threatened having one. My statements at the time were clear and no weapon was ever used or found in connection to the robberies. There-fore, nothing on the tape revealed it was my intention to threaten the use of a weapon. In order to prove their case for a first degree robbery conviction, the prosecutor needed Timson to paint a different picture during his testimony. In other words, the officer perjured himself under oath.

Timson stated before the jury that during the interview I told him I had my hand in my jacket to make the tellers think I had a gun. Supposedly, I told officers from other jurisdictions the same thing. They never produced those witnesses and they never provided taped evidence of those statements, even though every other comment during the interrogation was recorded. When asked why this was not on the tape, Timson said, "We made a mistake and the recorder wasn't on."

The most critical part of their case against me to convict for first degree robbery were those statements, yet they had no evidence of them. My attorneys should have jumped on this. They didn't. Wouldn't a good trial lawyer question what other mistakes might the detective have made? Wasn't it convenient for the prosecution the recorder wasn't on during this very important stage of the interview, but every other part of it had been captured?

I remember when the question was asked in the middle of my interrogation. My answer was, "I had my hand in my jacket pocket so I would not leave any prints." I later testi-fied to this. It would have been clear to the jury if the prose-cution hadn't erased that part of the interview.

The defense wasn't allowed to review the tape beforehand. The first time I heard it was during the trial. It was a clear example of withholding evidence. I filed a pro se pretrial motion to review the tape under the precedence of Brady v. Maryland, but my motion was never heard by the court. I asked my attorneys to object, but they didn't. They failed miserably time after time to defend me.

The vice president, Smarner, of one of the banks testified for the prosecution. He looked every bit the part of a banking executive. With his tailored suit, finely groomed haircut and Florida tan, Smarner told how he knew I was the Boonie Hat Bandit. He followed me out of the bank after the twelfth bank robbery so he could get a description of the vehicle and the plate number. Even though his actions broke bank proto-col, it was clear Smarner saw himself as every bit the hero.

The final witness presented was the uniformed cop, Des-mond, who had followed my car after the last robbery. Des-mond was brought in to grandstand about the 'high speed' chase that happened when I was apprehended. The prosecu-tion argued I didn't cooperate with police. I did. I hadn't eluded police. Other than not acknowledging any photo-graphs they had of me during robberies, I cooperated fully during my arrest and during the interrogation.

During witness testimony, I listened intently and formulated a plan for appeal. I wasn't anxious or nervous. I was amazed by some of the things said and even more so by things that were not said when they needed to be. What I would say once I was on the stand to tell my side of what happened?

When I gave my testimony, just as the robberies themselves were, it was surreal. I was relaxed and I concentrated on re-maining calm and collected for what I knew would come. Montgomery tried to rattle me in an effort to portray me as I was something I was not: angry, hot-tempered, dangerous and violent. I needed to address the jury directly and make eye contact with them. I got no advice from my attorneys before my testimony.

Certain issues needed to be raised during my testimony. My attorneys were not going to bring them up, so I had to. Double jeopardy, duel sovereignty and the jury's right to nullify needed to be brought up. I did, which lit a spark in both the judge and the prosecutor. This brought on what one reporter would later describe as "a spar" between Montgomery and me.

Montgomery said maybe I should work on my law degree. He badgered me about my legal knowledge and several other items. When asked if the police were lying, I said, "Yes, that's what I am saying." They were. As the prosecutorial attack continued, Judge Perkins should have stepped in and stopped this line of questioning. My attorneys should have objected to what Montgomery was doing. No one did a thing.

The F.B.I. agent who had been present during my interrogation wasn't at the trial to testify. The State claimed he had to maintain his anonymity for safety reasons. This didn't jive with the fact he and three other agents had taken part in a press conference during the robbery spree asking the public for information and offering a reward for my arrest. Suddenly, when my life depended upon it, the agent didn't want to be identified. However, the prosecution readily put words in the mouth of this non-existent witness, and asked me if I was calling the agent a liar. Since anonymity wasn't a real issue, I can only wonder if the agent refused to perjure himself on the stand so the prosecutor could get his conviction. Instead, he was turned into a "strawman witness" whose words were used against me while they were never uttered in the courtroom. Hearsay isn't supposed to be allowed as evidence.

My attorneys should have stepped in and defended me at several junctures, but they did not. Montgomery misrepresented the law to the jury. He gave the impression the federal crime of robbery of a financial institution and the state crime of robbery in the first degree were different crimes. Given his explanation, double jeopardy wasn't at play. They are the same crime with the same elements. The state could use my guilty plea and conviction in federal court for bank robbery against me, but suddenly they were utterly different crimes than what the state was prosecuting me for?

Montgomery held up the federal plea agreement to the jury and said by signing it I had agreed it "did not preclude any government agency from prosecuting me for these crimes." This was another misrepresentation of the truth. The agreement I signed states on the first page "government." However, the "government" the document refers to is the federal government, including agencies such as the I.R.S. The plea agreement was a deal between myself and the federal government. The state was not a consideration in that contract. Montgomery said I waved my 5th Amendment right to protection from double jeopardy by reaching an agreement with the federal government. I had not.

The first point I countered him on, but the second one got past me. My attorneys should have stepped in and made the law and plea agreement clear to the jury. Once again, they failed me. I should have been tried by the facts, not on faulty premises the prosecution decided to feed the jury. Most regular citizens know little about the law. I didn't know detailed specifics before my life depended on it. The jurors didn't know to question what the prosecutor, an officer of the court, was telling them. They didn't know they were being lied to and misled.

Many people claim when they step down from the stand they are relieved. Not me. I was angry and highly disappointed in my lawyers. I had so much more to say and a lot was left on the table. Part of the reason for telling this story now is to expose those issues.

During the trial there was controversy over what one of the police said or didn't say, in his statement. There was a break so Jerry could read the discovery. Had he ever read it before? Their utter lack of involvement wreaked.

During another break, Jerry and Scott pulled me into an empty jury room saying, "It's not going well out there. We talked to the judge. He is still willing to give you twenty years if you plea now." I refused.

I thought to myself, *No kidding it's not going well. They have a guilty plea from another court to show the jury and those two don't seem to have a clue of what they are doing.* Were they throwing this trial? The prosecution, the judge and my own attorneys were hostile toward me.

The closing arguments were basic. Montgomery said I deserved a first degree conviction, I was guilty of robbery in the first degree due to the testimony given and because I pled guilty to these crimes in federal court. The defense said I was a desperate father who made a mistake. My attorneys told the jury to choose the crime of robbery in the second degree.

The lawyers then went into chambers with Judge Perkins to discuss and choose jury instructions. When they came back, I was told we had a choice of three versions. Both the prosecution and the defense must agree upon them. Again, I was not privy to these discussions. That, too, is under appeal.

The jury was read the instructions, then deliberated. I was taken down to the holding cell. While hoping for a verdict of second degree, I was not very confident. I prayed for nullification, but I knew the chances were slim. An hour later, the verdict was given: guilty of robbery in the first degree on all seven counts. The guilty verdict was no surprise, but the choice of first degree robbery was disappointing.

Once the guilty verdict was read, I was put in handcuffs. It was a symbolic gesture to show my guilt. Now the wait began for the jury's sentencing recommendation.

Chapter Nineteen

The Sentencing

Keith

It was late afternoon and the jury was brought back in to hear arguments on sentencing. The perimeters were ten to thirty years or they could give me life. Scott would be doing the sentencing phase of the trial, but I asked Jerry if he would please continue to present to the jury. Scott had zero trial experience. I was not keen to the idea of my life being used as a training ground for him.

Neither one wanted to represent me, but Jerry was the lesser of the two evils. They were both angry with me, but Jerry was less likely to screw this up. Plus, Jerry was more charming and compassionate sounding than Scott. As it turned out, neither would be a huge factor in my sentencing. Elise and Marissa were the stars.

During the guilt phase of the trial, the prosecution put on a display of theatrics and subtle dramatics. They were experts in presentation. They paraded their witnesses in one-by-one to give their testimony, giving the effect they were confident of the outcome. For the police officers, it left the impression they were too busy to stay because they had to rush back to serve the public.

With the tellers, of course, Montgomery wanted to give the appearance the entire experience was traumatic. The tellers appeared so traumatized they could not bear to stay and watch the entire trial. Two of them left crying, with tissue in hand. I have to admit, the prosecution was very skilled at presenting their side in the most compelling ways possible.

Our turn came to gain some compassion from the jury. Like everything else, ours was unrehearsed and it was the plain truth. One benefit of the lack of representation I received was that all of our witness testimony was genuine and un-coached. No one took the time to create any illusions or to slant testimony one way or the other. What people saw on that day was straightforward and heartfelt by the people who testified on my behalf.

Jerry did a fairly good job of asking Elise and Marissa the right questions, letting them express their thoughts and feelings. He questioned them like victims, just like a prosecutor.

Marissa's testimony was fairly short. She told how loving and caring I was and about how gentle of a person I am. She described me as a cuddly teddy bear. Leave it to my little girl to say something like that. In good times and difficult times, she needed me with her. Time has proven that to be true.

Elise was much more candid and emotional. Her comments were along the same lines as Marissa's, but in more detail. She said I was active in their school lives and in their interests. Elise described me as an attentive and involved parent, then talked about the fears she had living life without a father anymore. The exchange between Elise and Montgomery became a little heated. He claimed Elise wouldn't really be losing me. He argued our relationship would be okay because she could still visit me when I was in prison. Elise didn't agree with him at all. She said she needed to be able to have me in her everyday life; that it was ridiculous to insinuate prison visits would substitute for normal interaction with me.

Elise and Marissa's testimonies were compelling. After the trial, some of the jury panel told them what a great job they did. I was proud of them. Not only was I thankful for their testimony, but I remember thinking, *They just saved my ass.* It was the only real help we had. If not for my testimony, and that of Elise and Marissa, the outcome would have been much worse.

Closing arguments in the sentencing phase were made after the girls testified. Jerry half-heartedly attempted to bring up the federal sentence. He told jurors I received twelve seventy-six month sentences in federal court, without mentioning they were run concurrently. If sentenced to thirty years, Jerry said the judge could give me two hundred and ten years. He never even asked for the minimum ten year sentence. While not likely, it should have been on the table. His one shining moment occurred when he used a soft, sad tone to ask the jury whether they thought I should die in prison. That was pretty good, I must say.

Montgomery argued that six years was not enough prison time for twelve bank robberies. Neither Jerry nor the judge stepped in and pointed out the jury was only there to consider seven of those robberies. This wasn't the federal hearing. Missouri only charged me with seven of the robberies and the other crimes should not have been included when considering my punishment. The jury had it planted in their minds they were sentencing me for twelve robberies, not seven. The prosecution put it on the state jurors to make up for the fed's "mistake."

Statistics can say anything. The prosecutor used creative statistics to claim that seventy-six months only amounted to six months for each robbery committed. Montgomery said it wasn't enough for twelve bank robberies. In reality, each of the federal charges carried the six year and four month sentence.

Finally, Montgomery said he wasn't asking the jury to give me life. He just wanted them to take one count and give me thirty years for it. He wanted them to give me and the victims, justice. This statement was misleading because, under the sentencing standards for Missouri, thirty years and life are essentially the same. A person is eligible for parole in Missouri at practically the same time whether he has a life or a thirty-year sentence. In some cases, people with life sentences go before the parole board before someone who has been given thirty years. So, to claim they wouldn't be giving me a life sentence by sending me away for thirty years was a semantic trick. Juries in Missouri are not privy to these facts, nor are they instructed in the difference in parole eligibility between the different classes of crimes. Frequently the jurors are unaware of what the true outcome of their decision will be.

Both parties rested and the jury went into deliberation to decide my fate. During this time, I was placed by myself in a rectangular holding cell. A toilet was in the back of the cell and concrete benches ran along the wall to the left. I never sat down for obvious reasons. The room was filthy. Dried toilet paper stuck to the walls. Urine and feces were splattered all over the walls, floor and toilet. The stench was extreme.

I shouldn't have been surprised by the conditions in the cell, the entire courthouse smelled like a dump and the courtrooms and hallways were in need of cleaning and repairs. The smell of stale cigarette smoke came from the judge's chambers, even though this was, by law, a non-smoking building.

The cell was located directly across the hall from the room containing the deliberating jurors for my case. A steel door on the cell with a small eye-level window covered with steel mesh allowed me to view part of the hallway. An elevator door was right next to the cell and I suspect it went to the employee parking garage because I could hear people coming and going.

A guard was stationed between the two doors. It was late afternoon or early evening and I saw and heard the guard saying goodnight to judges and other court employees, but could not hear anything going on in the jury room across the hallway and the door was just out of my view through the small screen window. I could only pace and wait.

About two-thirds of the way through the deliberation, one of the jury members told the guard they needed to see the judge. Judge Perkins made his way to the jury room a few minutes later. I could hear the door shut. I don't know what was discussed in there, but I have my suspicions based on the sentence they returned with.

I believe the jury asked the judge what the maximum sentence was for robbery in the second degree. Maybe there were disagreements over whether the actual elements of these crimes met a first degree charge. That was a legitimate question. No weapon was used. No threat of a weapon was ever uttered.

There was an important piece of information the jury didn't know. Time served is vastly different for a first degree conviction as opposed to a second degree. The mandatory minimum for second degree robbery is 40%, whereas first degree robbery carries an 85% mandatory minimum. Without this information, does a jury really understand what they are sentencing a defendant to? Under current law, like the issue of jury nullification, the jury can't be told this information during the trial. Jurors must have this knowledge on their own before a trial begins if it is to be known at all. This should be changed. Juries should know a sentence means two totally different things depending on whether it is first degree or second degree.

While in the holding cell, I prayed intensely for God's will to be the minimum sentence of ten years. I also prayed they would not decide on thirty years or life. As always with God, prayers are answered according to His will.

About an hour went by before the jury reached an agreement on a sentence recommendation. This hour seemed like days. Those were, and still are by far, the most intense moments I spent during this entire process. Not even prison and the robberies themselves caused this much stress. It was the only time I felt pure anxiety.

Finally, it was time for the jury's recommendation to be announced in court. I was taken back down the hall and into the courtroom. Upon entering, I saw the looks of worry and stress on the girls' faces. They looked so attentive and grown up. Many people were still in the courtroom, but from that point on, to me, there were only the three of us.

Judge Perkins called for the jury to enter the courtroom and be seated. Next, their decision was handed to him. The judge read over the sentence for each of the seven counts, one by one. This added to the anxiety. The jury foreman began to read, count-by-count, what the sentence recommendations were. Hearing fifteen years for the first count was a relief. Then, when the foreman was finished with all seven counts at fifteen years, I thought *It could have been better, but it could have been much worse.* Disappointment was all over Montgomery's face. He considered this a loss. He wanted me to get the absolute maximum. He still had a chance.

The judge dismissed the jury, thanking them for their service. Perkins announced a final judgment and sentencing hearing would be held on September 10, 2010. The courtroom cleared out and the officer let me speak to the girls for a few minutes. Jerry and Scott went out the back door of the courtroom without saying a word to me.

Elise and Marissa were relieved at the fifteen-year sentence. I saw it on their faces. Elise said if I received life or even twenty-five years she would have lost it. Both girls were angry about the ugly comments Montgomery made about me when he didn't know me. He called me a narcissist in his closing statement. It upset the girls to hear me attacked. I told Marissa and Elise I would call them later and there were tears as we expressed our love to each other. I could feel and see their love for me. It was a rough time for the three of us.

On their way out, reporters caught my daughters in the courthouse lobby. Elise told them the sentence was "fair" and justice was served. Jurors told reporters the girls did a great job. That was affirmation Elise and Marissa saved my bacon.

Later, I heard a couple of the male jurors wanted to give me thirty years. The rest of them insisted on lighter sentences. I thank them for their mercy. The difference in those sentences made a huge impact on my children and me. My daughters were responsible for any leniency I received.

Before I went before Judge Perkins for the final judgment on September 10, I had a forty-five minute interview with a Probation and Parole investigator, Ms. Livington. It was the formal pre-sentencing interview conducted by the department to determine how long I should be incarcerated. Once again, I was alone with no legal representation present.

The conversation with Ms. Livingston had a rough beginning. Not only wasn't she sympathetic; she was borderline confrontational. She had done hundreds of interviews in her career, and she wasn't in the business of being chummy with convicted felons.

That attitude lasted for the first ten or fifteen minutes. As we spoke, however, she began to lighten up. By the end of the conversation, she saw I wasn't a threat to society. In fact,

Ms. Livingston told me she was going to recommend that I either be given the minimum ten-year sentence or that I be given a suspended sentence altogether. The professional opinion of the person paid to make these determinations was that I should not be in prison any longer than the minimum required.

Chapter Twenty

Final Judgment

Keith

The next time I saw Jerry was the day after the trial. The first thing he said was, "Well, the jury didn't believe you."

I didn't even respond to his comment. I told him, "I guess I have to be concerned about the judge running the sentences consecutively."

Jerry said, "Don't worry about that. He will run them concurrently." Then he left saying, "See you on the 10th."

I trusted no one, but I was fairly confident he was right about the sentences being run concurrently. Federal court handled my sentences that way and I hoped the state would follow suit.

On September 10, 2010, I was taken up to the courtroom. Several lawyers mingled around as well as a few other defendants. I overheard a conversation between Jerry and one of those attorneys, Henderson. He asked Jerry what he had going on that day. Jerry told Henderson a sentence was being handed down by the judge today after a trial he had. When asked how he thought it would go, Jerry said, "Well, the jury recommended fifteen years on a robbery first degree case."

Henderson said, "Wow! You did a really good job for a jury trial."

Jerry smiled and took the compliment and the credit. All I could think of was how little Jerry had done in his defense of me. Elise and Marissa's testimony softened the hearts of the jurors. Jerry did next to nothing the entire time he represented me, and certainly didn't deserve any credit for a job well done.

Of course, Mystery Lady sat in the gallery. Who was she? Why was she so interested? I never found the answers to those questions. On that day, no one was in court to show support for me. Elise was back at college and I told Marissa she did not need to be there. We thought it was a formality.

I was the last person to be sentenced that day. I witnessed every other defendant receive his sentence as I sat awaiting my fate. Some of the sentences were unbelievable. One woman, for example, was given probation for beating someone with a baseball bat. I saw some people get off lightly for committing violent crimes and I saw other people sent to prison for decades for crimes in which no one was even touched. I tried to remain calm because I already knew my fate. The jury recommended fifteen years and I sat waiting for the inevitable.

After a couple of hours, Jerry came out to speak with me. He said, "The judge wants to give you thirty years. You pissed him off. We are talking to him now."

Another surprise. I stood up for my rights. That's all I did and I would do it again. I refused a blind plea which could have given me life in prison, but I wasn't belligerent to the court. I was polite and respectful. Judge Perkins had no reason to be angry at me for defending myself.

When Judge Perkins finally took the bench and called us forward, almost everyone had left the courtroom for the day. Even Mystery Lady was gone. I guess she could not wait. I was allowed to make a statement before sentencing. Jerry, Scott and the prosecutor stood to my left. I made the same apology I made in federal court, recognizing the victims and expressing my earnest regret for the harm I caused.

Judge Perkins rendered his judgment. He said he had read the pre-sentencing report written by Ms. Livingston, but he didn't agree with it. I had never seen a copy of her report, but my attorneys assured me she had been true to her word. I believe she was. He also brought up the other five crimes the state hadn't prosecuted me for as a factor in his decision. I should have only been sentenced for the crimes I was convicted of in court. Why would a judge sentence me for crimes that weren't before him? The only answer I can come up with is that he had a personal grudge against me. Instead, he was giving me ten years on counts one and seven and fifteen years on counts two through six. Due to "aggravated circumstances" he ran counts one and seven consecutively while counts two through six ran concurrently.

I said, "That's twenty years."

He said, "I wanted to give you thirty years! Thank your lawyers for talking me out of it." I believe he made that "on the record" comment in an attempt to stop any claims I would later have of ineffective counsel. Judge Perkins wanted to make it appear as though my attorneys had done something for me, when in reality they hadn't. If they did talk him out of anything, it was for their benefit in the public eye, not for me. Scott had already told me he was going to make sure I spent the rest of my life in prison. To have that actually happen may have been bad for future business.

So much for Scott's assurances when he wanted me to enter a blind plea. The judge wanted to give me much more time and most likely would have had I pled. Furthermore, Judge Perkins wasn't satisfied with the fifteen years the jury recommended, so he manipulated the sentences. He was determined, even if he had to bend the sentences, to make it happen.

The "aggravated circumstances" Judge Perkins referred to were questionable. One teller said she almost peed her pants during the robbery. Another teller was pregnant at the time, but since I couldn't see that from behind the counter, I hadn't realized it. I would have chosen a different line if I had known she was pregnant. Flimsy as these "aggravated circumstances" were, Judge Perkins used them to stretch the fifteen years the jury recommended into twenty. People nearly pee their pants in haunted houses at Halloween or during horror films, or even from laughing too hard. I was given five years of prison time on the excuse of that one comment. One would think "aggravated circumstances" would mean that some sort of bodily harm had been done during those two robberies that were different than what had occurred in the other ten. At least in Judge Perkins's opinion, that was not true for me. Judge Perkins was obviously grasping at straws to find ways to give me more time than the jury recommended.

Judge Perkins asked if my lawyers did everything I asked them. I said, "No, they did not." He asked if they made any promises they did not keep. I said, "Yes, they did." I saw the air come out of the judge and Montgomery. Their shoulders slumped.

Judge Perkins inquired what those were and I told him. He saw no grounds for ineffective assistance of counsel and I told him, on the record, I planned to appeal this issue. Perkins said I had that right and ten days to file a notice of appeal. I filed it later the same day. This was the last I ever saw any of them.

Chapter Twenty-One

Which One Are You?

Keith

Sitting in the courtroom awaiting my verdict, I realized that while there were many people in the room, there were only two who were on my side: Marissa and Elise. This thought caused me to consider all of the people who either abandoned me in my time of desperate need, or who kept just close enough to get some enjoyment from the limelight. With my life in the balance, I knew only my children were outwardly in my corner. It was a sobering realization. This chapter is dedicated, so to speak, to the people who appeared to be friends in the past but who proved to be as fair weather as they come. I don't need to mention names. They know as well as I do who they are.

When I was arrested, people I had helped out financially and with my time acted as though they didn't know me. When I was in financial straits, I still loaned them money. When my life was in turmoil, I was still a helping hand to them. When their lives were in shambles, they turned to me. Everyone loved Keith when I had something to give them. Now that I was on trial, I had become one of the classless untouchables.

Crisis is an isolating thing, and I have never felt more alone than I did during that period of my life. Prior to my arrest, I had at least the illusion of friendships and family ties while I went through my inward struggles.

A feeling of isolation played a part in my crimes.

After my arrest, people disappeared completely from my life. Over the years, I have been rundown and maligned in nearly every way imaginable, including being accused of my own mother's death. Children in the family were told, "Keith killed Grandma." My mother did die after my arrest, but she was in her eighties and suffered from congestive heart failure. To indoctrinate the children I was close to with the belief that I killed their grandmother was an unbearable stab.

Everyone is likely to experience abandonment in their lifetime to some degree. Sometimes friends and relatives are unmistakably absent during a crisis because, truthfully, the person in crisis doesn't fit into their everyday lives anymore. Divorce, job loss, medical conditions, family crises, even legal problems can take an individual out of the circle of friends. No longer serving a purpose in their daily lives eliminates the need for their attention. That hit me squarely in the jaw as I sat in that courtroom.

I found out some people feared what others would think of them if we remained friends. I had phone calls with a few people who told me they couldn't pass greetings onto mutual friends because they hadn't told anyone they were speaking to me. Being someone's dirty little secret certainly undermined the value of the conversations I had with them. I was a faithful friend to them, regardless of what mess their lives had been at times. When I needed support, they made it clear I was a liability. However, they wanted me to know that in reality they were "there" for me, as long as no one knew, of course.

In addition to fair weather friends, another group was as damaging in its own way. Some people acted as though they cared, but in reality they were hoping for a front row seat to the train wreck my life had become. By being close to me, they thought they would get the inside scoop. They would find out juicy details, be in the limelight and maybe get some time on camera. My problems were their attention-getting device. Many of them wanted to absorb themselves with my drama so they felt better about their own lives. *At least their lives weren't as screwed up as mine*, they thought.

Some people love gossip. It makes them feel important. They know something juicy, and they relish the attention they will get by being "in the know." Too many people are willing to give the gossiper exactly what he is seeking: attention and a forum. People came out of the woodwork to be interviewed about me. One former acquaintance who barely knew me referred to me as "odd." His comments were based on the fact that I was often standing outside my house talking on the telephone. I worked from home. That isn't odd behavior for a person who works from home. In reality, he didn't know me at all. Before I made a comment like that, I would have politely told the reporter that I didn't know the person well enough to make a comment. Instead, this gentleman gave out useless information in an effort to make me look bad.

Family members are not immune to being in the spotlight. If the situation is sensational enough, they gain prominence by being associated with the big story. This happened to me. Family members were unwilling to lend a hand, but they enjoyed getting some of the paparazzi's attention. Some used my crisis as an opportunity to grandstand and make people think they were the hero who was going to save the day for me and my children. They didn't follow through, but they had their moment in the public eye. All people remembered were the grand promises. They never saw the lack of follow through. Old jealousies and unresolved issues within the family made this more insidious than the bystanders seeking attention. Why? Because there is an unwritten code that family will be there. They will support. They will defend. They will fight off attackers when no one else will. For the most part, this didn't happen for me.

People made a lot of excuses for their inaction. I commonly heard, "I just don't know what to do." That might have been the case, but a shoulder to cry on or a hand to hold during the darkest days would have been sufficient. I needed to know they were there for me even if there was nothing that could be done. Most of the time during a crisis, there *is* something that can be done to help. Phone calls, financial assistance and networking for specialized services are things a friend might be able to help with. I realized it wasn't that they didn't know *what* to do. They didn't *want* to do anything. Few people wanted anyone to expect anything out of them.

The only people I had confidence in to do any legwork for me after I was arrested were my two daughters, and at times Roger. Unfortunately, my daughters were only seventeen and were in no way able to do what needed to be done. It would have been too much to ask of them. They were children. I ask, however, "Where were the adults?

As the youngest in my family, I was a people pleaser. I always helped out any way I could when my family and friends were in need. Once I was incarcerated, I found out I wasted a lot of time and energy on people who were only concerned about themselves and what I could give them. In a friendship, everyone has the opportunity to choose if he will be a giver, a taker, a fair weather friend, or a spectator. Consider this question: Which one are you?

Chapter Twenty-Two

Publicity and the Media

Keith

My experience with the publicity and media surrounding the robberies and my capture could be described as a "give and take" relationship. There were benefits for all parties involved. As always, key items were left out of news reports, leaving people to make their own decisions on a verdict without all of the information. The role of the media in this story may not be finished, but I can give my thoughts about the effects it has had on my case from a legal standpoint and I can address the effects it has had on me as an individual.

From the outset, the publicity created a mixed bag of results. Many comments were made in interviews and on news blog sites online. Most of the interviews given by friends and neighbors were fairly accurate portrayals of who I am. On the other hand, a few others involved personal glorification, grandstanding and pure assumption by the people interviewed. Some wanted to be on television so badly they were willing to twist what they knew or had observed. Over-exaggerations and outright lies were told.

I admire and appreciate those who told the truth. I respect those who relayed their true feelings or those who gave no comment at all. Some said nothing because they either knew nothing or they wanted to remain neutral. Not everyone wanted to be a part of the media frenzy taking place after my arrest.

Until this event, I hadn't stopped to think about how little we know about our acquaintances. It's easy to assume we know someone because we work with them or live in the same neighborhood. It's also easy to try to make sense out of an event based on our own personal view of the world. I've always been a very private person and people who knew very little about me gave their take on me based on one event while the cameras rolled. One event or period of time in someone's life shouldn't define who he is. The media tends to miss that point.

The police and other law enforcement officials often led the public and media to believe they knew more than what they did. This is not an uncommon tactic by law enforcement. It began with misinformation regarding the description of me and my vehicle during the robberies. It continued after I was arrested.

One of the detectives interviewed said, "I could tell Mr. Giammanco is relieved this is all over." I never said that. In reality, I was thinking about my children and other family members and how the arrest would affect them. This ordeal was only the beginning of the hardships to come. I wasn't relieved, but the detective led the public to believe I was.

Lawyers use the media to put their spin on the message being given to the public. They like to come up with coy one-liners to detract attention from what is at stake. Instead of dealing with the specifics or truths of a case, lawyers shut down debate by becoming glib.

In a response to an interview I did with *The St. Louis Post Dispatch*, the St. Louis County Prosecuting Attorney, Bob

McCulloch, said I was a loser on the double jeopardy issue because Missouri is a separate sovereignty. The prosecutor's comments were spread in the media before the issue was decided in the courts. In the interview, I said if I was prosecuted twice for the same crimes, it was a clear indicator the constitutional rights of citizens had dissolved right before our eyes. Furthermore, taxpayers' hard-earned money was wasted by convicting me a second time.

In that same interview, McCulloch quipped, "Well, he may be a nice guy, but we can't have people going around robbing banks." I don't disagree with his statement, but it was a diversion from the obvious: I was already stopped. I pled guilty in federal court and was given a prison sentence. McCulloch pursued a second conviction out of his own self-interest. To the credit of the columnist who did the interview, the last sentence of his article pointed out that the United States Constitution says a person cannot be convicted twice for the same crime.

Media organizations from all over the country contacted my family members for several weeks after my arrest. While my mother, sisters and other relatives declined to speak to the press about the case, my daughters did. Elise and Marissa acted with great bravery and courage by speaking to reporters. They were criticized and attacked for their willingness to stand by me. I am touched by their portrayal of me. Speaking to the media did them some good, though, because they found support from the community that recognized their plight. Our church set up a trust fund to help my daughters and some kind people gave donations to keep them afloat while they finished their senior year of high school. For that, I am eternally thankful.

Some of the blog comments about my daughters were outrageous, cruel and spiteful. The girls were accused of being snobs who had "grown up with silver spoons in their mouths." Marissa and Elise were far from spoiled rich kids.

They grew up in a modest neighborhood and we weren't ever rich. They had no expectations from me or the world and never considered themselves privileged.

Attacks against my daughters were senseless. Elise and Marissa had no knowledge of what I was doing and they should never be condemned for it. They committed no crimes and to be attacked because I did was unnecessary and cold-hearted. My daughters were already paying a huge price. No one should face public ridicule for the mistakes of others.

That being said, many supportive, sympathetic and empathetic comments came from people who genuinely cared for the girls. To this day, people will ask us how Elise and Marissa are doing and most people recognized they were innocent bystanders of the media spectacle that hit our family. Regardless of what anyone may think of me or my actions, I appreciate the kindnesses some offered my daughters.

My personal feelings about the publicity and media coverage are surprising to some. I was the only one during the robbery spree who knew what was going on. I've been asked if I would watch the F.B.I. and local police scramble to catch me with some kind of pride or boastfulness. I didn't gloat and I didn't worry or fret to a great extent either. I watched the local news once after each robbery. I approached it as a business, albeit an illegal one. I needed to know what the bank camera photos of me looked like and what was being said by law enforcement. I needed to know whether or not anyone saw me leave the scene, if they had a description of the vehicle I was using or if there were any other clues they may have obtained. I wasn't watching to glorify myself. I was watching to see if there was anything I needed to change in my methods. Once I learned what I needed to from the local broadcast, I stopped watching the reports.

After one of the robberies in St. Charles County, I tuned into the 10:00 P.M local news broadcast. At the top of the news, the reporter said, "Authorities say they have a description of the getaway vehicle driven by who is believed to be the Boonie Hat Bandit after the robbery of a Bank of America in St. Peters."

I watched as the piece ran and they said the robber left the bank parking lot in a late 90s model white Pontiac Grand Am. Then and there, I knew they had gotten nowhere in their investigation. The description of the vehicle was not even in the ballpark and I walked away from the bank to a nearby fast food restaurant where my vehicle was parked. After seeing the report, I was able to go about business knowing I need not make any adjustments. Each time I realized they had no solid leads, I did feel a sense of relief, no differently than I would with any business decision that went well.

Publicity surrounded my crime spree and it followed me after my arrest. Immediately after settling into the St. Louis County Jail, I received a variant of contact from media corporations, reporters and others interested in getting a story. Contact came in the form of phone calls fielded by jail caseworkers. Some came in letters. Reporters showed up in person requesting interviews. Both local and national outlets wanted to be first to get my reaction to unfolding events. Authors who wanted to buy the rights to my story wrote to me.

Throughout this experience I made my own decisions as to if, where, how and when I shared my story. During the first several months in county jail, requests were steady at one or two per week. With other topics in the news and with legal proceedings coming to a standstill, interest died down after a while. Two national networks and one local television station were persistent to get interviews throughout. They kept in touch with me about once every month to six weeks. My response was always the same, "Not at this time, but I am not ruling it out."

I got all kinds of advice on how to handle the media requests and my newfound infamy. Some said I should keep quiet and never talk to the media. Some said I should wait until the court proceedings were over. Others said I should talk to the media immediately to gain more public sympathy. I was even told I should start talking to the media in an attempt to taint the jury pool so I could receive a change of venue.

Jerry and Scott gave me advice as well. They told me not to give any comments. I was to tell the reporters to speak to my attorneys. Ironically, I eventually gave interviews to discuss the inaction and ineptitude of my attorneys. Those interviews happened before my case was completely prosecuted in both federal and state courts. Someone had to speak up for me and for my defense since my counsel was lacking.

Another attorney gave me some of the most interesting advice I received. It came during the interview process while I sought an attorney I could afford and who would represent me. One of the most highly-regarded criminal defense attorneys in the St. Louis area, Martin Spires, gave a very short but interesting comment regarding the media. Mr. Spires said, "At first the media attention will hurt you, but later it will help you." I am still not sure what the full meaning of his comment was, but I believe he was right.

A few months after the federal sentencing, I realized the St. Louis County prosecutor was not going to drop the state charges against me. I contemplated contacting the media. I reached an impasse with my attorneys and I was steadfast in my vow to not plea or accept punishment for the same crimes a second time. A trial date was finally set, almost two years after my arrest. It was time I spoke up in the early spring of 2010.

I selected two reporters and wrote each of them a letter telling them I was ready to do an interview. One was and still is, a national television reporter from ABC News who did stories for *20/20* and *Good Morning America*. My case garnered national attention and doing a nationally broadcast interview was the most effective strategy.

The other was the columnist for the *St. Louis Post Dispatch* whose article I referenced earlier. This columnist had a reputation of putting a witty yet lighthearted spin on both human interest and local government stories. He was known to be somewhat critical of local government, law enforcement and court systems. Ironically, he never asked me to do an interview. To serve my purpose for getting my points across, he was the best choice to do the interview.

Both reporters responded upon receipt of my letters. I did a total of four interviews, one interview with each of the reporters I had chosen before the trial. The other two interviews I gave to a local FOX News reporter whom I promised I would talk with should I decide to speak to the media. She did one interview before the state trial and one interview after it.

That same FOX News reporter returned the favor by participating in an effort by the prosecution to smear me. During the twenty-three months I was at the county jail, I had hundreds of visits and phone conversations with close friends and my daughters. Visits were always in a booth separated by glass. We spoke using a telephone, and all conversations were recorded. During one of my conversations with Roger, we had a lighthearted moment about naming a racehorse "Robbin Da Bank." How many of us haven't tried to find something to laugh about during a time of stress? We certainly wouldn't want our reputations or characters gauged solely on a lighthearted moment. That is exactly what the prosecution wanted. Out of all of the hours of tape they could have put on the air, the prosecution (with the help of the FOX reporter who opened the segment as though it was an interview she had with me), used that one short conversation to make me sound as though I was delusional. The segment was aired before my trial and during it in an effort to discredit me in the eyes of the public and the jury. The clip didn't even identify the other speaker correctly, claiming it was my brother. My brother had died years before I was arrested. Truth and reality aren't necessary when ratings or agendas are in action.

The interviews were no different than what I expected. I had the advantage of not being careful with my answers. I already pled guilty and was sentenced in federal court, so there was no need to protect myself. I did not have to refuse any questions. I could be honest and be myself. Although the questions were predictable, the national reporter gathered much more material and was more creative with her questions. The reporters were professional yet casual and easygoing at the same time. We were all relaxed.

The main focus of the two television reporters was the human interest side of the story. They wanted to know how I felt, what led up to the crimes and how my arrest affected us as a family. They asked about my children, how I pulled the crimes off and how I thought the tellers felt. The usual topics I expected were asked.

While there was an ongoing human interest story involved, I took the chance to expose some legal points as well. I showed what I considered serious flaws in our legal system. My goal was for the interviews to be printed and aired on television, both locally and nationally. I wanted to educate the jury panel and also to expose the legal system for what it was.

I wanted to send a message to my attorneys and all attorneys for that matter, telling them, "If you don't do your job, you will be exposed for who you are, for what you are and for what you represent." I was only somewhat successful in doing so. The printed column and local television interviews came out before the trial, but the national interviews with ABC did not air until shortly after the state trial.

The interviews did get indirect reactions from the judge and my attorneys. Most of what I said about lawyers, laws and the legal system was not aired or printed. I believe what little of it was, was effective. The media members never promised those comments would be aired, but I was told more of them would be than what actually were. This was not surprising, though, because the media gets most of its inside crime information from law enforcement. The media does not want to bite the hand giving them their information for future storylines.

Bank robbery brings with it an additional element to the publicity and media coverage. Over the past one hundred and fifty years or so, publicity surrounding train or bank robberies has been different than that of other types of crimes. A level of romantic mystique and folklore is associated with bank and train robbery. Everyone knows who Jesse James was. Everyone knows who Bonnie and Clyde were. Whether they go down in a blazing shootout, they never get captured or their story falls somewhere in between, there is a heightened interest in bank robbers. They are placed at a higher status than other criminals. People want to know what makes them tick so the public can be sympathetic to their sprees.

From the time I was captured, my experience was no different than that of other notorious bank robbers. I can't recall outright condemnation for the crimes I committed, with the obvious exception of the legal system. I was treated differently by other criminals in jail and in prison. The same is true of my treatment by most staff at the St. Louis County Jail and in the Missouri Department of Corrections. Even the arresting police officers were caught up in the mystique. A high-profile bank robber is asked different questions and is treated with more respect. Celebrity status exists. Right or wrong, it's real and I experienced this effect from the first day I was arrested.

Publicity and the media have hurt me and helped me. I used it to my advantage at times. During the crimes, I was able to get a handle on what law enforcement knew through the media. When going to trial, I used it to give my side of the story to the public. The legal system used the media to prosecute me in the publics' eyes and the local media always made sure the prosecution got the last word. Many people tried to gain a moment of fame through association with me in the media. I can neither condemn nor praise the role of the media in my case. The press's job is to find stories that increase viewers or readership. No matter how compelling a human interest story or how brutally someone is maligned in the media, in the end, it's just business. Publicity is nothing personal.

Chapter Twenty-Three

Bonne Terre

Keith

My life was about to go through another change. Going to prison is an eye-opening experience, and thankfully not one most people encounter firsthand. Many people are interested in prison and they watch television shows giving a glimpse behind the prison walls. This is my account of what it is like to live there.

After my conviction in state court, I was transported from the St. Louis County Jail to the Missouri Department of Corrections intake diagnostic center at Bonne Terre, Missouri. All inmates entering the system are tested for disease and other physical ailments. Batteries of tests given to gauge aptitude, psychological fitness and basic education skills. D.N.A samples are given and the identification photos for the Department of Corrections are taken at the diagnostic center.

Tests are administered before placing an inmate in an institution, theoretically, to match the inmate with the institution best meeting the requirement of the crime committed as well as any educational or medical needs the inmate has. With all of the resources used for this placement, it's not always very effective. Some people who specifically ask for educational services are not placed in prisons with schools. Some people who have medical or psychological issues are not placed in what may be a better institution for their needs. Safety for everyone involved, staff and inmate, along with a fair opportunity for true rehabilitation, should be the top priorities. If an inmate wants to rehabilitate and they ask for educational services, for example, the focus should be placing willing individuals in prisons offering those opportunities. Tax dollars are spent to incarcerate these people anyway. The money may as well be used to rehabilitate those who are willing. All states could do a better job with this very important task.

On the fourteenth day of my stay at the diagnostic center, I was called in to see a caseworker. She informed me, due to the length of my sentence, I would be placed at one of the state's seven maximum security prisons. Contrary to Judge Stewart's wish at my federal sentencing, I would not be going to a lower level prison. I would be incarcerated with the most hardened criminals the State of Missouri had to offer. Anyone sentenced to ten or more years in Missouri is sent to a maximum security prison, regardless of any other personality traits or circumstances.

Placement based solely on the amount of time someone is sentenced to is a huge mistake by the Department of Corrections, in my opinion. Other factors, such as prior criminal behavior, psychological state and willingness to reform should be weighed in the decision. Huge sentencing variations exist between jurisdictions and courts depending on the county. One judge may give the minimum sentence or probation and another may give thirty years for the same crime. Because all things are not equal in sentencing, length of incarceration shouldn't be the only or primary determining factor in where an inmate is placed. Contrary to popular belief, not all inmates are the same.

The caseworker gave me some rather surprising news. She said, "They will be shipping you out soon. You have a relative working here."

I said, "I don't believe I do."

"Yes, an aunt."

I only had two aunts still alive, and they were both pushing eighty-years-of-age. They weren't employed by the prison system or anywhere else for that matter. I told her I didn't see how it was possible for either of my aunts to be there. She gave me a name I recognized as an aunt of my ex-wife.

This turned out to be a blessing. The diagnostic center is not a pleasant place. Take it from someone who spent two years in a county jail, and who has spent years in maximum security prisons, the diagnostic center is not someplace you want to linger. It has even less freedom and fewer privileges than the county jail does. The average stay for an inmate at Bonne Terre's diagnostic center before going to a maximum security prison is six to ten months. As bad as county jail had been, this place was worse.

The one joy at the diagnostic center was the ability to walk outside in the late September weather. I could do this while going to and from the testing sites and the dining hall. It was my first time outside in nearly two years. It may not sound like a big deal to many, but it was important to me. In everyday life on the outside, we take nature for granted. Even if we live in the city, we see trees, walk in green grass, hear birds singing and enjoy the sights and sounds of the seasons. After being inside month after month, dragging on into years, I realized the value of the little things I took for granted when free. I was so overjoyed at being outside that I called Elise my second day at Bonne Terre. One of the first things I told her was, "I got to go outside!"

As she started to cry, she said, "Oh, Dad, I am so happy for you!"

I described to her how nice it felt breathing fresh air and stepping off the sidewalk to feel grass under my feet again. Elise understood and appreciated the significance to me.

For the short time I was at Bonne Terre, I was paired up in a cell with a young Hispanic man named Marcos. He was twenty-two-years-old and was sentenced to three years in prison for driving while intoxicated. It was his first offense, but a collision badly injured someone in the other vehicle. I read his sentencing and judgment documents at his request. Marcos wanted me to explain them to him. He could speak almost no English; just a few words were the extent of his vocabulary.

As it turned out, Marcos was due to see the parole board in a few weeks. On the type of felony he was convicted of, he would only be required to serve 15% to 33% of his sentence. He had already been there for several months. An interpreter was provided for his court hearings, but his legal counsel did not speak Spanish. That counsel was provided by the Missouri Public Defender System. He understood very little of what his court documents said and at that late date he hoped I could help him know what happened.

Shortly after I arrived at Bonne Terre, Marcos, asked if I would help him learn to speak English. He understood more English than he could speak, but he could read very little. Marcos had a girlfriend with whom he was in very close contact and who spoke both English and Spanish. She accepted phone calls from him and made sure he had money on his inmate account so he could buy snack items and phone time from the canteen. Since his English skills weren't good, conversation was difficult. He would show me his artwork in an effort to communicate. Some inmates are amazingly talented artists. I can barely draw a straight line, so I am impressed by the artistic abilities others have. Art gave Marcos the opportunity to share a little bit about who he was as a person when his English skills put limitations on his conversations.

Marcos's previous cellmate was "helping" him learn English. When I looked at the words he was teaching him, I was appalled. The cellmate was Marcos's age and thought it was funny to teach him lewd, crude and vulgar phrases involving sex, women's body parts and curse words. Marcos didn't need those words if he wanted to have conversations with other people.

It was sad and sickening to know someone pulled such a cruel hoax on someone who genuinely looked for assistance for the sake of entertainment. It wasn't the last time I heard or saw this in prison. I got him on the right track with useful, simple English words and phrases, and learned some Spanish words in the process. Helping Marcos learn English was a fun and useful way to pass the time.

Since canteen was only available every two weeks at Bonne Terre, I had no snacks to eat. In the evenings, Marcos was kind enough to share his peanut butter, graham crackers and candy bars with me. I never got the opportunity to repay him for the snacks. Two days before I left Bonne Terre, I filled out a canteen order to be picked up on Friday. I left that Thursday. I apologized to him for not being able to return the favor.

On the night of my fifteenth day at Bonne Terre, I learned I would ship out at 4:00 o'clock the next morning. I considered it a blessing that by random coincidence I was able to get out of the diagnostic center months ahead of the normal schedule. As I was getting ready to leave Bonne Terre, I was told I would be going to the South Central Correctional Center in Licking, Missouri. People in the system know it as "S Triple C." I spent the next three years and five months of my life at S.C.C.C.

Chapter Twenty-Four

Welcome to S.C.C.C.

Keith

The trip to South Central began on an old, gray school bus with bars on the windows. The inmates who were no strangers to the system called it the "Gray Goose." Like all D.O.C. vehicles, its license plate began with the number thirteen. I guess the state believes that unlucky number is befitting anything transporting inmates.

The bus was full and the inmates were handcuffed and leg shackled while in route to various prisons throughout the state. The first stop was the transfer hub at the Jefferson City Correctional Center. There, smaller groups of inmates were transported by full-sized vans to their assigned institutions.

The bus ride took a few hours since J.C.C.C. was almost half way across the state from Bonne Terre. During the long trip, many of the offenders chose to sleep or talk. I chose to peer out the window at the beautiful countryside. I grew up in Missouri and it was treat to get to see familiar sights as well as beautiful scenery. Through the winding back roads, I saw spring-fed streams, wooded hillsides, farms and wildlife. I knew I had better take advantage of this opportunity because who knew when I would be allowed a ride through the countryside next.

Once transferred into the van heading to the South Central Correctional Center, it was another two-hour ride before myself and the six other inmates traveling with me arrived at our destination. The van arrived at S.C.C.C., but for the next year and a half I struggled to find my way.

We got to the prison around 2:00 in the afternoon and were walked through the rear door of the indoor recreation area. Over the next forty months I would get to know that place very well, but at the time everyone and everything was completely new and unfamiliar to me. Unlike many of the other inmates I arrived with, I had never experienced the prison environment. I didn't have any relatives, acquaintances or friends in the system. I knew absolutely no one. That changed as time went by, but on that day it was totally foreign.

They took me into a hallway where they removed my cuffs and leg shackles. From there, I went into a small room connected to the gymnasium. Three folding tables were set up with a nurse and two prison officials seated at them. The nurse asked a few basic health questions. Was I taking any medication? Was I feeling sick or poorly in any way? At the next table, I was given an institutional rule book and a few other general information handouts. At the final table, I was given my housing assignment. I was assigned to Housing Unit 6, Wing C, Cell 155.

As a first-time inmate, I was struck by the realization of where I was. It was difficult to believe I was in a maximum security prison. The reality of how I would now be thought of and treated began to sink in. Officially, employees are told to set a good example for inmates. Many do not.

When I said, "Hello," I got no response. The same went for "please" or "thank you."

If I asked a legitimate question, I was given an "I don't know" or "You will find out."

The rest of the inmates with me were treated similarly. Civility was nonexistent. I understood that I committed a crime, but I was still a human being and doing my best to be polite and respectful in an uncomfortable situation. I had never been treated this way. It was an eye opener.

What does dehumanizing treatment do to someone exposed to it for years? What impact did rudeness and the lack of common courtesy have on a man? What does this do to rehabilitate an offender? Many offenders already have issues with low self-esteem. Right away, I could tell the system had no interest in rehabilitation.

To be honest, this negative beginning wasn't reflective of every interaction I had with staff, but it was a dismal way to start. Some professionals in the Department of Corrections set good examples for the offenders to follow. The negative people make it as difficult for the professionals to operate as they do the inmates. Negative people make it more dangerous for staff and inmates since they antagonize people. We've all heard the old expression about one bad apple ruining the bushel. Proportionately, there are more bad apples than just one per bushel working for the D.O.C. In spite of that, it would be unfair to say there are no good employees in the system.

I learned a lot at the next stop in the intake process. I was sent into the gymnasium to be sized for the standard state clothing and boots issued to all inmates. The young woman in charge of clothing issue was friendly and pleasant to me. She continued to be throughout my stay at S.C.C.C. She and her inmate employee showed me the ropes and explained the logistics of some of the inmates and staff at the camp.

When I first met her, I did what I had always done upon meeting someone new: I offered my hand to her for an introductory handshake. She looked at it like she understood but explained something new to me, "We are not allowed to shake hands or have any physical contact with offenders."

I get not wanting sexually-based contact between employees and inmates, but it seemed foreign to me that a standard social handshake was not allowed. It's part of common courtesy. The department needed to keep the lines distinct so no one could later call it an assault. Well, that policy goes overboard.

I turned to the inmate worker, Barker, and offered to shake hands with him. We did, introducing ourselves to each other. All three of us joked about how it was okay for Barker and me to shake hands. A lighthearted moment was much appreciated.

After our introductions, Barker and I walked down the main walk to the property-clothing issue department. The sidewalk is always called "the walk" in prison. I waited a few minutes there for my name and Department of Corrections I.D. number to be ironed onto my state-issued dry goods. It read "Giammanco, D. #1214070."

I was issued three sets of gray shirts and long pants, one pair of gray shorts, three undershirts, five pairs of boxer shorts, five pair of socks, one pair of boots, one pillow, one pillowcase, two sheets and two gray blankets. These items I put in a light brown 3'x2'x2' steel footlocker issued to me at that time. The footlocker also donned my new identity, my name with the identification number following it, written in permanent black marker.

Then it was off to Housing Unit 6 where I spent the next six months. Barker lived in my housing unit. It was the end of his day, so we walked together. By the time we walked the side "walk" to the housing unit, the outdoor recreation period had ended and there were very few people moving about the prison yard.

As Barker and I reached the front of the house, I noticed three doors. The door on the far right led to the sally port for entering wings A and B of the housing unit. The center door was the entrance to the Central Unit, also known as "the bubble." The door on the right gave access to the C and D wings of the unit. That would be the door I entered, pulling the cart with my footlocker perched on it behind me.

I stopped at the unit control window opening. The officer working unit control asked me for my identification card. She took it from me and placed a blue dot sticker on it. The dot signified I was assigned to Housing Unit 6. She then pointed to the door for C wing and instructed me to go on into the wing.

Entering, I spotted cell 155. It was the first cell on the left-hand side at ground level. A short, thin man named Lewis was standing in the half-opened doorway of the cell. He had a curious look on his face as I walked towards him. He came forward and asked if I was given cell 155 and I told him I was.

Lewis was my first of nine cellmates at S.C.C.C. He was happy to hear we would be rooming together and immediately began helping me unload the footlocker and setting it inside the cell. Lewis was one of the good cellmates I would have. He moved to an honor house in less than two weeks after I arrived at S.C.C.C. and was relieved to see he had someone decent to cell with for the last few weeks he was in a regular housing unit. When I later moved to an honor house, we talked and played softball together. Lewis was sentenced to life without parole.

When he left for the honor house, I got a new cellmate who was straight from serving time in disciplinary segregation (known as "the hole"). He was a tall, slender, young African-American named Kirk. He was my cellmate for about one month.

Compatible cellmates are difficult to find in prison. The structure of the living conditions and the cells themselves are one issue. Simple compatibility issues between human beings are others. People can be hard to live with anywhere. In a 9'x12'x8' room, that difficulty is dramatically increased.

Overcrowding is a main problem at the maximum security institutions in Missouri. Cells are constructed for one person to be housed. They are not designed to have two persons crammed into them. Missouri isn't alone when it comes to prison overcrowding, as prisons across the United States are facing the same dilemma.

 The housing units at South Central (and a few of the other prisons around Missouri) have an unsettling design feature. Each of the housing wings is in the shape of a coffin. I don't know if many people notice this, but it is a morbid touch to add to the architectural blueprints. I doubt it happened accidentally. Someone planned it that way. It's part of a perverse cruelty in the system, telling us we are essentially dead to the rest of the world.

Cells are equipped with one sink, one toilet and one desk. Two plastic chairs are thrown in. Two identical bunks are against the back wall. The bottom bunk is bolted to the floor and the top bunk is makeshift bolted to the bottom bunk. Looking at them, it's obvious they were not made to be stacked like they are, proving the cells were designed for a single person. Each bunk has a thin four-inch vinyl-covered fiber mattress.

The walls are concrete, as are the floor and ceiling. A secure non-breakable window is on the back wall of each cell. It measures 4½'x 2' with a steel frame and a support/security bar running vertically, giving the appearance of two 1' wide panes. The window is practically blocked by the top bunk. The door is solid steel equipped with electronic locks that can be engaged and opened from the housing unit bubble. Locks can also be opened manually by using a key. A 2'x 8" wide unbreakable window is installed in the upper right portion of each cell door.

Light is provided by two 4' florescent lights enclosed in steel and unbreakable glass. The light fixture is mounted above the steel desk, wedged where the wall and ceiling meet. Two standard electrical outlets are in each cell: one above the sink, the other near the desk. One cable television outlet is available for those with that privilege. A round hole in the wall by the toilet is used as a toilet paper holder. A steel mirror is mounted above the sink in each cell. A touch sensor switch operates the light.

An important feature in each cell is a wall-mounted medical emergency panic button. This sends a signal to unit control making them aware an inmate has a problem in their cell. Emergency buttons are often misused by both the institutions and the inmates. At S.C.C.C., if one of the buttons is pushed in a general population housing unit, an immediate response by staff takes place, acting accordingly to the type of emergency. If an inmate pushes one of these buttons having no real emergency, he will be reprimanded.

Living conditions are cramped for two full-grown men. For anyone believing we deserve these conditions, keep a few things in mind. This environment breeds many things that have a direct effect on society. The spread of illness drives up medical costs to taxpayers. Injuries and deaths are caused by the tension of housing two inmates in such close quarters. In lockdown conditions, using the toilet can cause violence.

Close living quarters provide a situation ripe for rape and rampant homosexuality along with the violence and disease that comes with those. Rape is an ugly thing, in or out of prison and the current housing system is tantamount to promoting and encouraging it. Young inmates are especially vulnerable to rape and sexual exploitation.

Flaring tempers due to the stress of living this way make it an even more dangerous environment for the staff working in a prison. Cells were designed to house violent felons in twenty-three-hour lockdown conditions as single-man cells for the protection of staff and inmates. I am not an engineer or an architect, but it does not take one to see the State of Missouri misuses the design of these institutions to house an exorbitant number of inmates. Overcrowding is a real problem and as a result of that problem, many other problems are created.

Inmates in the Missouri prison system are afforded some privileges not given in many other states or even in the federal prison system. One of which is the availability of televisions with basic cable programming in the cells. I even heard of times in the past when gaming systems and video games were sold in the canteen. Those were taken away before my arrival.

Some may disagree with inmates having privileges. Some may think, *I can't even afford cable television. Those criminals don't deserve television in their cells or at all for that matter.* That's a judgment call, an opinion, and everyone has a right to feel whichever way he wants to about it.

Missouri gives its inmates access to television, C.D. players and radios for a reason. Think about this. How many of us have given a baby a binky? How many of us have taken one for a ride in the car when they wouldn't sleep because of colic or restlessness? How many of us have bought a fussy toddler a candy bar or have gotten a grade school child a box of sweet cereal at the market just to keep them quiet? I could go on and on about dealing with teenagers or even a spouse.

The televisions and the other so-called privileges are pacifiers. They cut down on tension and strife between inmates and between inmates and staff. Radios and televisions pacify years of free time. Missouri practices lengthy sentences for maximum security inmates with no chance of good time behavior credit. First time offenders are in prison for decades. Thousands of men are warehoused for years on end. In order to keep them quiet and occupied, the state decided televisions were a great babysitter.

It isn't this way in every state. In the neighboring state of Arkansas, inmates are given hard labor. A prisoner is too tired to watch television after a hard day's labor in the farm fields, on the cattle ranch or from doing road work. The difference is the amount of time served in Arkansas.

With an armed robbery charge in Arkansas, an inmate can get out of prison after three years of hard labor and good behavior. In Missouri, that same inmate would be given a twenty-year sentence for a first degree crime and under current law he would not be eligible for parole for seventeen years, which is 85% of the time sentenced. I would trade my television for fourteen years of my life.

As a new person at the prison, I had what one might call several welcoming encounters. Some were by individuals and others were by committee. These were efforts to feel out or test the new inmate. The first of these encounters came on my second day at the prison. Housing Unit 6 went to canteen once a week. Two days could be chosen from, either Tuesday or Thursday. The institution has since gone to only allowing one canteen day per housing unit each week.

Since I arrived at the camp too late on a Thursday to go to canteen, I thought I had missed the opportunity to go there until the next week. Friday morning, Lewis and I saw the sergeant working the housing unit standing outside during morning recreation.

Lewis said, "Hey, go tell the sergeant you just got here yesterday and ask if you can go to canteen today. He will probably let you go." I did just that.

The sergeant looked at his watch and saw it was about 10:00 A.M. He said, "Go fill out a small order and I will call up there and tell them you're coming. They close at 10:30, so hurry up." It was kind of him to make those arrangements, especially since many employees would not have done that. I made tracks and did as he told me.

After I picked up my first canteen order, while on the 150-yard walk back to the housing unit, I took the right-hand turn down the walk and around the handball courts. There I encountered three inmates walking towards me. They were younger men in their twenties who looked like they knew the prison life. All of them had tattoos, shaved heads and facial hair of some sort. They were hardened and comfortable in the environment they were in.

As they approached me, they stopped and one of them said, "Why don't we just take this old man's canteen?" The other two laughed as all three of them were eyeing the bag in my hand.

I needed to act since they were half-heartedly blocking the walk in front of me. That's when I chuckled and told them, "You can try to take it, but you will remember that you tried."

They looked at me, then looked at each other and finally one said, "Come on, man, let's go."

Although my heart was racing, I shrugged my shoulders and smiled as I headed toward the housing unit. This was my first "new inmate test" at the prison.

I learned fast in the county jail it is important to stand your ground and to not be run over. Defense is part of the prison culture. Some inmates are such cowards that they support themselves by frightening and doing harm to the old and weak. They work through intimidation and veiled threats until they find their prey, whether they are after food, coffee, tobacco, phone time or even sex. They will find the weak and will repeatedly press and rape them of belongings or their manhood. Those who are weak become their punk or bitch. It really is a sick scenario. There are human trafficking elements to this practice. The weak are traded as commodities by some. The young, the old and those who have physical or mental disabilities are easy prey in prison. Ironically, some of the people who approach a new inmate demanding payment for protection are not qualified to provide any protection at all. They are simply scamming someone.

At about the same time I had my run-in over canteen items, I knew of another man who was pressed in the same way. He gave in. For the next several months, he turned over his canteen order to other inmates because he did not stand up for himself in the beginning. Being in good physical condition and staying alert are extremely important in prison. If the situation arises, you have to be ready to defend yourself and your belongings.

There is an interesting, yet inaccurate, stereotyping made when a man of my age and appearance enters the prison population. It is assumed by many, especially by young men, that if you are an older, clean-cut white man, you must be a child molester (or "chomo" as they are called in prison).

That became ever so clear to me only a few days after arriving at S.C.C.C. The rumors of me being convicted of sex crimes against children started being spread by a group of young Hispanic men and they quickly spread throughout the housing unit. Lewis informed me of these rumors and he had told them they were wrong. It hadn't changed their minds; they still had this idea in their heads. The word was they were going to jump me out on the yard.

The next time everyone was out of their cells for recreation in the wing, I came out of the cell and got everyone's attention. I yelled out a few choice words directed at all of those who were spreading the rumors and also for the benefit of those who believed them. I slapped my Sentencing and Judgment documents down on one of the recreation tables and said, "There you go! For anyone who is concerned about what I am in here for. Now, let me see or hear what you are all in here for! Let's see if any of you have the balls or guts to do what I did!" There was dead silence.

A couple of the inmates went over to the table and looked at the papers after I had walked over to use one of the telephones in the wing. Later, a few inmates told me they were from the St. Louis area and remembered who I was. Others heard the stories on television or read about them in the newspapers. With some, I was back to being a celebrity and they wanted all of the details.

I did not hear anything more about being a child molester until I moved to a different housing unit and then several times again later after I started working with Caroline as a tutor at the school. On at least one occasion I know of, Caroline stepped in and set people straight on the facts surrounding why I was in prison. Otherwise, I would tell them what I was in for and then I would ask them what they were in for. That question usually had three results: they shut up, they told the truth or they lied. Most inmates won't or can't talk freely about their crimes unless they know someone. My crimes have never been a secret; no one's are in reality.

The young men who accused me of being a child molester after my arrival at South Central thought they were doing society a favor. They got their kicks by passing judgment on others instead of looking at their own iniquities. Not long after they accused me, they found their prey right there in C Wing of Housing Unit 6. Several of them beat the man outside of his cell on the walk of the top tier of the wing. I never even noticed the man before. I sure noticed when they carted him off to medical to treat his injuries. After reviewing the tapes from the cameras in the wing, the attackers were taken to the hole. I don't know if they were charged with assault or not.

I certainly don't have a place in my heart for anyone who preys upon children. In fact, I find those behaviors despicable and appalling. That being said, no crime or sin is anything to be proud of, including my own. We all have our crosses to bear as humans.

At the same time, I don't condone the actions of people who take it upon themselves to physically punish someone else for their crimes. One man judging another is a risky spiritual proposition in my opinion. It can also be risky in the physical sense, too, especially if the vigilante is himself incarcerated for crimes against society. Glass houses can be built anywhere, including inside prison cells. The beaten man, whatever he had done, was put into prison for his punishment. I know from personal experience, having your freedom, family, friends and way of life taken from you is very hard to cope with in itself.

I am also sympathetic to the victims of the crimes and the suffering they experienced. Some have died and some are scarred for life. I recognize and appreciate the needs of the victims to see justice served. I am not diminishing those facts.

In light of that, I do want to make the point that, right or wrong, the justice system sets and doles out the punishment. People are sent to prison for their crimes. Separation from society and their loved ones is the penance, not the arbitrary vengeance of fellow inmates or staff. No one should be abused and tormented by someone who feels the need to get their kicks and punches in. It's hypocritical of people who are also incarcerated to think they can or should pass judgment on anyone, and it's unprofessional for staff to do so.

The first fight I witnessed at S.C.C.C. was only a few days after my arrival and it was quite the spectacle. I never saw one like it before or since. A fully-clothed inmate went into a shower stall and carried out an attack on another inmate while he was showering. As the showering inmate began to fight back, the fight made its way to the open floor of the wing. So, there was one clothed (but wet) inmate as well as a completely naked inmate throwing blows in the middle of the wing. After both got a few licks in, staff members came in and stopped the fight. They let the naked man put on a set of boxer shorts before taking them both to the hole.

This must have been a shocking experience for the guards who broke up the fight. I think of the two female guards who were on duty then and I can only imagine what they thought of the incident. Some of the inmates even thought it was odd. I know it shocked me.

Housing Unit 6 at S.C.C.C. is not an honor dorm, so time out of the cell is limited. Time to use the telephone for contact with family and friends, the same as in the county jail, is short. This makes the telephone a natural source of conflict. Not long after I arrived in the housing unit, this conflict surfaced between an established inmate in C Wing and myself.

Only four telephones were available in each wing. Since we were only out of our cells for a total of one and a half hours per day to use the phones, take showers or handle other matters, phone privileges were valued. In three one-half hour periods (morning, afternoon and evening), nine cells were let out at a time. Four phones were available for up to eighteen people who could possibly want to use them. The rule was to use the phone for fifteen minutes then let someone else use it. That was, unless no one else wanted to use the phone.

One morning, I rushed out of the cell to get a telephone so I could talk to both of my children for a few minutes each. I talked to one of the girls for more than five minutes when I heard this rough, gravelly voice say, "Hey, I need to use that phone, Dog." I turned around to see a short, overweight, much older man named Burke leaning on a cane. I politely informed him he could use the phone when I was finished.

In the meantime, another phone opened up and I saw him use that one. When our recreation period was over, as I was walking the short way back to the cell, I noticed Burke was walking behind me. It turned out he lived in the cell next door to mine in C-156.

Burke yelled to me from behind, "Hey, you're going to get your head split open over that phone, Dog."

I turned around, looked him over from head-to-toe-to-head again and said, "Well, it sure as hell isn't going to be you that does it." Burke mumbled something as we were both entering our cells and closing the doors.

The next day, the same exact scenario occurred. Only this time, I held the telephone up over my shoulder, as if I could use it to strike him with and said, "If you want this phone, come and take it from me!" At that point, Burke waved his hand in the air, as if to blow me off and walked away.

That was the end of the phone conflicts with him. Yet, he seemed to follow me through the camp as I would later move to different housing units over the next three years. We never did speak again, though. I overheard Burke one day (you couldn't miss him since he was fairly loud) telling someone what year he was born in. He was three years younger than I am. Burke appeared to be much, much older; clearly showed the hard life he has lived. In prison you must stand your ground and also protect yourself, your health and your appearance to others.

Chapter Twenty-Five

Adjustment Time

Keith

I have always been hopeful and prayerful I will be released from prison before the completion of the redundant state sentence I was given. I put a lot of effort and footwork into getting that accomplished. Even though release from prison has been my number one agenda from the beginning, a prisoner needs to keep things in perspective.

The wheels of the justice system turn very slowly and the playing field is slanted. After I realized my release was not going to occur overnight, the only healthy option I had was to settle into my environment and to do so without becoming a part of it or without letting it change who I am as a person. Shortly after I arrived at S.C.C.C., I began to work on that.

Using my experience at the county jail, along with my observations of South Central, I knew there was only one way I could cope with this situation. I didn't want this experience to ruin me as a person. I also wanted to use it as an avenue to make me an even better, more useful and more productive person than I had been. I put walls up to block out all of the negatives in the prison environment. I tried to look at all of the blessings and positives there are in life in general. Remember, the first chapter of this book is called 'Count All Things Joy'? I try to live by that.

This is easier said than done, that is true. There have been times when those walls have cracked. But after a few small repairs here and there, for the most part, those walls have stood very strong and have done their job. Not too far into my incarceration, those walls would double in height and strength and they would withstand everything thrown their way.

Passing time in prison is important. "How you do your time" and "knowing how to jail" are phrases often used by inmates. Another saying many in prison are familiar with is "Do your time; don't let it do you." It basically means to keep yourself busy in a productive manner and to, most importantly, keep your head on straight. Don't let the place or the people get to you. Don't go crazy and don't do things that will make your sentence even longer or harder to get through. It was now time, a couple of months into my incarceration at S.C.C.C., to begin that process. The question was, "How?"

A little more than six months after I arrived at South Central, I qualified to move into the honor house, also known as a privilege dorm. If an inmate had good behavior, he qualified to move to one of these dorms after six months at the institution. I was lucky, blessed and responsible enough to meet those requirements.

The honor house provides a much better lifestyle as far as prison goes. An inmate gets more recreation time, more hours to use the gym and library, more time to have outdoor field and yard activities. Honor inmates get more time to use the telephone to keep in touch with family and friends. The inmates in the honor house are not confined to their cells for almost all of the days and evenings.

Microwave ovens in each honor wing allow men to warm up or cook items from the canteen. For those of us fortunate enough to have family and friends send money or to have a paying job at the prison, cooking gives a much greater choice of food items to buy from the canteen list. Having the ability to cook in the wing and to buy a greater variety of food items made the honor house a healthier place to be.

The honor house also gave more time and freedom to do the basics of life like taking showers, doing legal work and playing cards or board games with others. I used my free time in a number of ways. I did legal work for myself and others. I kept in contact with my daughters, family and friends. I worked on my fitness either in the gym or by playing pickup basketball games. I also played on one of the softball teams in the summertime. The recreation department at S.C.C.C. did a good job providing activities and equipment to help keep us fit and busy.

In the honor house, inmates are out of the cell more so, therefore, having less time with a cellmate. This cuts tension and strife dramatically compared to living in twenty-three or twenty-hour lockdown conditions. Living in the honor house increases one's chances of getting one of the more desirable or better-paying jobs at the camp. "They" say it is not a consideration, but believe me, it is. The more well-behaved and responsible inmate gets the better job in most cases. There are few exceptions. Placement in an honor house is a good indicator to employers an inmate is trustworthy and responsible.

My first move from Housing Unit 6 was to one of the "limited" honor wings in Housing Unit 4. This wing had most of the same privileges as the full honor house. It had a little less open freedom and two hours less of gym and library time per week. Although I qualified for a straight trip to Housing Unit 3 (the full honor house), I put in to move to Housing Unit 4 as a favor to someone.

This turned into my first experience of learning real men of their word are hard to find in prison. An inmate, Greeson, who had moved to Housing Unit 4 from Housing Unit 6 was in a bad situation with his cellmate. He needed someone new to live with him, so I agreed to move to Housing Unit 4 to share a cell with him. When I moved down there, Greeson said the cellmate he disliked moved out and that now he was happy with his new one. Now I had a different cellmate whom I didn't care for while moving into a housing unit I didn't need to be in. Once Greeson told me he had no plans for a move, I put in a request to move to Housing Unit 3. It would take two months to find a replacement cellmate for the one I disliked in Housing Unit 4. After four months and two cellmates, I finally got the call to move to Housing Unit 3.

To live in the honor house, an inmate must have a job, must be enrolled in certain programs or must be enrolled in the required G.E.D. classes. In Missouri, G.E.D. classes are mandatory for those who do not have a high school diploma or a G.E.D. already. Since I had a high school diploma, I was not required to attend those classes. I realized getting a job would be a good way to occupy my time. After all, I wanted to do my time and not let it do me.

While living in Housing Unit 4, I was called to work in the prison kitchen. All inmates at the South Central Correctional Center must work in the kitchen for at least ninety days. In many institutions, working in food service is a sought after job that pays very well by prison standards. It is a hard job to get. That is not the case at S.C.C.C.

I applied for other jobs on the camp prior to working in the kitchen, but I was never hired. I later found out from other inmates that no one can get a job anywhere on the camp without working in the kitchen first. At South Central, for those inmates who do not have at least a G.E.D., they must work in food service for no pay. Zero. That is, until they earned their diploma. Inmates with their G.E.D. or diploma were given "pay slots." I worked utility in the kitchen. It paid ten dollars a month. That was only a dollar and fifty cents more than an inmate gets for their "state tip." Sitting in a cell doing nothing doesn't pay much less.

I have a problem with S.C.C.C. mandating ninety days of work in food service. Nowhere in my sentencing and judgment documents does it say I am sentenced to labor. I am aware many states, like Arkansas, have hard labor and job assignments required in their systems. I am not against working. I am against being treated as slave labor and getting nothing out of it. When sitting in your cell pays as much as a job does, it doesn't encourage people to better themselves. It's a lot like the current problem we have with the welfare system in our country.

Other inmates told me food service was not a desirable place to work on the camp. The pay was minimal and some of the staff treated workers like dogs. Staff would not hesitate to put someone in the hole for the slightest violation. What constituted grounds for a write up was arbitrary and discipline was not handed out fairly. If a food item was missing from a work area in the kitchen, instead of finding out who did it, they sent every inmate working in the area to the hole. I knew one man who was sent to the hole for reading his pocket-sized Bible on a break.

When going into and leaving work in the kitchen, there was a disgraceful, dehumanizing and invasive strip search of each inmate which happened every shift. I was more than happy to resign after my required ninety days. My next job proved to be much more rewarding.

I only had a few weeks left in my stint working in food service when I made the move to Housing Unit 3. All four wings in that housing unit were privilege or honor wings. Inmates in the honor house were, almost to the person, like myself. They wanted to do their time with as little drama and trouble as possible. The residents of Housing Unit 3 did our best to avoid the prison mindset. That attitude is one of pre-requisites for getting into the honor house in the first place.

As always, a few bad apples made their way onto the cart. Those inmates usually screwed up what they had earned and were shipped back to one of the other housing units. For the most part, Housing Unit 3 was made up of inmates who knew how to do their time and who did so with a certain de-gree of peace and coexistence with others. Many older in-mates as well as those with disabilities were housed in this unit. Some younger inmates were in the mix as well.

Housing Unit 3 had a number of nicknames across the camp such as "The Cupcake House" or "The White House." The cupcake comment implied honor inmates were weaker or softer than those in the other houses. Some called it "The White House" claiming it was made up of mostly white or Caucasian inmates. I found that to be untrue. In society at large, some people go out of their way to cause racial ten-sion. In prison, that behavior is on steroids.

Placement into the honor house was based on one's behav-ior. Many inmates who badmouth the honor house or system are simply angry and resentful because they don't have the self-control to get there themselves. I have run across a few inmates who, for whatever reason, have chosen not to move to an honor unit when they had the opportunity to do so.

After moving to Housing Unit 3 and getting settled in there, I began applying for jobs across the camp. I applied for near-ly every job posted: the furniture factory, the library, the law library, the Captain's Crew and several others. I applied for a tutoring job in the education department. I applied for a con-tinuing education program offered by the Missouri State University School of Business. I was turned down for everything. I was frustrated because I knew I was a good candidate for all of the things I applied for.

Since I didn't have a job yet, I spent a lot of time going to the gym, playing basketball and softball and doing law work to appeal my case. Even though I was persistent in applying for work, I was determined to be accepted into the college program at the camp, too. Little did I know the college program was extremely hard to get into and many men who were on the camp much longer than I had been were waiting to be accepted as well. To remain in the honor house, I was required to be in school, working or enrolled in the D.O.C. rehabilitation programs that were offered. I am not a fan of those programs and, with a mandatory minimum sentence, they were useless to me in many ways. Somehow, I had to have something going to keep my honor status and to stay in Housing Unit 3.

As I continued my quest to find something meaningful and productive to occupy my time, in the autumn of 2011 I had a breakthrough. A posting announced openings for the Introduction to Business courses given by Missouri State Universiity. I applied and this time I was accepted into the program which began in the winter-spring semester of 2012.

The first class I took was Business Math. Since math wasn't my favorite subject, I needed to study and work hard to get everything I could out of the class. Classwork became my outlet and my challenge to focus my time on. I concentrated hard and used all of the study time I could get in the prison library. On one of those trips to the library in late January or early February 2012, something amazing happened. At about 1:15 one afternoon, my life changed forever.

The prison library is located in the same hallway as the school for the G.E.D. program. Across from the library entrance is a guards' desk and what most would describe as a reception area. The school's educational supervisor and the secretary's office were in that area, as well as the copy machine for the school.

I was standing in the library doorway, waiting for the ten-minute controlled movement window to open so I could return to my housing unit. As I looked across the hallway, standing at the copy machine, talking to someone while she waited for her copies to finish running, I spotted the most beautiful woman I had ever seen. Then, for a brief moment, our eyes met. I thought, *Wow! Who is that? She is so pretty!*

I assumed she was a teacher and wanted to meet her and work in her classroom. More than anything, I wanted to go over and say hello to her, but I felt it would be improper in that environment. What would she think? I wouldn't want her to assume I was just another creepy inmate who had no business approaching her. I'm naturally shy and didn't want to stand there staring. So, at that point, I retreated into the library and waited for the movement window to open. Going back into the library was no easy task for me. She was beautiful and I wanted to meet her, but I thought it was the best thing to do. When the movement window opened, I left the library. She was no longer standing there.

As I walked back to the housing unit, I could not stop thinking about her. I never have and I never will. Little did I know that this brief encounter, when our eyes met for the first time and no words were spoken, would be one of the most memorable moments of my life. It was the first step in finding the whole.

Chapter Twenty-Six

Classroom 10

Keith

When I was a young boy in the early- and mid-1970s growing up in the St. Louis area, the game of hockey was beginning to take hold there. With the expansion of the National Hockey League in 1967, the St. Louis Blues was one of the new franchises taking the league from six to twelve North American cities. I immediately loved and was fascinated by the game.

Playing in that era was a flashy Montreal Canadien center iceman by the name of Guy La Fleur. He was a talented scorer. Fast, sleek and glamorous, playing back in the day of helmetless players, he motored around the ice gracefully with free-flowing shoulder-length blonde hair common in the 1970s. He was a superstar. I wanted to play like him and to be like him. I even had a replica of his red, white and blue Canadien sweater. His surname was French for "the flower." He donned the number ten on his sweater. No one has worn it since. It hangs in the rafters of the Bell Center in Montreal.

Many years passed since the number ten meant so much to me. The same goes for the phrase "the flower." Those would come back to me in a more significant manner than ever before, beginning in March 2012.

After going through the interview process, I was hired by Caroline as a tutor in the G.E.D. program at South Central. Her classes were held in Classroom 10. My first day of work was March 29, 2012, one day after the interview. I was eager to get started.

Being a tutor can be a very gratifying and fulfilling position. I truly wanted to help the other guys at the institution achieve something substantial, do something that would give them confidence and that would help them move forward with their lives. After a life of crime, they needed something positive to work toward. It was to society's advantage for these men to become productive members of our communities since nearly every inmate will be released at some point.

All of those are noble reasons, right? Well, truth be told, the most important reason was to be close to Caroline. From the moment I saw her at the copy machine, I needed to know this incredible woman. We hit it off the moment we met. My first impressions of her at the copier were surpassed by speaking with her during our hour-long interview. I felt the need to be with her in any capacity. Working so closely with Caroline would be the greatest experience of my life. I learned more than I thought possible both academically and about who I am and can be.

Working in Classroom 10 with "the flower" of my life allowed me to bloom into the person I always should have been. For most of my life I kept the real me hidden behind a curtain, always afraid of what others thought. Caroline took that fear away and because of her I am able to celebrate life. Classroom 10 was where I finally found my footing in life and it was because I found the only person I felt safe around. It's ironic to know my first taste of true safety and freedom in life happened inside a maximum security prison.

I interviewed on a Wednesday and I had been told I wouldn't start work until the next week. Teachers only worked Monday through Thursday at the school. It was a pleasant surprise to be called in for work the very next day. I soon found out why.

Classrooms were supposed to have two tutors, but Caroline's was operating with only one. I later learned from Caroline, her tutor, an older man named Johnson, was having personality conflicts with a few of the younger students in class. They realized they could get under his skin, so they did what they could to drive him to distraction. Some of their tactics with Johnson were worse than simply irritating him.

Her other tutor left a month earlier to take a higher paying job in the prison, leaving Johnson as the only tutor. Johnson declared he wanted to get out of the tutoring business, so it was imperative Caroline got a replacement tutor as soon as possible. My arrival helped him be on his way and his departure was a joy to me. He left for good at lunch time on my first day. His desk next to Caroline was vacated and I planted myself there immediately after his departure.

After settling into my new perch, it was time to learn the ropes of prison G.E.D. tutoring. Since I was now the only tutor in the room, it was a baptism by fire. Learning the grading system, answering random one-on-one questions from students about their assignments, familiarizing myself with the curriculum and learning the filing system was a wonderful change of pace for me, but it was a little overwhelming starting out. Caroline made me feel very comfortable. I had no classroom teaching experience and her help, patience and kindness were crucial.

Caroline's experience in the classroom made it easy for me. I observed her teaching skills and her calm teaching methods. Her assignment preparation and classroom organization were impeccable and the learning curve was easier because I worked with someone possessing a lot of patience and experience in the classroom. Caroline gave me confidence in my abilities with just one sentence, "The best way to learn is to teach." It was true and soon I was able to help the students without having to double check with Caroline. I had a great role model when I did run into difficulty explaining a concept to a student. Caroline's way of teaching was clear and concise.

Her desktop (if you could ever see any of it) was a whole other story. This was a source of humor for us throughout our time working together. It still is. Caroline was a good sport and had no problem poking fun at herself. She always knew exactly where everything was; could find it in an instant if it was needed. Her desk drove me crazy.

After not being in a classroom since I graduated myself, teaching high school curriculum was intimidating. It took me a while to refresh myself on the English and advanced math. Spelling, at this stage, is a lost cause for me. My spelling skills are a disaster. Like Caroline's desk, my spelling became another ongoing source of comedy for us.

My poor spelling skills are partially responsible for Caroline writing this book. I hadn't worked for her more than a couple of weeks when she said, "If you ever want to write a book or a screenplay, you might want to have me edit it for you." We laughed but agreed on the spot I would. As time went by, the idea turned from a simple editing job to her being the author of my story. No one knows me better and no one could express my thoughts and feelings like she can.

As enjoyable as it was to work with Caroline, it wasn't easy to be an inmate tutor in a prison. Gaining the respect of the inmate students is difficult. Convincing them another inmate can teach them anything is a challenge. Why should they listen to another inmate? We all wear grey, right? Getting over that stubbornness and pride isn't easy. Both the young and the old suffered from this attitude. Exacerbating this is the fact the education program at the South Central Correctional

Center is mandatory. Any inmate who doesn't have his high school diploma or equivalency must attend school. By and large, the prison classroom doesn't have a motivated crowd.

Many students went to school thinking it was idle time for them to be social. Some resented being forced to attend school when they didn't want to. School most likely hadn't been a bright spot in their lives prior to prison and there's a good chance school wasn't the highlight of their days at the prison. Caroline's job was to teach them and to keep them on task. She had to motivate them to get their G.E.D.s. My job was to help her do this.

Caroline, like all of the other teachers at S.C.C.C., was the only person of authority in the classroom. No guards stood in the room to maintain order. Her classroom management skills were good and we seldom had anyone cause serious trouble in Classroom 10. Chitchat was the biggest hurdle. Friends who lived in different housing units wanted to catch up with people they normally didn't get to socialize with.

Caroline used her authority to discipline students when she needed to. Few of them crossed her once she put an end to an issue. Those who did continue were written conduct violations, but overall the students were orderly. I had no part in classroom discipline. Inmates do not (and should not) take an authority position over other inmates. Some in prison forget that, but it's a good rule to live by.

Some students were eager to learn and we had some positive experiences. There are good stories to tell and I will. It should be clear, there were challenges to teaching in a prison.

I had to verbally defend myself several times while working in the education department. It never escalated into a physical defense, but I had to stick up for myself. The usual accusations of being a child molester surfaced. I was accused of being a snitch and of being a "lame" because I was unwilling to steal classroom supplies for some of them. The latter is what led to Johnson leaving once I was hired. In addition to irritating him, some younger students were trying to strong arm him into stealing for them. Pens, folders and writing paper, items that either weren't offered at the canteen or that could be sold on the yard, were in high demand.

A few students were pushier than others. One day, with Caroline present, I was accused of being a child molester. The young man loudly claimed he had seen my paperwork confirming I was one. Caroline stepped in and flatly told him what I was in prison for.

Working with Caroline was a joy, but the constant perverted statements made by some students were bothersome to me. Much of it was directed toward Caroline when she would step out of the room for a moment. Private conversations about her in hushed voices occurred all the time, but when she left the room for any reason it became a public display of reckless, lewd, crude and classless comments about her. It was disgusting and it would make most people's skin crawl. It did mine.

Several different students, regardless of age or demographic, made comments. Most of them were guys younger than Caroline's own children. Some sat in front of her desk pretending to want help with their assignments, but really they were there to fire on her.

One day when Caroline left the room to run copies, one student bragged of his intentions. I simply looked at him and asked, "What makes you think you could ever have a woman like that?" He got up and walked to his desk with no comment.

Another time, a student repeatedly went to her desk and asked her to get him a different assignment. The assignments he asked for were in the two bottom drawers of the filing cabinet. As I followed his eyes, I realized what he was doing. Other students began asking for the same assignments. They were hoping to look down Caroline's blouse as she reached for the lessons. Caroline dressed professionally and in good taste, so they weren't successful, but I let her know what was happening. I told her I would get them their assignments when they asked and lo and behold, they were no longer interested in getting more of that work.

Caroline and I immediately worked as a team and there was a comfortableness in our conversations from the very beginning. Because of that, I could talk with her about situations with confidence knowing she wouldn't misinterpret my concern. She knew I was making sure her safety was secure.

In the same way, she knew she could defend me verbally about my crimes to inmates without worrying I would be offended. Most inmates don't want a staff member talking about their personal information. I'm one of those inmates. If it had been anyone but Caroline, I would have been uncomfortable with it.

The lewd behavior was not limited to the inmates. The regular desk guard, Presley, made sexual comments about Caroline and another good-looking teacher to inmates. He made fun of overweight, less-attractive teachers behind their backs to inmates, too. Because he was sexually depraved in his own right, he disregarded the safety of the teachers. It was hard to tell who was worse inside the prison: the inmates or the employees. Presley's color-coded counting system and his insistence that he treated everyone the same didn't save him from having zero class. For all of his efforts to put on the appearance of being professional, it was clear he wasn't.

Presley wasn't the only inappropriate "professional" at the school. The interim school administrator never took his eyes off of Caroline's chest when he spoke to her. I saw him doing it. Besides being perverted, he was inept at his job and didn't know how to lead an organization. Others were unprofessional as well and those ranged from the secretary to the major of the camp.

It was a difficult position for me to be in. I could see the inappropriate behavior of staff and inmates toward Caroline and there was nothing I could say or do about it. Outwardly, I had to act as though none of it bothered me. Inwardly, I was angry at what I saw and heard. I told Caroline early on in our working relationship I would never do anything to hurt her or to put her livelihood in jeopardy. I kept my word.

Some might say I shouldn't have felt this way about Caroline in the first place. Well, our love and relationship is completely natural and God is at the center of our relationship. There is no turning it on and off. Neither one of us planned to find love inside a prison. Caroline didn't take her job looking for it and I didn't rob banks trying to find it. It just is.

For about a month, I was the only tutor in Caroline's classroom. When there was a tutor job opening at the school, the position was advertised and then teachers interviewed the candidates. Caroline believed it was important we operate as a team to bring about student success, so when she interviewed new tutors she asked my opinion about the candidates. She didn't want to bring someone in who wouldn't get along with me or who had behavior problems out on the yard. She knew I saw how people acted in the general population and not just how they behaved during an interview. I appreciated that she wanted my opinion.

During my time in Classroom 10, there were two tutors who were hired for our room. Both had different styles of teaching. One, Crawford, was extremely excited about teaching math. The drawback was it was all done on a one-on-one basis at his desk. He had a phobia about doing lessons in front of everyone at the board. Math wasn't one of our favorite topics to teach, so Caroline tried to get someone who enjoyed math as her second tutor. Caroline and I would do the lessons at the board, but Crawford was very good at helping students individually.

The other man hired I knew through the Missouri State University School of Business program we both were enrolled in. Having Caroline for a boss was a bonus to both of us because she proofread and edited our papers for class. We worked well together in the college classes and I knew he would be a positive addition to our classroom team. Joe was a great coworker. He was, until he got himself in trouble outside of our classroom. Tutors had to be write-up free and the outside incident cost him his job. On the day he was written up, he came to Classroom 10 to apologize to Caroline. We admired his consideration of the impact his departure would have on the classroom.

While I vowed to never harm Caroline's career, others had different intentions. The school secretary, Barbara Mason, had petty jealousies toward Caroline from when she first began. Caroline and the education supervisor, Randy Turner, were good friends and it drove the secretary insane (more so than she already was) that she was not the only person the supervisor looked to for input. Working conditions were okay as long as Randy was there, but after he was called away to military duty, Caroline's interactions with the secretary went downhill.

Barbara openly insulted Caroline in front of other staff and students. She looked at Caroline and said, "I am a vindictive person and I go after anyone who crosses me." She refused to order supplies for Caroline. Barbara made sexually harassing statements to Caroline. She basically did everything she could to make Caroline's life miserable while she was at work. Even the acting education supervisor admitted to Caroline he was afraid to stand up to Barbara because she would make his life hell if he said anything to her. Caroline was left to fend for herself.

This was the kind of working environment Caroline had to put up with and it was painful for me to see what she went through. It might have been easier for me to remove myself from such a heated environment, but I would do it again a thousand times over.

Working in Classroom 10 wasn't all bad. There were many good experiences and accomplishments. Working together was fun and our classroom was dedicated to getting the students their educations. Although some students had no intention of getting a G.E.D., there were some who would work hard to make progress. Knowing we were helping them brought a lot of satisfaction to us.

At the school, there were three levels of classes: low, medium and high. Classroom 10 was a medium-level classroom. Each classroom had three sessions of students per day lasting three hours each. The curriculum was from a state-approved set of books. When Caroline took over Classroom 10, there hadn't been much emphasis on student performance. Caroline worked diligently to put together sets of classroom assignments for each subject. All three sessions worked on the same assignments and progressed as a group. We gave them individual help and did short board lessons. It worked. Students moved on to the higher level classrooms at a rapid rate based on their test scores. Testing was done every few months to monitor progress. Because of the positive rapport we had with the students, many of them asked to remain in Classroom 10 even after they tested into the higher level classes.

Part of having success in the classroom was providing a positive environment. Wherever a classroom may be, students want to learn where they feel valued and encouraged. Caroline had good classroom management and students knew what behavior was expected, but it was also a lighthearted place to be. The students liked knowing they were treated with human dignity in her classroom and it was okay to have a sense of humor in there. The guys knew our team wanted them to succeed. That made a difference in their attitudes and their actions.

It was gratifying to see men who struggled academically their entire lives have success. The look on someone's face who finally understood how to multiply fractions or who now could write a solid five-paragraph essay was wonderful. It made the job rewarding for both Caroline and me.

One gentleman, Parsons, could barely read when he entered Classroom 10. He was in his fifties and hadn't been in prison all that long. Caroline worked individually with him, helping him read his assignments out loud to her. Over time, he gained enough trust in me that he would work with me also. As we developed our rapport with him, Parsons confided that he was in prison for forcing out at gun point some drug dealers who stopped paying rent on his house. They had filed charges and this middle-aged husband and father was now spending time in a maximum security prison. He was determined to create something good out of his situation, wanting desperately to become literate. Even though Parsons could have gone to the low-level classroom, he asked to stay in Classroom 10 because he trusted us and was making progress.

Some of the students had learning disabilities and some had limited academic skills. Some were bright but never earned a high school diploma. These men hadn't experienced academic success before for a variety of reasons. Some came from inner city schools where education wasn't a top priority. Some made poor life choices and wasted their time when in public schools. The one commonality was they were incarcerated and now were expected to get their high school equivalency.

Many of our students went to prison when they were young and had little life experience outside of prison. We answered questions about basic household finances, current events and other topics our students wanted to know about. The state needs a more intensive readiness program for inmates. Before release, inmates need to know how to interview, how to bank and do other daily financial planning and how to pay utility bills. These are important skills for all of us to have. Someone who spends a decade or more in prison or who went to prison at a young age needs to have these skills to be successful when they go back to our communities. We did what we could to help them with the basics in addition to bringing them up to speed academically to pass the G.E.D.

Some teachers and staff truly wanted their students to succeed, but some didn't put much effort into it. While we all need to earn a paycheck, some of them were there for just that. They had no real investment in the success of the students. Some of the teachers were better suited to be guards. They were more interested in writing conduct violations and belittling students than in teaching them. Having students in the classroom was an inconvenience to them. Students could focus on getting their education in Classroom 10 because they knew Caroline's goal was to educate them. She wasn't there to argue with them or to find a reason to write them up.

I have worked at a number of places and I have had positions of responsibility at my job sites. I can recognize professionalism and it was lacking in the education department. A few staff members had personalities unsuited to being in a volatile environment like a prison. Some were there to get personal glory or to have a power trip. Some were simply there to collect a state paycheck. I won't go into great detail about all of them, but I will tell about a few of them.

The teacher who ran the test preparation class, Christy Massey, looked for self-glorification. When students worked hard in other classrooms and earned their way to the final stage before taking the G.E.D., she was hell-bent on taking all of the credit for their success. Students who made it to Massey's classroom were already academically prepared. She thought all of the attention should be given to her for her accomplishments. At the graduation ceremonies, an outside observer would swear this woman single-handedly took these students all the way from illiteracy to being college bound. No one had to ask her. Christy Massey was more than happy to go on and on about it to the audience.

Massey was held to a different set of rules than the other teachers. She would supply candy for her tutors. She kept it in her desk and it was common knowledge by staff and inmates that she gave it out. She made physical contact with tutors, like stroking their arms during conversations. She hugged students when they graduated. These were major violations of the staff handbook, but Massey's husband was a sergeant, so thought herself above the rules.

Another teacher, Sandra Jennings, constantly came to our classroom and asked Caroline what the correct answer was to basic grammar or math questions. She knew nothing about the curriculum and would teach her students the wrong way to do assignments. Caroline one time had to go to Jennings's classroom (at her request) and re-teach them the grammar lesson they were working on because Jennings was too confused to explain it to them. Jennings worked there for years, steadily drawing a paycheck. Right before we left South Central, Jennings was voted "Teacher of the Year" by the education department staff. At least that is what everyone was told.

It was an interesting environment. Caroline made the best of the difficult situation she was working in and tried her best to make her students successful. I worked hard to help her accomplish that. In a perfect world, we should all have a job we look forward to going to every day. I had that in Classroom 10. It was the most enjoyable work experience I ever had. Yes, it was because of Caroline.

The environment in Classroom 10 made up for all of the craziness we dealt with from students and staff. Learning the ins and outs of teaching in Classroom 10 taught me many things. Good and bad things happen in life. God is in charge. I made poor choices in the past, but God gave me the opportunity to help others, allowed me to finally find the love and happiness I had searched for my entire life. I became whole in Classroom 10.

Chapter Twenty-Seven

Finding the Whole

Keith

When I first laid eyes on Caroline at the copier, I felt a change begin, one which evolved and accelerated during the interview and as we worked together. It is something intangible I can't put into words, but it is real and continues to grow inside me.

While teaching in Classroom 10, Caroline and I ran across a math assignment that became important to us. I've already said math isn't our favorite subject to teach, so I know it sounds strange that we became so engrossed, but we did. In this series of course work, students had to learn how to find the parts of numbers; the percentage of a number and the whole of a number. One lesson was called "Finding the Whole." We looked at each other and both of us said, "We have spent our lives trying to find the whole and now we finally have!"

After wandering through life for forty-seven years as a half of a person, with Caroline I could finally feel myself becoming whole. I'm not saying wonderful things didn't happen in the past. I went many places and I have had some great experiences, but there seemed to be nothing to tie them together. I was scattered and broken. Now, since finding the whole, everything is bonded together. Even the not-so-good things, both past and present, can be considered a joy. That's what Caroline's entry into my life has provided. Life makes sense now and it has purpose and explanation. It is the same for Caroline. It's the most peaceful and certain thing we have ever encountered in life.

We made an immediate connection. The first Monday after I was hired, the staff and the inmates were called into separate meetings with the wardens. Because of some issues that happened previously in the education department, the wardens wanted to lay down the law about staff-inmate relations. It was the only time I would see the wardens in the school. They seldom were around the general population of inmates. They were sufficiently embarrassed by prior events to deem it necessary to make their way to the education department that day.

After lunch, Caroline and I got to speak for the first time about our respective meetings. I looked at her and said, "No one is going to tell me who my friends are."

She smiled and said, "Good for you."

We knew we already considered ourselves friends. Right from the start, a partnership was formed.

A few weeks after I started working at the school, Caroline suffered a major injury. She tore the A.C.L. in her right knee and five weeks later she had to have surgery to replace it. A.C.L. replacement surgery is painful and it requires a lot of rehabilitation. She was gone for six weeks, and then for another three months she left early three days a week in order to do physical therapy. Her third session of students was eliminated during that time because otherwise they would only meet once a week. I missed her terribly during her six week recovery after surgery, but I enjoyed having a little extra time after lunch to talk with her while we worked in the classroom before she left for therapy.

On one of those days, we talked about the stigma people have about former convicts. People are judgmental and some people will use past incarceration as a hammer to hold over the ex-con's head. Caroline told me she hoped when I got out of prison I never ended up with someone who would use it as a weapon against me. Every time I went to the grocery store or was late getting home, she didn't want someone grilling me about committing a crime. She didn't want me to be punished by someone for crimes I already paid for. As we talked, we stood by the filing cabinet where I was putting assignments away. As she was getting ready to leave, we had a moment. As we stared into each other's eyes, she told me she could tell there was something I wanted to say. There was. I wanted to say, "You know, someday I'm going to marry you." I didn't say it. We just stared into each other's eyes and then she said she needed to leave to get to her appointment. It's something Caroline and I will never forget.

That happened in August. It wouldn't be until the next April that I told Caroline I loved her. I have done a lot of things in life that required nerve. Robbing banks is one of them. I have never been as nervous as I was the day I told Caroline how I felt. The greater the reward, the more risk it requires. There was no greater reward I could ever have than to gain Caroline's love and respect. Therefore, it was the greatest risk I had ever taken.

I planned so carefully what I was going to say to her that I broke it up into four points. Caroline jokingly called it "The Business Plan." I guess I did sound like an entrepreneur trying to pitch his new idea to investors, but everything I said was heartfelt. I could tell Caroline was emotional as I told her how I felt, so I let her know these were my feelings; she wasn't responsible for them. I could see the relief sweep across her face. When I was done with my presentation, I finished it by telling her, "I love you and I will never, ever stop." That's something I repeat to her every single day.

By the time I told her how I felt, it was time for lunch. I knew she needed some time to process it all. It was a huge step for both of us. After she came back from lunch, Caroline let me know she felt the same way I did. From that day forward, we faced the world as a team. We became whole. For all of the fears and struggles we would go through, we weren't alone anymore.

We supported each other through every heartache or difficulty that came up since. The summer before we left Classroom 10, Caroline's youngest son was critically wounded in Afghanistan. She's told me I was the only thing holding her together during that traumatic time. When she spent four weeks in Washington, D.C. with him as he began his recovery, it was tough being apart, but we knew we loved and supported each other.

Caroline and I don't have what outsiders would consider an "easy" relationship, but it is. There is nothing truer or easier for us than loving each other. As Caroline explained to a few of her friends, we have a great relationship. I just happen to be incarcerated right now. Our faith in God and our amazing connection to each other, make the inconveniences of our separation possible to bear.

For years I searched for what was missing and finally found what I was looking for. I can endure the prison atmosphere. I can face the challenges ahead. I can be happy in this moment. All because I have the love of the one person who makes me whole.

Phone calls and letters are what we have right now. We are working on getting me home sooner, but our certainty lets us know we will be okay no matter what. We will be married someday. I long for the day when our vows seal our sense of oneness even further. We are hoping it won't be inside a prison, but we will do that if need be. Caroline is writing this book as Caroline Giammanco because of our certainty that we are united now and forever. I love her and I will never, ever stop.

Chapter Twenty-Eight

The Island of Misfit Toys

Caroline

I began working at the South Central Correctional Center in July 2011. It wasn't my first pick for a job, but teaching positions were hard to come by in southern Missouri at the time. I had experience working in alternative high schools and working around adult felons wasn't much different than working with eighteen-year-old delinquents.

I quickly learned a lot of hard truths at S.C.C.C. No one should think working in a prison was easy and it wasn't. Within a few months, my life was threatened multiple times by an inmate and I received next-to-no support from the staff. I encountered coworkers who lied and intimidated to get what they wanted. I went into the job knowing the inmates might harm me. I found out a staff member was just as likely to stab me in the back.

We all have heard that absolute power corrupts absolutely. A combination of superiors who did nothing for the betterment of the organization and of others working for their own agendas created a situation that led to me leaving the prison.

In the prison system, inmates are not supposed to be given special privileges. Those are understandable rules, as long as everyone follows them, but not everyone follows the rules. When the overstepping staff member is the head of custody and when the offender is threatening and violent, it escalates into a dangerous situation. It completely undermines the safety and security of the institution.

In a penitentiary where smuggled drugs and contraband were a serious problem, it was commonplace for all employees to undergo searches. Every time we entered or left, our belongings were scanned, we went through a metal detector and we could be pat searched at any time. Everyone was used to the routine.

Ironically, the head of custody, Major Joe Jenkins, told officers he was exempt from searches. He walked around the search lines, bypassing the metal detector. He didn't do this to test the determination of his staff to enforce the rules. Instead, it was the assertion of his own self-importance. When an officer insisted the major obey the rules, he was glared at and reprimanded. What kind of example did it set for the employees when the superior officer refused to follow the rules? What kind of questions did it raise?

In the spring of 2013, Major Jenkins insisted the education department hire a particular offender as the porter (janitor). Offender Kessler was a favorite of the major and it was obvious he could do anything he wanted to on the camp. He was big, aggressive and immune from discipline. That was not a healthy combination in a maximum security prison.

Soon Kessler caused safety concerns in the education department, and because he was the major's pet, no one was willing to do anything about it. Offender Kessler was in fights and never went to the hole. He bragged that the major gave him all the food he wanted from luncheons. He wouldn't wear his prison uniform to work. He told people he didn't have to follow the rules because he worked for the major and not for the education department.

In his housing unit he was given special privileges. By order of the major, he was allowed to stay out in the wing long after every other offender was locked down. While on the loose in the wing, he went from cell to cell to cell. To the bystander, it sure looked like business was being conducted. Two years later, Major Jenkins was arrested for drug distribution during a raid conducted by outside law enforcement officials. Many of us weren't surprised.

Offender Kessler acted friendly to me when he began working at the school. Really friendly. He found excuses to come into my room, even though his duties didn't have anything to do with my class. Our tutors were responsible for cleaning the classroom, but Kessler ordered my tutors to clean other rooms, so he could be in mine, alone with me. He had no authority to order anyone to do anything. He was an inmate. Keith was not going to leave me alone with Kessler. My other tutor, Crawford, was also no fan of the porter. The three of us made sure I was never left alone with Kessler.

I began to hear from other teachers and tutors that Kessler was threatening them. He bullied them and gave them menacing stares. One of my co-workers reported his threatening behavior, but nothing happened. Her concerns were completely ignored. Kessler had only worked there a few weeks and it was already an alarming situation.

When Kessler saw I had no interest in him, his demeanor changed. Jealousy reared its ugly head. After I told Kessler to stay out of my classroom, Keith and I heard from other offenders that rumors were being spread about us. Kessler and a tutor were telling people we were holding hands in class. We were not. Having the accusations made in that environment was serious.

Our regular education supervisor, Randy Turner, was on military assignment, so one of the teachers was made the acting education supervisor. His name was Richard Blake. The tutor spreading rumors about us, Offender Reese, worked for Blake. He had a reputation throughout the camp of stirring trouble. He caused uproars in the church group. He bad-mouthed the education supervisor in his absence. He even criticized the chaplain. Reese had a life sentence and being a snitch and an agitator was the prison persona he had developed over time. It made him feel important.

Some coworkers told me to brush off the comments made by Kessler and Reese. After all, those two were "only offenders." Kessler and Reese were offenders who had the ears of the major and my supervisor. That made their comments more alarming.

In June, I addressed the issue with Offender Reese. I made a general comment to him that someone was spreading rumors about staff members. He immediately became defensive. Reese took my general comment and made it very specific. He said all of the women teachers were talked about having sexual misconduct with offenders and it wasn't just me being discussed. Funny, I never mentioned offenders, let alone the idea of sexual misconduct. Reese, of course, claimed he was trying to put a stop to the rumors. It was obvious he knew why I brought this up to him. His own comments proved his guilt.

Reese had the protection of Richard Blake. I spoke to Reese in the mid-morning and by lunchtime, Blake pulled me aside into his office. He wanted to know about the "argument" I had with Reese and why I was "mad" at Reese. I told him there wasn't any argument at all. Blake said I needed to understand Reese "hadn't been himself" lately. Blake gave a laundry list of family and personal issues Reese was facing. By policy, we weren't supposed to discuss personal issues with inmates, yet he knew so much about Reese's personal life.

Of course, it was common for teachers to talk with our tutors. We spent hours and hours together each day. It was hypocritical for the supervisor to be so blatantly defensive about Reese when the department loved to use "overfamiliarity with staff" as a reason to fire employees. The rule applied only when it suited the whims of the department. Obviously, Blake could get away with it. The major was a glaring example of favoritism gone wild.

It was irregular for a supervisor to intercede on an inmate's behalf. Blake cared more about protecting Reese than he did finding out if his employee was causing trouble for a staff member. He wasn't concerned about my well-being. His mindset became important as events unfolded in the months ahead.

Word kept coming to Keith and me that Kessler was running his mouth. He told people on the walk that he and the major were going to make sure I was fired. We were told Kessler was jealous because I avoided speaking to him whenever I could. I had nothing to say to him. Kessler told other tutors in the education department that every day he looked for a way to get Keith fired. We were targeted by the offenders who got special privileges from the authorities. Those authorities themselves believed they were above the rules of the prison. As we would later find out, they believed they were above the law in general.

Months went by and we were not the only victims of Kessler's bullying. He continued to threaten other students and offenders. He made life uncomfortable for staff members. Several times my coworker, Michael Vaughn and I spoke to Richard Blake about this. We spoke to him privately and in staff meetings, every time requesting Kessler be fired. Any one of his instances of bad behavior would have gotten other prison workers fired. Richard Blake never removed Kessler and ignored our requests.

The apprehension and fear in the school was felt by everyone. The officers assigned to our hallway witnessed his threatening behavior, but they did nothing about it. Kessler sat in the guard's chair drinking coffee while the guard stood. Kessler came and went as he pleased around the camp. Students came into class saying they heard the officers joining in with Kessler, laughing about "getting that bitch walked out." That was me they were talking about. Not only did the guards do nothing to maintain safety in the school, but they joined in on threats toward staff. Supposedly, everything in the prison system is done to "insure the safety and security of the institution." Obviously, that wasn't reality at S.C.C.C.

On September 23, 2013, Kessler threatened to beat up Offender Teague, the tutor who worked in the classroom across the hall from me. The entire incident happened in front of the education officer, Officer Ballard. Nothing happened to Kessler. Days went by. Nothing. Finally, nine days after the incident, I asked Blake if he had spoken to Offender Teague about the threats he received. He said, "No, I've been busy." I reminded him that nine days had gone by. At the end of the day, Mr. Blake still had not spoken to the victim. He never spoke to him.

On October 2, 2013, Michael Vaughn approached me after lunch and told me he had spoken with Assistant Warden Eleanor Heath regarding the porter. She told him she couldn't act based on his word alone. She asked Mike if anyone else who knew about the situation. He told her I did and Assistant Warden Heath wanted me to email her a report of what I knew. This was the beginning of the end of my employment at the prison.

I wrote a lengthy email to Assistant Warden Heath outlining the problems we faced with Kessler. In detail, I explained how he threatened and intimidated offenders and staff. I told how he stole from the department without any punishment. I told how he created a hostile work environment for staff, students and workers. I listed aggressive encounter after aggressive encounter the school endured since Kessler began working there. He was not required to follow the rules the other offenders followed. I made a point to only mention behavior directly dealing with our department. I left out what happened in the housing unit and I didn't tell about the fights he had been in. If the wardens wanted to look into his behavior, they could do that, but I focused on the impact he was having on the school. As it was, the email was pages long. Assistant Warden Heath had plenty to consider. Mike and I thought some relief was in sight.

I stuck my neck out by sending the email, but I also was told to report to the assistant warden. Clearly, someone needed to let her know what was going on. Mike did what he thought was the right thing by reporting the situation to the wardens. I did what I thought was right by telling what I knew. Mike and I carpooled to work and on many of those trips we discussed how we should handle the volatile situation in the education department. We felt there were no other options at this point. The difference was Mike Vaughn didn't put anything in writing. I did.

The next day at work I went to the office area to use the copy machine. Major Jenkins was sitting in the office chair at the guard station. It was clear he knew about the email. His icy glare was an attempt at intimidation. If he could have felt my blood running through his fingers, he would have killed me on the spot.

A few hours later, after the major had left, Blake called me into his office and told me to shut the door. He said, "I want to say thank you and congratulations."

I asked him, "For what?"

He said, "Whoever you talked to about the major and Kessler sure made an impact." He assumed I had spoken to Eleanor Heath. Given his past behavior as a snake in the grass, I knew where this conversation was going. He was fishing for information. I needed to be cautious.

I told him, "I never actually spoke to anyone. Someone else did and I was asked to email what I knew, so I did." I tried to keep my comments controlled.

For good reason, I didn't trust Blake. Over the past several months he had proven he was self-serving and spineless. He told me he was impressed. He was all smiles and tried to reassure me he was my friend. Blake knew I had been put through the wringer during my time at the prison. He said, "After all you've had to put up with the past two years, it's time you got some thumbs up."

I told him, "This isn't about me. Someone has been going around threatening people and my supervisor asked for information."

He kept pressing, saying I had gotten the major into a lot of trouble. I told Blake I didn't say the major did anything. Offender Kessler went around saying he works for the major and not for the education department. I asked who ordered his release when he was caught stealing the cheese from the G.E.D. lunches. If the wardens wanted to do an investigation into it that was for them to do. I only asked a question. Unlike what was done to me, I didn't participate in a smear campaign. I told the truth when the warden asked for my input.

Blake said, "Well, I certainly hope you don't think I haven't done anything about it."

I just stared at him. After months and months of his refusal to do anything to resolve the dangerous situation, I was incredulous. I didn't even bother responding. He allowed fear and intimidation to run rampant in his department and now he was concerned about how he might be perceived.

"Well, I can tell you that Offender Teague was threatened in front of Officer Ballard and he did nothing about it," I said.

Blake leaned forward, smiling and said, "You know he has been put on leave without pay?"

I said, "Ballard?"

He said, "No, the major."

Blake wanted to shake my hand because I had gotten the major into hot water. If the major was in trouble, it was because of his own actions, not mine.

I reminded Blake of an incident from the summer before. Sandra Jennings called a meeting with Major Jenkins because none of the write ups by teachers were acted on. The major sat in her classroom and blackmailed the entire staff. Jenkins told all of the teachers we were free to question what he did or how he operated. We could complain if we wanted to. However, he was accumulating damning information on all of us. If we questioned him, he would use that information against us. Blake sat in on that meeting. He didn't say a word in defense of the staff.

The major's threat went against D.O.C. policy which states employees have a duty to report any misconduct they are aware of. The major's failure to report, if he did have incriminating evidence against anyone, meant he could lose his job for breaking policy. Furthermore, his comments constituted blackmail. That is a crime whether you are inside or outside a prison.

I gave Blake few details about my email to Assistant Warden Heath.

He said, "I wish you had sent me a copy of your email, too."

I'm sure he did. Why would I share the email with Blake when he was one of the problems with the way things ran around there? The porter still wasn't fired. I had no confidence in Blake at all.

The next week, Kessler was still working at the school. One morning before work I said to Blake, "I notice that the major is still walking around."

He said, "Why wouldn't he be?"

Stunned, I looked at him and said, "Because you told me last week he was put on suspension without pay."

He looked at me condescendingly and said, "Oh, that. Well that suspension was a long time ago, like last month."

That is not how he had presented it to me in his office the week before. Who asks to shake the hand of someone for a suspension happening a month earlier for an unrelated issue? The constant lies were disturbing. My fear was rising and I was becoming more certain I was in danger of reprisal.

Finally, Offender Kessler was removed from the education department. He was never officially fired. They simply advertised his job in the housing units. For a few days, it seemed like the ugliness was over.

Then after work on October 17, I was told disturbing news by an officer working in Kessler's housing unit. Word had it Kessler now worked for the major and Assistant Warden Heath. The same warden who told me to report his bad behavior was now Kessler's boss. Either he was promoted after my report or they were simply more honest about whom he worked for the entire time. I was in a very dire situation.

The next morning was a Friday and normally I wouldn't have to work, but this week began with the Columbus Day holiday and we always worked the Friday of a holiday week.

No students would be at school that day, but the staff was expected to work in their classrooms.

I arrived at work worried and stressed. Retaliation was a certainty and it had kept me up all night. I talked to my good friend and coworker, Kelly Rainer, about my concerns. We went to my room so she could read the email I sent to Heath. It was only a matter of time before I was retaliated against and I wanted Kelly to know what was in the email before I left the prison for good. While Kelly read it, Blake quietly walked into my classroom and began peering over Kelly's shoulder to see what she was reading. He had a habit of being rude like that. Kelly, once she realized what he was doing, jumped up and left.

Blake sat down across from me asking if anything was wrong and if I wanted to talk to him. I didn't and I told him so. Like usual, he couldn't look me in the eye when we spoke. His eyes always gravitated to my chest. He persisted asking repeatedly if there was anything I wanted to talk with him about. At that point, I figured *Why not tell him what's on my mind? My days are numbered here anyway.*

I began by saying, "Richard, I never should have been the one who had to handle the situation with the porter. Now I am in a very bad position. You know retaliation is likely."

He agreed and responded, "I know, I should have been the one who took care of that."

The time for holding my tongue was over and I said, "Damn right you should have been! We told you for months it was a serious problem and you did nothing about it. Now I have a target on my back."

We discussed instance after instance of hostile work conditions I'd endured at the prison. The secretary, Barbara, did everything she could to undermine me, the guards were sexually harassing and my safety had been threatened more than once with no support from the staff or administration.

Blake admitted I was treated unfairly. What had happened to me over those two-and-a-half years was so bad he broke down in tears in my classroom, apologizing for not doing anything to help me. Imagine that. My employment and safety were in jeopardy and I had to give him tissues because it was all so horrible.

He apologized several times and promised to do better in the future. I didn't put much stock in it based on his past behaviors and my gut feeling proved true once again as time went by. I stuck my neck out for the safety and security of the education department and no one in the department came to my defense or aid when I was bullied or mistreated. Blake admitted he was more concerned about making his life easier than he was taking responsibility for what happened at the school. It was all a little too late.

Later that morning, I called Keith up from his housing unit so he knew what happened. For his own safety, he needed to be aware Kessler was hired by the major and the assistant warden. Knowledge is power, as they say, and he was at risk if he wasn't aware.

The next week it was a matter of time before the axe fell. As stressful as it was, it was fortunate the players showed their hands for months. It gave Keith and me the opportunity to talk about how things would most likely play out. Keith always said their first move would be against him. He was the easiest to get to. They already had him.

Sure enough, on Wednesday afternoon of that week, it happened. Officer Presley came to my classroom door as third session students were arriving. He gruffly told Keith to grab his coat and go up front. Everyone knew he was going to be locked up and I couldn't help but think they did it during a movement window so as many people as possible on the camp could watch the spectacle.

Keith never had a write up the entire time he had been in prison and there was no doubt he was locked up to get to me. The sneers on the faces of the officers proved it, clearly implying his head was on a platter and mine was going to be next. I'd had enough. Without hesitation, I knew I was walking out of that place for the last time. I shined light on some of their darkness and they put Keith in the hole in retaliation. I wasn't going to spend one minute pretending it was okay.

I stopped Blake in the hall and, pointing to my classroom, said, "You and I both know what that is about. We talked about this last Friday. The retaliation has started. I want a letter of recommendation because I am done with this place." He agreed and told me he would need my email address so he could write me a letter that night.

I gathered some of my personal belongings as the last session of the day unfolded and I walked out that evening knowing I would never go back. Michael Vaughn walked with me through the Administration Building to the parking lot as we did every day after work. It was a very sad and solemn car ride back home. He knew I was taking the brunt of our efforts to make the school a safer place.

That night I received via email a glowing letter of recommendation from Richard Blake. It was the kind of recommendation employees hope for from an employer. He talked about my contributions to the school as the Professional Development Chairperson, my dedication to providing a high quality education to my students and my pleasant and professional manner. I thanked him for it. His true colors showed the next day when he blocked me on Facebook. That's the kind of "friendship" I had gotten all along from him.

I wrote a letter of resignation effective immediately and mailed it to both Jefferson City and to Blake at the South Central Correctional Center. I was done being a part of that system.

Chapter Twenty-Nine

Truth or Consequences

Caroline

The shock was intense. We knew retaliation was likely, but when it happened, it was still a blow. The major would follow through on his threats to attack anyone who stood up to him. I stood up to him. They found the most vicious things to accuse us of and plenty of people to lie about us so they could be part of the feeding frenzy.

In prison it is a game for some inmates to get staff fired. Some inmates do this by manipulating employees into sexual affairs. Others spread rumor and innuendo. Some plant false evidence to be used against the staff member. Plenty of people were already participating in this game against us and Major Jenkins thought he had plenty he could crucify me with. Thankfully, Keith and I were careful. We didn't have contact, we didn't write each other notes and we didn't exchange contraband.

I quit because the powers that be would do their best to make a spectacle out of me. Fired staff are walked out by the authorities in a very embarrassing public display. It's big news and nearly everyone on the camp wants to watch it happen when it does. I hadn't done anything and I possessed enough self-respect that I wasn't going to be paraded through camp like I had anything to be ashamed of.

I was concerned for my safety. Being stabbed crossed my mind. Being raped was in the forefront. Immediately upon Keith's lock up, the entire school was on fire with word that Keith and I were having sexual contact in our classroom. Not only was my authority as staff swept away by those accusations, but dozens of the inmates were now looking at me as prey. They wanted to be next in line if I was giving out favors. I saw it in their eyes.

I could not stay under those conditions. I reported wrongdoing and now an all-out character assassination was in full swing against me. The major announced it would happen at the faculty meeting that summer. He may be corrupt, but in this instance, he was a man of his word.

The rumors flying around the prison in the coming days and weeks were mortifying. The worst ones were spread by staff. I had contacts and friends within the prison walls, so I heard what was said about me. One of the officers in the administrative bubble told people coming and going through the prison I was caught having sex and was walked out. Presley in education told other staff I was writing notes to multiple inmates and my desk was full of love letters. Because he was the education officer, people believed him. He would know, right? In reality, no one but the prison investigator was allowed to search my room and desk. Presley made up lies to sound important and to degrade me. The wildest rumors possible were spread. Everyone wanted a moment of fame by adding to the juicy gossip.

I wasn't only worried about me, though. As dire as my circumstances were, Keith was in real danger. He had enemies from many different sides of this situation who would be menacing him. Administrative Segregation, or "the hole," is not solitary confinement. Keith was with some truly violent and vile people; some would feel compelled to threaten him. Keith was aware of the threats he would face. We talked about the possibilities in the days and weeks leading up to their move against me.

I was concerned about the inmates with perverted intentions toward me. The guys who made lewd comments about me behind my back, the ones who had delusions they would count me as a conquest were angry at Keith for my departure. They would make him pay if they could.

I worried about the staff members. I mentioned in the preface I was on the verge of getting out of an unhappy marriage that died years before. I purposely avoided bringing the other half of that unhappy union into this story because our marital problems were not connected to anything that happened after I began working at the prison. The marriage had died in 2009 and we were simply strangers living in the same house for years. I mention him now for one reason only: he also worked at S.C.C.C. He wouldn't exact punishment on Keith. He wasn't a violent man. I was concerned other staff members might mistakenly show "blue solidarity" and let something happen to Keith, though. With all of the rumors flying, an officer might assume Keith was the reason for the dead marriage. Keith had nothing to do with that failure. I didn't want him to pay the price for some officer's misplaced loyalties.

The third possibility was the most frightening. I was afraid the authorities who retaliated against me might be better served if Keith never spoke to anyone again. My concern wasn't unfounded. Things happen to people in the hole. I had little confidence something wouldn't happen to Keith to keep him quiet. Quiet whispers in the camp told about the time the major tried to kill the former chaplain by running him off the road late one night. If he would try to kill a man of God, he'd have no qualms about having an inmate killed.

About a week after I resigned, I received a letter from the Department of Corrections. It came from the state's capitol of Jefferson City. The letter stated, "This letter is to acknowledge your written notification of resignation dated October 24, 2013, wherein you indicate you are resigning from your position as an Academic Teacher III to be effective immediately on October 24, 2013. Your written notice of resignation is accepted in bad standing as you did not provide fifteen calendar days' notice....In an effort to evaluate our operations and to assist in future retention of employees, please make arrangements to meet with your immediate supervisor for an exit interview which shall be held in accordance with D2-3.5 Exit Interview. Thank you for your service to the Department of Corrections." It was signed by the Director of the Division of Offender Rehabilitative Services.

After all of the hell I went through, I was placed in bad standing because I didn't give them enough notice when my life was in danger? After spending weeks with my injured son, I didn't have vacation days left. I was on FMLA (Family Medical Leave Act) status and I had no vacation or sick days to use for a two-week notice. As dangerous as the situation was, there was no way I could go back to work for two more weeks. I had no choice but to walk out on the spot.

The department wanted me to schedule an exit interview with Blake who knew exactly why I walked out on October 23? That was absurd. If they wanted my input, I was going to give it to them.

I called the director's office. He was in a meeting, but I talked to his administrative assistant for over an hour. She connected me to his direct subordinate, Mr. Rader, with whom I also had a lengthy conversation.

I told Rader, in detail, of the events leading up to my resignation. He asked if I was aware an investigation was launched against me. Mike Vaughn let me know an investigator went through my classroom the day after I quit. I let Rader know, considering what Mike told me, that I was fully aware an investigation was being conducted.

I said, "If they want to investigate me, that's fine. I know I haven't done anything wrong. But, if we're going to have an investigation, why don't we investigate everyone involved? I am not the one who has allowed an inmate special privileges while he has threatened and abused other inmates. It's the major who has done that. So, go ahead and investigate me, but why don't you look into the person who actually has played favorites with offenders?"

Mr. Rader said, "You're right. That needs to be looked into."

In the week between my resignation and my phone call to Jefferson City, I told close friends of mine about my concern for Keith's safety. Some told me, "Well, there's nothing you can do about it but pray." I believe in prayer, but I wasn't going to sit on my hands. I was going to be the only advocate Keith had and his safety was hanging in the balance.

While I spoke to Mr. Rader, I told him about the dangerous conditions in the hole. I let him know about the instances I was aware of and I let him know it was a real concern. He was shocked.

I said, "I am telling you right now, no harm had better come to Mr. Giammanco. Considering the major might be better served if he never speaks again, I will make sure every tax-payer in the state of Missouri knows all about that place if anything happens to him."

I was on a campaign to ensure Keith's safety. After Rader and I hung up, I called the director's office back and made sure they were aware of the same information I told Rader. It was time for the truth to come out.

I kept documentation for months about the hostile work environment I faced in the prison. I let everyone I spoke with know there thirty typed pages of documentation outlining the behavior of individuals at S.C.C.C. was available for anyone to read. Later, an investigator from the Investigator General's office contacted me requesting a copy of my documentation, which I sent to her. Within two hours of my conversation with Mr. Rader, Kessler was put in the hole under investigation. After the state investigator received my documentation, Kessler was transferred to another prison.

After I left the prison, I was in contact with Keith's daughter, Elise, through Facebook. One of the heart wrenching aspects of Keith's lock up on October 23rd was that his twin daughters' birthday was the very next day. There was no way for him to contact them, and when they didn't hear from their dad on their birthday, they would panic. Keith, a very attentive father, would never miss contacting them on their big day. The girls needed to be aware of what was going on. After finding out, Elise sent Keith a postcard with her new phone number. All we could do was wait to hear from him.

His only call for November came on the 9th. Before then, we didn't know how he was or what was happening with him. It was a stressful and traumatic time for the girls and me. Contact was limited, and over time I wrote Keith, using the nickname he gave me a long time ago. The investigator would most certainly know it was me writing to him, but we weren't sure what the rules were about having written contact. I used an alias because the less my name was visible by anyone who might handle the mail at the prison, the better it would be all the way around for us and especially for Keith. All correspondence went through Elise, so the return address was hers.

Prior to my conversation with Mr. Rader, I contacted Keith's public defender, Jenna McCalester. She was useful on two fronts. First, the prison couldn't refuse to let his attorney speak with him. She could schedule a phone conversation with him; attorney calls are confidential. Keith would be able to speak freely with her. I explained our situation in detail when I contacted her, so McCalester knew who I was and why I was concerned. The second way she was helpful was now the prison knew a lawyer was aware Keith was in the hole. If he was invisible, if they believed no one would notice he was in the hole, he wouldn't be as safe. Having an attorney check on him would let the prison know he had people watching out for him. Jenna McCalester agreed with my line of thinking.

The months of stress were difficult. We knew from Keith's letters that conditions were harsh in the hole. Food was short and temperatures were cold. We weren't sure what threats he was facing. He couldn't express those in letters or else he would have been put in protective custody. For the majority of inmates, P.C. is not something they want to be labeled as. Sometimes people find themselves in dangerous situations and it's a must. Protective custody has a bad stigma, and no one wants to be viewed as a pushover in prison. It's usually better to handle business and not go P.C.

In mid-December, I moved to Kansas City to stay with family and to look for employment. Rural Missouri is not a good place to find work in a pinch and I needed to go where I could have a paycheck. The added emotional support from family members helped and it provided a safe haven for me to collect myself after all of the trauma I went through.

Early on, Keith and I agreed our best course of action was to tell the truth. We didn't have to coach each other on what to say. The truth was we loved each other. We had nothing to gain by lying. First of all, we weren't ashamed about loving each other. We hadn't done anything criminal by loving each other. Secondly, for Keith's safety, a transfer to another camp was best. If we lied about our relationship, he might not get a transfer. We also felt it was important to be totally honest. If we wanted the truth to come out about the prison, we needed to show our integrity by owning up to any short-comings the prison perceived us to have. The truth had to come out.

Finally, on December 20th, I received a call from Jim Marshall, an investigator at South Central. He talked to Keith the day before; had already talked to Kelly and Michael, my friends and coworkers. They knew me better than anyone else at the prison. If there was something to be known, they would know it. I had no problem with that. I had nothing to hide.

Jim began by telling me what a nice conversation he had with Keith; repeated several times that Keith was a really nice guy; said Keith was honest in his conversation.

I told him, "I expected him to be."

Jim was testing the waters and continued singing Keith's praises.

I finally said, "I think the world of Keith."

Jim replied, "Well, he says he *loves* you."

I surprised him by saying, "Yes, he does and I love him, too." I could almost hear the air escape from Jim's lungs.

He paused and then said, "Oh."

He wasn't expecting that answer, but it was the only honest answer I could give him.

The tone of our conversation shifted for the better after that exchange. Jim appreciated our honesty. He said 95% of the people he investigated lied to him or hid things. It was a pleasant shock for him that Keith and I were forthright and willing to cooperate. His investigation turned up no evidence against us.

He said, "There was nothing on the cameras. There were no notes. There was nothing. The worst anyone could say about you was that you two spent too much time together."

We were cleared in the investigation.

Jim and I discussed the retaliation issue and I told him my concerns for Keith's safety. At first he said there wasn't anything he could do about a transfer, but as we talked and went into greater detail about my concerns, his opinion changed.

I told him, "Keith and I did nothing wrong. I am willing to take my lumps for anything I did do, but I am not going to be punished for things we didn't do. The worst they can say about us is that we love each other. If the D.O.C wants to try to regulate emotions, good luck. We love each other, but we never acted on it. If you investigate further, you will see there *are* people there who have done things that are wrong. If anything happens to Keith because someone there allowed or encouraged it to happen, then that is not only wrong, it's criminal."

Jim said, "Yes, it would be criminal."

I said, "If anything happens to Keith, I will make sure everyone in the state of Missouri knows about those people."

Jim's next words were, "I'm going to recommend a transfer."

After this business was taken care of, Jim and I had a more lighthearted conversation. Jim laughed and told me stories about their conversation. Keith was not the average inmate and Jim was impressed by what a genuinely nice guy he was. Several times he mentioned how easy it was to talk to Keith.

I said, "Be careful. Look what happened to me because he's so easy to talk to." We both got a good laugh out of it.

Jim told me Keith and I were free to write to each other directly as much as we wanted to and when Keith had phone privileges he could call me directly. I was very relieved. We talked about why I used a nickname when writing Keith earlier. He understood my concerns, but assured me that as soon as I resigned we had been free to contact each other. Jim was going to finish his report and send it on to the Investigator General's office in Jefferson City. Later, a report would be sent to the warden for review.

Jim told me to call him if I ever had any questions or needed to talk to him. I only called him a couple of times, and he was as pleasant as he was during our tape recorded interview. He helped with information he knew, and when he didn't know the answers, Jim suggested whom I could talk to. Jim contended his investigation cleared us and our visiting rights would be established as soon as the six-month waiting period was over. He was confident of it. Our occasional phone calls lasted until someone else answered the phone when I called one day. She told me she was instructed to field any calls from me for Jim. Obviously, the department wasn't happy with his honest cooperation with me. Over a year later I spoke to Jim outside of the prison and learned he had no idea my calls to him were being intercepted. Prison is chock full of lies and deception, even within offices.

Keith and I were glad the investigation was over. Writing directly to one another was a treat. We were able to catch up on things that happened since we last saw each other on October 23rd. On January 4th, Keith was able to make his first phone call from Administrative Segregation to me. I was in New York with my son who was still recovering from his injuries. Keith was only allowed one fifteen minute call a month. It was too short for our liking, but we were ecstatic to hear each other's voices.

We thought the end of the investigation meant he would be released from the hole. That wouldn't happen for nearly two more months.

Chapter Thirty

A Change of Scenery

Keith

Most people who have never been in prison or in a prisoner of war camp are still familiar with the term "the hole." They have heard stories or been given depictions in movies or in books. Those of us who have been in any type of prison have heard many stories, and many of us have a story of our own to tell about the hole. This is mine.

In the State of Missouri, the hole is officially referred to as Administrative Segregation or Ad-Seg for short. There are two levels of Ad-Seg. The first level lands you in a cell with another inmate who has also gotten into trouble. At South Central, Housing Unit 2 is used for this purpose. The highest level of segregation consists of solitary confinement. That is reserved for people who have committed extremely violent acts. Housing Unit 1 is used for that level of segregation. Neither is a good environment. Housing Unit 1 may be isolating, but Housing Unit 2 is dangerous because you can be celled with highly agitated and violent people, even if you are in for a nonviolent offense.

In the Missouri prison system, a prisoner may be placed in Administrative Segregation for many reasons. Fighting will

land someone a stint in the hole. Any major conduct violation such as assault (of staff or inmate), sexual assault, arson,
drug possession or drug distribution will do it. Any major or
minor violation may send you to the hole.

Sometimes all it takes is the wind blowing the right direction and someone can end up there. If an inmate writes an
anonymous "kite" (note) accusing another of wrongdoing, it
will immediately result in a trip to the hole. In the court system, nothing a defendant says is taken as the truth. Defendants on trial are looked at as liars who aren't to be trusted.
Once convicted, any anonymous tip made by an inmate is
treated like gospel. A random false accusation will send another inmate to the hole indefinitely.

There are people who choose to do a great deal, if not all, of
their prison time in the hole. Some are weak and frail, and
some can't control their mouths, so it is safer for them in the
hole. Some people crossed the wrong person or group and it
is no longer safe for them to be around other inmates. Those
individuals are put in protective custody. Groups of homo-
sexuals can engage in their activities freely with one another
on a constant basis in the hole. The hole is also a place for
individuals or groups (gangs in particular) to rotate in and
out for "business" dealings. For whatever reason, many can't
make it out on the yard in the general population, so they are
permanent residents of segregation. The same is true of some
staff members. Some prefer to work in those housing units.
Some are placed there intentionally.

Believe it or not, an inmate can do time in the hole for doing
absolutely nothing wrong. That's what happened to me. The
D.O.C. uses the term "investigation" to justify taking someone to the hole even if there is no conduct violation pending
against him. On October 23, 2013, I was placed in the hole
under investigation. I knew what they were trying to do.
Caroline and I saw it coming. If they put me in the hole and
made my life miserable, they thought I would turn on Caro-

line. That wasn't going to happen. As the investigator later told me, I was considered the "victim." I was expected to tell him how Caroline had manipulated me. I let him know I didn't feel like a victim. Caroline hadn't done anything wrong. The people victimizing both of us were members of the system.

As things became more stressful and dangerous in the education department, Caroline and I agreed at some point I would end up in the hole. Our discussions began a few months prior to it becoming a reality. We could sense it coming. We could feel something in the air. By October 23rd, we could almost touch it.

I was an easy target. Both staff and inmates harbored jealousy over Caroline and me spending time working together. The major was sure to retaliate after the email Caroline sent to the assistant warden. The deck was stacked against us and time eventually ran out.

On that October afternoon, at about 2:00, the education desk officer came to the classroom and told me to grab my coat and come with him down the hallway. I remember a few minutes earlier the last thing I said to Caroline was, "I love you." As I left the classroom, not a word was spoken between us. We just looked at each other. I still have not laid eyes on her since that day.

When I made the short walk from Classroom 10 down the hall towards the outside doorway, I saw the sergeant waiting. I was sure when I saw the henchman standing there it was a done deal. This guy had it out for inmates ever since his wife was caught having sex with an offender in the kitchen freezer. She was a cook and the episode became big news across the camp. After that embarrassment, he'd become a real hard ass who delighted in finding any excuse to lock someone in the hole.

The sergeant walked me outside to a young guard named Taylor who was waiting. Taylor asked me to put my hands behind my back so he could put handcuffs on me. He gave me the routine pat search and took the pen I used to grade papers with out of my breast shirt pocket. We waited a few moments for the staff to get the walk secure to take me to Housing Unit 2. As we were waiting, Taylor asked if I had been fighting.

I said, "No, I don't know why I am going."

Taylor responded that if I didn't know, then it was most likely for investigation. He said, "Are you in school here?" When I told him I was a tutor, he replied, "Oh, it is for investigation then, I'm sure."

We took the 100-yard walk, then Taylor handed me off to a guard assigned to Housing Unit 2 outside the entrance. I was taken to the A Wing of the unit. As we walked in, I remember it sounded like a zoo.

Inmates yelled through the steel cell doors at me. They were jealous about Caroline and screamed, "It's about time they got you, you rat!" "We knew they'd get you someday," they shouted. Some anticipated Kessler following through on his threats and they enjoyed every bit of it.

They relished in the fact I came from an honor dorm, so I heard, "It's someone from 3 House!" There were more crude things said then and later. Threats were made.

I was placed in a steel cage about the size of a telephone booth. As I stood in the cage, the heckling from the inmates continued. I felt like an animal in that zoo, only the spectators were the ones out of control.

I recognized a couple of faces through the small glass windows of the cell doors. I found it odd, though, after being at that institution the better part of four years, hearing and seeing many faces and voices I had never seen or heard before. It is true I'm not much of a social bug inside or outside of prison. Many of them knew who I was, though. There are very few secrets anywhere in prison.

As I stood in that cage, although I knew chances were slim, I prayed someone with sense would get me out of there. I was guilty of nothing. Caroline wouldn't have any way of getting me out. If she tried, they would use it against us and it would make my release from the hole even more unlikely. It would make her life harder, too. We both knew that. I wasn't afraid, but I was concerned about what was happening to Caroline. She was in a bad situation and I was concerned for her safety.

It was between a half hour to an hour before a guard came in with some paper work and a plastic bag. First, he had me sign a paper stating I realized I was being placed in Ad-Seg.

I only asked him one question, "Why am I here?"

He gave the standard answer for most things in the Department of Corrections, "I don't know."

I was told to strip down to my boxer shorts, t-shirt and socks. Through a small hole he ordered me to give him my state gray uniform and my tennis shoes. He put them in the plastic bag to be kept with all of my personal property from my cell. That would be stored in my foot locker until I was sent back into the general population.

Next, I was told to strip down naked so they could check the remainder of my clothes and view my person to make sure I had no contraband before taking me to a cell. Some of those people I mentioned earlier who are frequent guests of Ad-Seg are "runners." They bring drugs and other contraband into the housing unit. Because of this, no matter why someone is sent to the hole, he is stripped naked and searched.

After I was stripped out and checked, two wing officers put cuffs on me while I was still in the cage. They hooked a tether (leash) to the cuffs and opened the cage. It was time to find a cell for me. I was taken to the other side of the housing unit to Wing C. I had the option of refusing a cell (or cellmate). Guards did not tell me this. I heard it from others who went to the hole. What I did not know was this could only be done once without consequences.

The first cell they brought me in front of was on the bottom tier. The door slid open to reveal the inside. My eyes were focused only on who occupied the cell. All I could see was a large body, under a blanket, on the bottom bunk. The cell was a mess and a foul smell rolled out into the wing.

I told one of the guards, "No, I'm not going in there."

He said, "Okay," and the other guard looked at a list. I assume it had the numbers of cells with open beds.

Choosing the right cellmate in the hole is important for many reasons. Compatibility is one, of course, but it's not the most important. Safety is the first and foremost reason. There are many horrifying truths about people going into the wrong cell with someone. This is even more prevalent in the hole. People have been beaten into comas or killed. It is a very dangerous and serious matter.

A couple of months before I was taken to the hole, a frightening incident occurred in the hole that made news across the camp. As the story goes, Frankie Fields, a white man from the honor house, was put into the hole under investigation. The guards put him in a cell with an agitated black man, Nelson, who shouted he would kill any white man they put in with him. Other inmates told Fields not to go in there with Nelson.

Fields said, "I won't refuse to go in. It will be okay."

Well, it was far from okay. For reasons only known to the perpetrator himself, Fields was severely beaten with a dinner tray after falling asleep. People who saw Fields while he was taken to medical on a stretcher said his face was unrecognizable. One of his eyes was hanging out of its socket. I lived only a few cells down from Fields in the housing unit before he went to the hole. I knew him fairly well by prison standards. I can't see him doing anything to provoke such an action.

It turned out Nelson had a history of doing this. At the time of this beating, he was facing charges of assault in the first degree for a similar occurrence at another Missouri prison. That's why he was transferred to S.C.C.C. He received twenty more years for the assault at the other prison. I don't know what happened to him because of Fields. From what I heard, Nelson was a few months from going home before the assault at the other prison. He must not have wanted to get out. It was a cruel way of staying.

This happens more often than one might think. Field's family was distraught. Supreme Court Justice Kennedy has come out against solitary confinement, but this is one reason to reconsider his opinion. It may be cruel and unusual to have someone in solitary confinement for years, but so is beating someone while they sleep until they are near death. It's better for people to be lonely than for them to be in mortal danger.

Looking into that first cell offering, there were too many unknowns. So, it was on to the next cell. The second cell they took me to was on the upper tier of the wing on the opposite side of the first cell. When the automatic door slid open, much to my surprise, I saw a familiar face. I said I would accept that cell and they asked the man in the cell if it was okay with him. The original occupant can refuse a new cellmate a guard brings to the door. A smile came to the man's face as he welcomed me in. The door slid closed while I turned my back to it. I put my hands through the chuckhole and the guard took the cuffs off and untethered me.

The young man's name was Martin; a former student in one of the classes Caroline and I had. We always got along very well with Martin since he tried hard in class. He was thirty-years-old and (in our experience) he was a happy guy. I learned much more about him in the next month and a half we occupied that cell together.

The cell was on the upper tier, on the backside of the housing unit. It was almost the same view as I had out the window of my cell in Housing Unit 3. This played an important role in my mental health and emotional well-being during the nearly four months I spent there. The view from the window kept my mind off of where I was at. Beyond the fence and razor wire, I saw the outside world. A working sawmill where they manufactured telephone poles was in plain sight. Trees and a field allowed me to see wildlife on occasion. An eagle and a family of deer gave me much-needed mental relief as I watched them throughout my stay in the hole. I saw cars and trucks passing on Missouri Highway 63 in the distance. Parts of Licking, Missouri were even viewable. A connection to the outside world made the hole less isolating.

The first moments in the cell were occupied by my thoughts and worries. The next day was Elise and Marissa's birthday and I was going to miss it. What would they think? There was also the ongoing concern over Caroline's well-being.

God blessed and protected me with three good cellmates during that four months. I think Caroline's efforts on the outside helped make that happen, too. My preference would have been to be in a cell alone, but since the D.O.C. is so overcrowded, that wasn't an option. The prison is so overcrowded on many occasions they put people in the hole for trivial violations to open up bed space in the general population. I am thankful to God and those three young men for providing me safety and peace of mind in my time there. They provided me some good conversation, too.

After I left the classroom, I wasn't sure what happened to Caroline. Was she still working there? Had she quit? Had she been fired? Was she safe? I heard rumors she left the prison. I heard she was fired, walked out in shame and that she quit. It was big talk around the whole camp. Staff and inmates were abuzz about us.

Martin and I figured out a way to be almost certain she was gone. I was pretty sure she was already. The day after I was put in the hole, I was outside in one of the dog pens used for recreation when in the hole. While out there, I could see the entrance to the prison. I saw Michael Vaughn leaving alone. Based on that, I had a good idea Caroline quit or was fired.

To make sure, though, over the next couple of days Martin and I came up with our plan. Caroline was attentive and concerned about her students' educational progress. When one of our students went to the hole, she prepared packets of work for them she would send through institutional mail. In this way, they could learn, keep their minds sharp and pass their time in the hole in a productive way. She was the only teacher at the school who did that. Many of our students sent her requests for work from the hole and appreciated having something productive to do. Martin agreed to send her a kite requesting one of those packets. I wrote the kite (so Caroline would see my handwriting and know I was okay) and Martin signed it.

A week or so later we had no response to our kite. We tried again in case she had not received the first one. Again, no reply. Since she knew my handwriting and that this student was serious about getting his G.E.D., I could confidently assume she was no longer employed there. I later learned the true story from Caroline of how events unfolded.

On November 9th, I was able to make one telephone call from the hole. We were allowed one fifteen-minute call per month. Since I did not have Caroline's number yet, I called Elise. We had a nice talk for about forty-five minutes. The guards forgot about me having the phone I guess, or maybe they wanted to see if I would say something over the phone that would help in their investigation of us.

Since we were still not sure of the policy regarding contact (and how it would affect our future visiting and so forth), Elise gave generalizations about how Caroline was. One of the sayings Caroline and I share is, "nothing changes." Elise let me know Caroline passed that message on to me. That's all I wanted and needed to hear. I knew Caroline still loved me just the same.

Elise agreed to be a go-between for us by sending letters from Caroline to me. It wasn't until December, when we talked with the investigator, that we found out it was okay for us to have contact all along after Caroline left the prison. We are thankful to Elise for her help. At the time, it was a huge blessing during a stressful time.

The conversation with Elise was a much-needed boost. She let me know Caroline sent her and Marissa birthday cards since I was in the hole. Knowing Caroline and I were on good terms after everything that transpired was an enormous relief. Knowing my daughters hadn't worried about me when their birthday passed was a weight off my heart. I could settle in with much more peace.

I could tell so many details about conditions in the hole: the food, the treatment of inmates by staff members, staff infighting and the potential for violence. Many events I witnessed while I there were shocking. It literally would take another book to do it justice. For posterity, I will give a few examples and a general idea of what it was like.

The vast majority of my time in the hole was spent reading books and the cherished letters I got from Caroline and my daughters. Those letters arrived almost every day. I spent a lot of time writing them letters in return. It took me a while to be able to purchase stamps, so getting word to them was slow.

I did my best to keep a regular sleep schedule. Many inmates sleep during the day and stay up all night. I tried to sleep at night for the most part. It's difficult to sleep in the hole because it is so noisy. The inmates are constantly talking or yelling to one another through the cell doors. Someone is almost constantly pounding, singing or rapping loudly. The staff doesn't mind all of the noise. In fact, they love to see inmates annoy each other. It's entertainment for them.

Staff were major participants in the noise themselves. They jingled their keys as loudly as possible. They talked to other staff and inmates at full volume in the middle of the night. They yelled often and they slammed every door as they went through. Noise was part of the fun for them.

The exception to this was if they were taking names for the once-a-month haircuts or if they were asking if you would like to go to the cages outside for recreation. They would be as quiet as a mouse then. If an inmate was sleeping, once they passed his door, it was a done deal and he missed out. For recreation, this was not much of a problem since it took place during afternoons and evenings. Just about everyone was awake at those times.

One task assigned to the evening shift was the book exchange. We didn't have a wide selection of books to read, but it was a way to pass the time and to keep sane during the long days in the hole. Two exchanges per week were supposed to take place, but it occurred only once per week a lot of times. Sometimes it was over a week before I got a new book to read. This was a task the guards did not like, so they were as quiet as possible so one might miss out. I remember overhearing grumblings between the afternoon and evening shifts over whose responsibility the book exchange was. Since the staff didn't like the job, they tried to make sure the fewest number of inmates heard them announce it.

I took advantage of the book exchange. I read many books in that four months. I thought of Caroline every time I read one; some we even shared after I got out of the hole. The book I liked best turned out to be one of Caroline's all-time favorites. We laughed after I wrote her a letter telling her about the book in detail and how she should read it, only to find out she knew it well. We weren't surprised we loved the same story.

The announcements for haircuts were the worst. One sergeant made the list of inmates who needed haircuts. This took place in the wing one Saturday per month at 7:00 at the start of the morning shift. On those mornings, the sergeant snuck into the wing, tip-toeing around, making sure no one was woken up. If he passed a cell unnoticed, that man would not get a haircut for the next month. This annoyed a lot of inmates and it resulted in arguments and conduct violations. It was done purposely to stir the pot.

I never bothered to get my hair cut in the hole. The only styles allowed were a complete head shave or a crew cut. Luckily, I had gotten a haircut at the camp barbershop about a week before going to the hole. I hadn't had a crew cut since I was a small boy in the 1960s and I wasn't going to try one as an adult.

These once-a-month barber trips were the only way to get a shave. No razors are allowed in the hole for safety and suicide prevention. I've never liked wearing a beard, so I made sure I was always awake and ready when the sergeant came in for haircuts. I wanted my shave; it was a relieving highlight. In those conditions, even the simplest parts of normal life were valued.

For many, occupying time in the hole is difficult. Once I realized I would be there for a while, I learned to do things to keep my sanity and to stay healthy. My biggest motivator was knowing I had Caroline and the girls out there praying for me, thinking about me and sending their love and support. With Caroline and the girls' support and certainty and with my trust and faith in God, I was able to get plenty of sleep while in the hole; peaceful rest was attainable for me, regardless of the distractions created by staff and inmates.

I made sure I got some type of exercise each day: pushups, sit-ups, jumping jacks, pull-up arm curls, ran in place and paced back and forth. I was in good shape before I went into the hole anyway. I played sports regularly and I didn't want to lose my conditioning.

I also knew I should not do too much activity while there, though, because the meals served were sparse and provided little nourishment. Unlike life in general population, no canteen food was allowed in the hole to supplement the meals provided from the camp food service. In the hole, we got the same food as was served out of the cafeteria, but it was smaller in portion. It was usually cold or lukewarm by the time it was served to us. Meals were served on a covered tray by the guards through a chuckhole in the cell door. Small portions of bad food guaranteed I didn't want to expend much energy on exercise or I would be hungry all the time. As it was, I lost several pounds during my four-month stay in Ad-Seg.

Time continued to tick by and several major holidays passed during my stint in the hole. Thanksgiving, Christmas and New Year's Day were spent in bad conditions with no way for me to talk with my loved ones. Not being able to talk with Caroline and my daughters was terrible. Holidays in prison are difficult no matter what, but in the hole the discomfort is multiplied.

The D.O.C. found a cruel way to twist the knife and make Christmas even more depressing for us. Normally, each inmate at S.C.C.C. received three holiday cards to mail out to family and friends. Cards were distributed a few weeks before Christmas so everyone had time to get them in the mail before the holiday. These were cards donated by an outside source and they cost the taxpayers nothing. Well, three days before Christmas, a sergeant brought around our cards and slid them under the doors. When I took a look at mine, they weren't Christmas cards. They were sympathy cards. The sergeant gave a smirking laugh when confronted with his cruel act. I don't know whose idea it was to give sympathy cards out, but it was appalling and pathetic. Knowing he took joy in carrying out the task was just plain sick. As a Christian who values Christmas for its spiritual importance, it was infuriating to have its significance mocked. It turned a sacred holiday into an opportunity to inflict pain and suffering.

The one and only highlight of being in the hole during the holidays had to do with food. We received the same holiday meals everyone else on the camp did on Thanksgiving and Christmas. These were much more of a blessing in the hole than when in general population. Holiday meals had a good taste and there was enough food to make it feel like it was a meal.

We also got the Christmas bag which was given to each inmate during the holidays by the D.O.C. It was such a welcome sight. Since there is no canteen or extra food allowed, these bags were truly a Godsend. Roughly thirty to forty packaged food items were in each bag. Cookies, snack cakes, candies, chips, beef sticks and other snack items made up the assortment. Unlike the general population, in the hole we were told we had thirty days to be finished with the contents of the bag. After that, it would be considered contraband.

Many inmates traded their items away for things like tobacco, stamps or a magazine. I conserved mine by eating one of the larger items or two of the smaller ones each evening. Since there were eleven to thirteen hours between dinner and breakfast, it was a welcome addition to my diet for those thirty days.

People may wonder how inmates get things from cell to cell to trade since there is no open contact or open movement between inmates. There are a number of ways this gets done. The first (and simplest) way is through "the Walkman." He is an inmate worker in the wings who is let out of his cell to do general cleanup. For his labor, he gets an extra food tray at mealtime. Usually a kiss-ass or snitch volunteers for this job. The Walkman passes things from one cell to another while guards are not looking. Some guards turn their heads and let this go on, others take punitive action if they catch it.

The second way is to "Cadillac" things from cell to cell with a weight and home spun string (which is usually made from state issued sheets). The name is derived from the weight at the leading end of the string called a "car." Inmates shoot their cars under cell doors, hook them together on the wing floors/upper tier walks and tie almost any item to the system and drag it from cell to cell. It is a unique, intelligent and interesting process. Some inmates become incredibly good at creating Cadillacs. Some guards let this go and others destroy and confiscate them.

The third (and least likely) way is to have a guard pass the goods. This doesn't happen very often and when it does, normally it's only books or hygiene products that are carried by guards. That's not to say other items aren't passed that way, too, but getting an employee to risk carrying contraband in plain sight is more difficult.

Finally, items are passed when inmates "check out" of a cell. When a suitable bed (in other words, one they want to get to) opens up in the unit, inmates will push their emergency button and claim they are in a dangerous situation in their current cells. By policy, the inmate will be removed from that cell. They will pack the items to be moved in their personal property or in or on their person and they will move to another cell.

There are a few problems with checking out. For one, it creates a "boy cries wolf" mentality. Since it is required guards move someone who is in danger, staff realizes most of the time it's just a ploy to transport goods or to select a suitable sexual partner. Because it happens so often, the guards become negligent in responding to the emergency buttons. They take their time or don't respond at all. People have been hurt very badly or even killed because of staff complacency.

Another problem with checking out is the inmate is required to sit for two hours, handcuffed with his hands behind him, on a steel bench with no back to it before he is offered another cell. There is also an automatic conduct violation written. Most of these people are long-time residents in the hole and they don't care about getting a violation.

While in the hole, regardless of the weather, inmates are given the opportunity to go outside every day for one hour in the cages in order to get fresh air. Only cellmates can occupy the same cage. Many spend the time outside pacing, doing push-ups and holding conversations with others. Like every other movement, inmates are transported there with cuffs and a leash while wearing an orange jumpsuit.

I learned quickly, weather is an important factor. Guards are required to supply coats for people in the cages during the winter. They distribute them after inmates are outside. One time I was left outside with temperatures in the teens for the better part of two hours. I was the only one without a coat. They claimed they ran out, but Caroline may be right that it was done intentionally because of our situation. It's hard to believe they were exactly one coat short. Of course, when the weather is nice, the one hour of recreation turns into forty-five minutes. When it's cold, raining, snowing or blazing hot, it turns into two hours. It's part of the mind games played by the staff. We are their entertainment after all.

If there is contraband in the cell, one inmate will refuse recreation, because if both go, the cell is sure to be searched. 'Searched' equals torn apart. Shower time is another opportunity for cell searches. Some inmates go for over a week without showering, even though showers are offered every three days. Cell searches cannot be completely avoided. At least once a week and sometimes many more, cells are ransacked and searched. While this happens, the occupants are handcuffed to the benches.

One time, one of the cell phones used for monthly inmate phone calls was misplaced. The staff started searching cells. They blamed an inmate for not returning it. It became a major ordeal. After tearing apart several cells, the guards found it in an area only occupied by staff.

Cells in the hole are the same as they are in general population, except there are no electrical outlets, no chairs and the automatic doors are thicker steel. The doors have chuckholes used for food and for securing (cuffing) inmates. The cells are decorated with gang graffiti, art work and some "Kilroy was here" type stuff. Some of it is lewd and crude. Some shows real talent.

Everyone in the hole is a badass. Since everyone is locked up or shackled (and many will never return to general population), even the biggest wimps in the prison will run their mouths with insults and threats to others. Caroline was concerned men would try to assault me because of their misguided opinions of me. Threats were made.

One incident was even comical. A former student, Clancy, was shackled on a nearby bench as I awaited my monthly review with the Ad-Seg committee. One day in class he had admitted he was a snitch; berated another student for not being one, too. At the time, we weren't sure if he was suicidal or what because normal people don't brag about snitching in a prison. He liked to brag he was in the know of everything in the education department and across the camp.

While sitting there shackled, Clancy began loudly spouting off at me. He said he told us this was going to happen, then went on about how I shouldn't have messed with Caroline's livelihood, how he had seen this coming and several other blowhard comments.

I looked at him and said, "You sure did tell us that, right before you went up and snitched on us about things that weren't true!"

Clancy frequently joined in the gossip mill of the school. He became very angry and told me how much he wanted to punch me in the face.

I told him, "Yeah, you are real tough shackled to that bench." We both knew that if he wasn't shackled to the bench, he wouldn't have done a thing.

Sitting next to Clancy was one of his followers who had bought into the persona he tried to portray. He was hanging on every word Clancy said. When I called Clancy short on his bluff, the look on the follower's face was one of incredulity. He turned and looked at Clancy with the realization he was nothing but a grandstander. Clancy was rolled from one camp to another for protective custody because he snitched so often. As far as we know, he is now in protective custody at S.C.C.C.

The monthly Ad-Seg meeting I waited for was uneventful. Nothing ever happened during those meetings. The three members of the panel brought an inmate in (dressed in nothing but his underwear even if the panel included women) and they asked if he had any statement to make. That concluded the "review." The staff then headed out for a smoke break. I saw this repeat time after time. The only staff member who was helpful was the wing caseworker who made an honest effort at doing her job.

Sexual perversion is widespread in Ad-Seg. Women employees who work in the hole are subjected to the worst behavior and comments one could imagine. They are shown male genitals often and they have to write numerous conduct violations for sexual misconduct. Those write ups become part of an inmate's permanent record. What I heard and witnessed disgusted me.

Homosexuality is rampant in the hole. There is constant talk about it and people partake of it on a regular basis. I lived in an upper tier cell. Looking out my cell door window, it was impossible to not see men either exposing their genitals or engaging in sexual behavior. As far as I'm concerned, people can do whatever they want to in private, but in the hole, all sexual behavior imaginable is on display.

On February 12, 2014, I was awoken at 4:30 in the morning and told I was transferring from S.C.C.C that morning. The eagle I watched on so many days was nowhere to be seen the day before and I thought it was my time to fly from there as well. I spent two nights in the hole at the prison in Bonne Terre and then on February 14th I arrived at the Southeast Correctional Center in Charleston, Missouri. It was about five hours from Licking and nearly four hundred miles away from Caroline. As things played out, it was obvious we were intentionally separated by as great of a distance as the D.O.C could arrange.

My first call after arriving at S.E.C.C. was to Caroline. It was especially fitting since it was Valentine's Day. It was wonderful to talk with her. We had made it through one of the worst hurdles. I was out of the hole and we could spend more time communicating. We were happy that in a little over two months, the six month waiting period for visits would be over and we could see each other once again. Since we were cleared in the investigation, we knew our visits would be approved. Jim Marshall told us there was no reason to not allow our visiting privileges since he found no evidence of wrongdoing in his investigation.

As I settled into S.E.C.C., I realized while the scenery was different, not much changed from life at South Central. As fans of the old Batman series will recall, it was "Same Bat Time; Same Bat Channel." There were the same Jokers and Riddlers. It was just a different episode with different faces.

As April 23rd, the end of our six month wait, drew near, Caroline applied for visiting rights. After a month of waiting for the approval, we were notified we were banned visits for five years. The D.O.C. used the excuses that Caroline left without giving a two week notice and that an investigation took place. It didn't matter we were cleared in the investigation. According to the policy, the fact there was an investigation at all was enough to ban us for five years. They knew the day they threw me in the hole under investigation they were sentencing us to five years apart. They didn't need to prove wrongdoing. They thought they had destroyed us simply by making sure we were separated.

We are separated physically, but we aren't separated in the most important ways. Caroline and I are committed and devoted to each other and we aren't going to let the arbitrary whims of the Missouri Department of Corrections interfere with the love we have waited our whole lives to have.

Chapter Thirty-One

Why

Keith

So far I told what led up to my crime spree, how I pulled off each robbery and what it's like to be in prison. What I haven't answered yet is probably the biggest question in everyone's mind: Why? Why would I rob banks? Why would I risk leaving my children? Why would I put myself in the degrading conditions of prison? It is a complicated issue, but here is my explanation.

Bank robberies have occurred throughout history for many reasons. People have robbed banks due to financial distress; the need to support drug habits and other addictions; the need to support a continued lifestyle for themselves or their family; the love of money; the desire to rob from the rich to give to the less fortunate; the need to express a political viewpoint or for a hatred of banks and the government. Finally, some did it for the thrill of it. Within each category, underlying factors and traits are seen by outside observers. Other more personal reasons can only be told and expressed by the person who committed the crime.

It was well-publicized these bank robberies were committed for reasons of financial distress. While there was anxiety, suffering and misfortune involved, the entire blame and responsibility can only be put on one person: myself. Now that this is clear, I can give deeper insight into what some people may already know and also into what no one except Caroline has known up until now.

Leading up to the first robbery I had a lot of overdue bills to pay. Many of us are quite familiar with that situation. As the press releases and interviews exposed, it is true I did it for my kids. I wanted them to have the same lifestyle they were accustomed to. I wanted to keep them in the home and neighborhood in which they were raised in. It was important they stay in the same private high school they attended, or at least I thought it was at the time. Later, Elise and Marissa told me it would have been okay for them to go to the public high school near our home. They also admitted that they received a better education and experienced a better social environment by attending the private high school.

I was fearful the financial despair, the desperation of owing back taxes, the default on the mortgage, the school tuition, the credit cards and the failure to make all of the other payments put all of the "good things" in their lives in jeopardy. I completely lost sight of what was important in our lives: being a family, together, with or without those things.

I want to make it clear, especially for the sake of my children, that all of the blame is on me and me alone. To say I did it for my children should not put any guilt on them. I was an adult and I chose to do things I shouldn't. My daughters bear no responsibility for what happened. While I understand the sympathetic tone of articles stressing my crimes were for my children, I never want anyone, especially them, to feel as though any of this is their fault.

My children are not demanding, spoiled brats. They were teenagers at the time who were grateful for the things their father provided them. They never gave me cause to think they wouldn't love me if I couldn't provide those things.

That was a fear I created in my own mind and in my own heart. My daughters have since proven to me they love me, as I love them, unconditionally.

I had a set dollar amount in mind when I started robbing banks. I wasn't doing it for the thrill of it and I wasn't going to continue once I got the money I needed. At the time I was arrested, I was $35,000 short of the amount I needed to resolve my debts. Had I never been caught, I still would have stopped when I reached that amount. I was doing this out of what I believed was necessity. Robbing banks was supposed to be a short-term fix to getting out of the financial hole I was in.

The financial distress and the need to provide for my children are the reasons most have heard about. Now that time has passed and I have had the opportunity to examine myself and my actions, I realize I committed the crimes for selfish reasons: self-image, pride and ego. It is shameful and it is nothing I am proud to admit. I was concerned with what others would think about me.

I was worried what my family, my friends and even strangers would think. I lived my life in a trap. I was always concerned about whether or not the people I was with or associated with were better off than I was or if their families had more than we did. I remember times of feeling extreme pressure to "keep up with the Joneses."

Maybe part of this compulsion was because my father left my mom to care for four children alone and I wanted to be a man who could do better than that. Maybe I placed too much emphasis on giving the appearance of having a good life instead of enjoying the one I had. Looking back, I can see how useless and shallow those concerns were. I sacrificed the real things in life in order to create the illusion of success.

When it came to closer relationships, I felt pressure to impress. Some of it was self-conceived, but at times it was put on me by others. Trying to impress my own family was important to me. I remember our mother saying, "I want to see my children have it better than me." Well, I want that, too, but in the quest to make it a reality I developed a self-consciousness. I had an overwhelming desire to show others and my family members I had done better. As the youngest in my family, I watched my siblings have successes and failures in life and sadly, I felt the need to out-do them and to make my mother proud. Not being honest with myself and others about keeping that standard is how I got in trouble.

I didn't want to admit defeat to my family members and friends. I didn't want to be the one others looked down upon. Sometimes, when a person is down on their luck, others take it as an opportunity to feel superior. I didn't want to ask for the help of others because I didn't want to be treated as second-rate. Part of this came from being the youngest, but I think it went beyond that.

Not many people want to be viewed as the family charity case. Not many people want to feel, since they had to borrow money from a family member, suddenly everyone has a right to judge every bit of food they eat, every purchase they make and every decision they make. I didn't want to be under someone else's thumb at the age of forty-three. I'm not saying I went about it the right way, but I was trying to save face with my family. It was an attempt to maintain some self-respect.

I think my fears have proven realistic, too. Since my arrest, I am considered a pariah by some in my family and former circle of friends. Many decided I am no longer a validated, complete human being. I heard through the grapevine what has been said about me at family gatherings. I am talked about as if I am an imbecile and a juvenile and many people made up their minds for me what I need to do when I get out.

They relegated what my standing (or lack thereof) will be in the family. I am no longer Keith. I am now their underling.

I would have been looked at that same way had I confessed to them the dire financial situation I was in. The gloating would have begun. The willingness to flaunt their superiority over me would have started. I didn't know what to do and I didn't feel I had any safe avenues to turn to for advice and support.

Fear and loneliness are a bad combination. They lead to desperation. One thing I definitely was during that time of my life was desperate. I would like to be able to say I had a family I felt safe being vulnerable to, but I can't.

The romantic relationships I had, unfortunately, also revolved around status and money. Talk about a recipe for failure, and they were. I chose relationships with people who focused on how much money I made or on what I provided for them. In one instance, I was told I had financial expectations to meet. In another, I wanted desperately to keep up with her success as a means of having value and fitting in. As a kid, I grew up feeling out of place and I turned into an adult who didn't trust in who I was. I didn't believe a relationship with me was adequate with or without material wealth.

The stress I felt over my financial problems was overwhelming. I tried so hard and for so long to prop up the life I wanted the world to think I had. I was living a double life. There was the inward me who was filled with turmoil. There was the outwardly successful Keith Giammanco who never let anyone see his struggles. I thought the robberies were the solution to my problems. Now I see they were, in reality, just a symptom of what was wrong in my life.

Contrary to the press releases stating I was "relieved" to be arrested, I wasn't. Knowing I faced years away from my family was not comforting at all. The stress had become so great to maintain the two lives I was living that, once I was in the county jail, there was a certain solace in knowing the cycle had ended. The cat was out of the bag, so to speak. I didn't have to try to impress anyone any more. The truth about my finances was on the front page of the newspaper. I could finally stop living in the shadows of my life.

I am not telling this because it is enjoyable or comfortable to admit these things about myself. It's a cautionary tale. I am not proud to admit how shallow my priorities were in the past. I believed in capitalism, the free market and in earning a good living. I still do. What was shallow was my mistaken belief that those had some impact on who I was and on my value as a person.

I realize some people will stand by me no matter what and others won't stand by me at all. I know I put too much effort into trying to avoid looking like a disappointment to people who weren't really there for me to begin with. I'm not the only one who has ever made that mistake, but it cost me dearly.

Chapter Thirty-Two

Sensible Justice

Caroline

"Politicians and inmates share a common bond: no one trusts them and no one believes a word they say." — Caroline

Once I was free from working for the Department of Corrections, and once Keith was transferred out of S.C.C.C., I got busy working on reform of the 85% mandatory minimums law in Missouri. When I worked for the prison system, I wasn't allowed to become involved in anything having to do with the improvement of inmate conditions. My situation changed, so it was time to act.

The prison system has employees under a gag order of sorts, which is why employees aren't often heard speaking out about conditions. Anyone voicing support of prison reform is viewed as a traitor and suspect.

I wasn't under those restrictions after I left in October, but as long as Keith was at S.C.C.C., his safety was the most important thing to me. I did not want to become involved in anything that drew negative attention to Keith. We already had plenty of that going on. I knew once I started working on the legislative effort, even more attention would be put on us. He needed to be out of S.C.C.C. before I could take any action. After his transfer in February, I immediately went to work.

Keith and I talked about the need for change many times and came up with a solid framework of how to begin. Keith knew the laws and statutes of Missouri very well. My college degree from the University of Arizona was in political science. Launching a legislative reform effort was second nature to me. Between the two of us, we had a good idea how to approach the problem given the political realities of our conservative state.

Keith became frustrated at times during this process. Trying to get anything done from behind prison walls is nearly impossible, and as our efforts continued, it was tough for him to be left out of the action. Even if he couldn't be in meetings personally, Keith was always with me. Someone once questioned Keith's involvement. I made it very clear to her there would be no effort if it wasn't for Keith. It is important people know Keith and many other inmates have something to offer the world. What most of them lack is someone with the determination I have to help them make it a reality on the outside.

I vowed to Keith we would leave no stone unturned in our efforts to bring him home sooner than the state sentence demanded. Fighting for a repeal of the 85% mandatory minimums law in Missouri was a good start. Not only would it help Keith, but it would bring relief to a lot of other first time offenders in the state. Taxpayers would save millions. Prisons would become less crowded and safer. Since, according to the Department of Corrections, 97% of all inmates eventually are released into society again, communities would be safer by encouraging rehabilitation of the inmates who qualified for early release.

Missouri's Truth in Sentencing Law took effect in 1994 when President Bill Clinton offered states federal funding to adopt the same 85% mandatory minimums the federal court system used. Prior to 1994, Class A felonies in Missouri (which include robbery, arson, assault, murder, rape, child molestation, kidnapping and elder abuse) carried mandatory minimums of 40%. After 1994, Missouri and many other states adopted the higher percentage so they could get the federal monies. This had a huge impact on the rate of incarceration and the overcrowding of prisons in our state. Much of the money was used to build prisons. It was a self-fulfilling prophecy. In the 1980s, Missouri's prison population was 5,000. It was seven times higher by 2015. The more prisons built, the more inmates were sent to them.

The federal funding has since gone away, leaving Missouri to foot the bill for the added weight of this mass incarceration. For a short-term benefit, Missouri and several other states, became entrapped in a sentencing law that would be unfunded in the future. The lengthy sentences still stood. The cost of incarceration grew multi-fold in the years between 1994 and 2015 across the nation.

President Clinton didn't encourage harsh sentencing laws because he had an extreme concern for public safety. It was done for political reasons. In the 1988 presidential election, Democrat Michael Dukakis lost the election largely because of the Willie Horton scandal. As governor, Dukakis allowed inmates out on work furloughs. One of those inmates, Horton, committed heinous crimes while out. Clinton knew his political career depended on being tough on crime. That spurred the creation of the increase in mandatory minimums. Today both Bill and Hillary Clinton admit the bill they pushed went overboard. They recognize that financially it isn't feasible to sustain such a level of incarceration. Financially it is a disaster for states and the human toll it has inflicted on inmates, their families, the states and communities is enormous.

The change in mandatory minimums associated with the 1994 legislation is substantial for individuals. If a young man breaks someone's jaw in a fight, he can be charged with first degree assault. A typical sentence is twenty years. Of that, he must serve seventeen years at 85% instead of the pre-1994 eight years at 40%. A clean criminal record doesn't matter. Once his conviction takes place, the next seventeen years will be spent in prison. If he never breaks a rule while in prison, once convicted, the soonest he can be released is seventeen years.

Missouri doesn't have good time behavior credit for those who are convicted of what are known as "dangerous" felonies. This is counterproductive. First time offenders have no incentive to practice good behavior in prison. Our communities deserve people who have shown rehabilitation before they are released, not simply someone who spent years locked in prison.

Some say criminals deserve what they get. In the abstract, it is easy to be harsh. When applying it to loved ones, most don't want one mistake sending their loved one to prison for decades. Many people ignore the need for criminal justice reform as long as it doesn't land on their front step.

While working in the prison, I saw what happened to first time offenders with no hope of getting out for years. Young men not equipped for the prison environment were vulnerable to change, and it wasn't positive change. If hope is taken away from someone, anger often steps in. A young man who must spend 85% of a lengthy sentence in prison will give up being nice for the sake of survival in the dangerous world of the prison.

Most violence in prison comes from hot-headed youth and one way to curb this violence is to give those people some control over their own destiny. A light at the end of the tunnel can do a lot to keep a flicker of hope and goodness going in someone. For what we spend to incarcerate people, I'd like to think we can get a better product coming out of the prison, not an angrier, more criminalized, version of the person who went in years before. By allowing first-time offenders the opportunity to go before a parole board at 50% instead of 85%, good behavior is encouraged and they have the hope needed to rehabilitate.

Taxpayers spend millions of dollars every year to incarcerate inmates. In Missouri, the low-end estimate is $21,000 a year for each inmate. The most current D.O.C. budget was $680 million for Missouri. There are 34,000 beds in Missouri's prisons and all of them are full. 11,000 convicted felons are housed in county jails awaiting bed space in the prison system. The state pays the counties for those bed spaces, but it causes overcrowding at the local level. If we reduce the number of first time offenders warehoused under the 85% mandatory minimums, space will free up and the overcrowding problem will be reduced.

Probation and parole offices will be helped because parole violators can be sent back to prison. Repeat violators are allowed to continue to walk our streets because there is no space to re-incarcerate them. The whole system has become upside down: first time offenders are imprisoned for decades while proven repeat offenders are allowed to remain in our communities.

Communities benefit from the release of first time offenders after they prove a pattern of good behavior, so releasing them before they worsen in the prison is a good idea. Under the current system, victimization will be more likely to continue. We don't need or want angry people victimized in prison or those who learned from the "pros" how to criminalize, coming back to our streets. The "corrections department" is supposed to correct behavior, not simply warehouse men and women. Nothing is gained by keeping first time offenders who have rehabilitated in prison under the 85% law.

Making a change in our system became a top priority for me. I started contacting organizations expressing interest in reforming the law.

I set up an email account, endminimums@yahoo.com , so citizens could contact me to find out more information. Early on, I attended an event by a somewhat well-known group holding a lobby day at the state capitol. Once there, a few of us noticed how unorganized the event and the organization were. It was clear we needed to take the effort in a different direction. It was at this event I met Justine Edwards. Our friendship and our commitment to change grew rapidly.

Justine is a pediatric nurse in the Kansas City area and her fiancé, Jeff Brooks, was incarcerated on a plea deal gone bad. He was originally charged with a Class C felony, but prosecutors threatened twenty years in prison for the Armed Criminal Action charge. Jeff used a flashlight to hit someone who sought out a confrontation with him. The victim had friends in high places in their community. In order to avoid prison time, Jeff agreed to a plea deal, accepting responsibility for a Class A assault, stipulating he would serve ten years if he violated probation. The judge increased the years to fifteen after Jeff signed the original agreement. He was seen drinking a beer in public and was sent to prison for fifteen years.

Justine and I quickly decided the best way to bring about change would be by uniting all the various organizations working separately on the issue. Many people across the state wanted change. They just didn't know how to go about getting it done or had been reinventing the wheel and working as separate entities.

In June 2014, Justine and I gave a presentation at a forum held in Springfield, Missouri and it was our first venture into publicly presenting on this topic. Years of teaching experience made giving public speeches easy for me. Justine did a fine job with her part of the presentation and was responsible for the power point.

Other organizations were presenting at the forum, including the N.A.A.C.P. Elston McCowan, the Missouri N.A.A.C.P. Prison Committee Chairman, approached me afterwards and said, "We need to join forces." Having a partnership with a major social-political organization was what we were looking for.

Justine created a website, www.End85.com . Interested citizens learned about mandatory minimums and our "Get Involved" page offered a registration link so people could join our fight. We posted news articles and videos pertaining to mandatory minimums. With the aid of another activist, we began the End 85% page on Facebook. Educating the public and law makers about the issue is critical.

Missouri is a very conservative state and during the 2014 state elections, the legislature became even more conservative. All of the Democratic state senators could fit into one passenger van. There were nine of them. Obviously, the key to passing legislation would be getting Republicans onboard. Some said there was no way we could do that, but it wasn't that difficult. Fiscal responsibility is dear to Republicans and they appreciate the opportunity to save tax dollars. In these tight economic times, saving money is appealing.

Getting over the knee-jerk reactions to phrases such as "violent" versus "non-violent" would be the stickier issue to navigate. No politician wants to run the risk of having a negative ad run in the next campaign cycle. No one wants to become another Michael Dukakis.

We gathered names and addresses of people interested in reform. We attended meetings and spoke to everyone we could about the issue. I lived in one corner of the state and Justine lived in the other, so between the two of us we reached a lot of people.

I came up with the idea of using postcards to promote our effort. In October 2014, we began our postcard campaign to the legislature. We sent postcards to legislators on behalf of the hundreds and hundreds of people in Missouri who gave us permission to voice their support. Nearly every district in the state had people on our list.

While historically this has been viewed as a Democratic issue, supporters came from all walks of life. Politicians needed to recognize prison and sentencing reform wasn't a partisan or black versus white issue. Supporters ranged from doctors, farmers, teachers, nurses, politicians, students, the old, the young, city dwellers, country people, black, white, Democrats and Republicans. Common sense appealed to everyone.

Let me qualify that last statement. Common sense appeals to everyone, except sometimes politicians. For all of their bold talk during the election season, politicians are by and large afraid of their own political shadows. They are afraid of what will influence their image in the next round of campaign ads. It's sad, but true. I can't tell you how many of the state legislators have told us they supported what we were doing, but they wouldn't sponsor a bill for it. Leaders lead, even when an issue is controversial. Our system runs the way it does because, like television shows, it's all about ratings. Few in politics have the willpower and courage to do what makes sense.

We were fortunate to have one Missouri representative willing to take on a challenge. Representative Don Phillips, a well-respected Republican from the conservative Ozarks area, sponsored our bill, House Bill 657. Don was a former highway patrolman and his background carried a lot of weight when it came to criminal justice issues. No one could accuse Don of being a soft-on-crime liberal. We were further boosted by the co-sponsorship of the bill by Representative Kenneth Wilson from Kansas City. He is another Republican and a former administrator for the Missouri Department of Corrections.

Past efforts to bring reform stalled, mainly because they were all-encompassing of every dangerous felony. Politicians made it clear they will not reduce sentences for rapists, child molesters and many of the other dangerous felonies. After speaking to many legislators one-on-one, we realized reform could only be done by starting small.

The bill introduced by Don Phillips, House Bill 657, made first time offenders of first degree arson, assault and robbery eligible for consideration for parole at 50%. The key word there is "eligible." It was not a guarantee of release. It would give the parole board the discretion to review the readiness and rehabilitation of first time offenders. If someone rehabilitated and could be a productive member of society, it made no fiscal sense for the state to pay to incarcerate him any longer, especially with a backlog of inmates awaiting prison space.

House Bill 657 was assigned to the Civil and Criminal Proceedings Committee. Justine and I testified at the March 30, 2015 public hearing of the bill before that committee. Also testifying in support were Keith's attorney, Kevin Schriener, as well as leaders of prominent organizations and a few parents of inmates who were affected by this legislation. Family members gave a human face to the incarcerated. Inmates as a category are easy to not care about. We needed people who revealed to the committee members inmates and their families as real people. The hearing lasted an hour and a half, which was a good sign, which we sorely needed.

Justine and I testified first. A few of the committee members were downright combative towards us. Galen Higdon, who had told me in his office a month before he would vote yes to pass it out of the committee, went on the attack immediately. He questioned the wisdom of releasing people who were first time offenders, insisting they had committed other crimes but they just hadn't been caught. Andrew McDaniel, who came from the district I lived in, was especially negative. He was a former county police officer and this was his first term in the legislature. In my opinion, he not only had tunnel vision on the issue, he had pinhole vision. It was not an easy question and answer session by any means, but we knew our facts and kept redirecting our "opponents" back to those facts. We had done our homework, using statistics from the Missouri Department of Corrections, the Missouri Highway Patrol Statistical Analysis Center and the Federal Crime Bureau.

Concerns about recidivism (re-offense) were among the top issues for the legislators. They worried about released felons committing new crimes. Lawmakers didn't want those felons used against them in future campaign ads. A few asked repeatedly how they would explain a yes vote to their constituents back home. They worried about easy punishments for crimes, claiming since prison had become so "easy" people didn't fear going back. We were able to counter those concerns using statistics from the Department of Corrections itself.

Representative Kimberly Gardner, a former prosecutor from the St. Louis area, was a powerful advocate for the bill during the public hearing, successfully rebutting comments made by her colleagues. She gave us the opportunity to address those issues. Her help was invaluable. Kimberly later joined as a co-sponsor of the bill.

Surprisingly, the crime firing up the committee most was the arson charge. We expected push back on both the assault and robbery charges, but we didn't anticipate the vehement response against arson.

We walked out of the hearing not sure what would happen next. Don Phillips was worried. I don't think he expected such vicious opposition from his own party members. Most of the committee members were respectful in their questions or they were silent. The display put on by a few legislators concerned us.

Before leaving the Capitol, I had a heart-to-heart talk with Don. It was time for us to throw the committee a few bones to settle their fears. We previously discussed possible concessions we could make if need be and I had already given Don a list of amendments we could use.

First on the chopping block was arson. Not many people are in prison for first degree arson and if it meant the difference between the bill dying or moving forward, arson could be taken off the table. Don agreed.

Next we addressed their concerns about recidivism and punishment. House Bill 657 was amended applying strict penalties to anyone benefitting from release at 50% who committed further crimes. Conviction of any additional felony resulted in the inmate going back to prison to serve 100% of their original sentence plus any time the new crime carried. That change satisfied their bloodlust, making sure sentences were tough and punitive. It also showed which offenders were truly rehabilitated. Those not committed to living crime free lives could opt to serve the original 85% of their sentences and not take the 50% option. Someone with no interest in future criminal activity would accept the conditions of the bill. Don agreed and the amendment was made.

I left Jefferson City unsure of what the future held. On the way home, I received a phone call from the legislative assistant of Representative Gina Mitten. She told me we had done an incredible job and our facts were impressively in order. She asked for more information about the bill and the origins of the 85% mandatory minimums in our state. I took this as an encouraging turn of events. If our bill was dead in the water, no legislator would be putting effort into finding out more information.

Things looked up once again a few days later when supporters forwarded me emails they received from Galen Higdon pledging his support of House Bill 657. I wondered all along if he was playing devil's advocate at the hearing. Maybe he wanted to see if we were able to stand up to some hard hits and low blows. Apparently, we passed his test. It was good to know, in spite of his public display, we had his vote in the committee.

Don Phillips and I kept in close email contact and about a week after the hearing we were gaining momentum. The removal of arson and the inclusion of the re-offense penalties had gained us support. The committee chairman told Don the bill had enough votes to pass out of committee. The hearing was scheduled for April 14, 2015.

Progress needed to start moving quickly. Only a month remained in the legislative session. Once the bill was out of the Civil and Criminal Proceedings Committee, it would go through the select committee and then to the House floor for a vote by the entire House of Representatives. Once through the process, it would go to the Senate.

As the date of the Civil and Criminal Proceedings Committee hearing approached, we were encouraged by the support of the chairman of the select committee. On the Senate side, people were expressing support and an eagerness to get it before them for a vote. The senators liked the cost savings to the state House Bill 657 provided.

A few days later, the Civil and Criminal Proceedings Committee voted 9-3 to pass the bill on to the Judiciary Select Committee. Passing by such a large margin was a boost forward. One former prosecutor was a no vote. The committee's vice chair voted against it. Then, of course, there was An-drew McDaniel. Next, it was on to the Select Committee on Judiciary.

Our bill kept rolling along. On April 22nd, it not only made its way out of the select committee, but the bill was voted out by a unanimous 10-0 vote. The chairman signed it and im-mediately passed it on its way to the House leader. It needed to be scheduled a slot on the calendar so the entire House could vote for it. The clock was ticking and Don immediate-ly went to work getting HB 657 on the House calendar. Jus-tine and I encouraged people to contact the Speaker of the House asking him to give HB 657 immediate attention.

House Bill 657 was put on the House floor for debate on April 29th. Justine and I drove to Jefferson City for the de-bate. We could sit in the gallery, but we would not be able to testify during this part of the process. Floor debate opened with the Speaker of the House calling the chamber to order at 10:00 A.M.

Debate began on a number of bills and it was disappointing to hear how much time was spent on soft issues. Lengthy debate was held on whether or not people eligible for Purple Heart license plates pay an additional fee for a special plate. The easy answer should be "No." Forty-five minutes of de-bate was held over a proposal for a state book for Missouri. The St. Louis delegation opposed it because it came from Kansas City. Another debate went on and on for an amend-ment to a bill dealing with fees impacting businesses with miniature golf and go-carts.

I looked at Justine and said, "Our bill is going to look like Godzilla at a preschool."

Finally, after 4 o'clock in the afternoon, HB 657 was brought to the floor for debate. We had reached the moment when this important bill would be fought for. Don Phillips introduced the bill with a short statement explaining it reduced parole eligibility to 50% for first time offenders of first degree robbery and first degree assault. Representative Galen Higdon stood up and voiced his support for the bill. Kimberly Gardner also stood up in support of the bill.

Representative Justin Hill, a brand new member of the House, ranted against the bill saying, "I will never vote for a bill that goes easy on someone who shoots a law enforcement officer!" His commentary went on and on. Another representative spoke up against it because she would not vote for a bill letting child molesters out early. The two representatives raged against those crimes. House Bill 657 did not apply to assault on law enforcement or child molestation. Totally different statutes cover those crimes.

This legislation was simple and clear-cut in reality, but fear and a lack of understanding got in the way of moving it forward. Legislators asked questions unrelated to the bill itself. I believe Don was surprised by the intensity of the attacks. Without understanding what they argued against, a few legislators brought the bill to a standstill.

Justine and I sat there, knowing all of the answers to the questions they were asking, but unable to say anything. We watched as the bill went down in flames. It was unreal after all of the work we had put into it. We anticipated heated debate. We anticipated difficult questions. We never considered the possibility the bill would be so misunderstood. How did that happen? We were stunned and sickened and there wasn't anything we could do.

The bill was pulled from the floor and laid over. While this seemed to be a major setback, in reality it was a blessing in disguise. The bill itself was clean and solid. Legislators needed a clear explanation of what the bill contained. It was better to pull HB 657 from the floor without a vote. In the future we wouldn't need to convince a legislator why they should vote for a bill they had already gone on record opposing.

Justine and I went to the third floor by the doors of the House Chamber. There I saw Don Phillips standing by Justin Hill. I approached Representative Hill and we talked about his concerns. Representatives Galen Higdon and Kenneth Wilson were busy finding the statutes so Hill could see his concerns were unfounded. Within a few moments, Justin Hill shook my hand saying he could support the bill as long as it clarified no injury happened to law enforcement or emergency personnel. When I explained the bill was for first time offenders of a fight or a robbery done out of desperation, his said, "Those people shouldn't rot in prison." How easy was that? Unfortunately, it was too late. The other members heard this bill gave breaks to child molesters and to those who try to kill police officers. The damage was done.

The next morning a whip count was conducted to determine support for the bill. There wasn't time to counteract the misinformation from the day before. Don Phillips told me he would not push the bill further if the whip count wasn't at least 70%. Not surprisingly, the results of the whip count were not good. Later that morning the final tally had been 46%. Even with the misinformation, nearly half of the representatives were still willing to vote for it. For now, however, House Bill 657 was dead.

The next evening, my phone rang. It was Representative Galen Higdon. He wanted to know if he could help. I asked if he would help garner support for next year. He not only wanted to do that, he was calling to say he wanted to sponsor the bill for the next year. We now had a new sponsor committed to the bill who would fight for it. Galen and I talked for quite a while. He said this legislation should have passed years ago. We simply cannot sustain increasing the prison population in this state. Galen pledged this legislation would be one of his top priorities for the new session. Our effort was alive.

Mandatory minimums are not the only legislative change we are working on. The practice of double jeopardy in our state must go. Twenty-five other states do not prosecute someone after a federal conviction and Missouri needs to be the next one to make that change. Granted, Keith and I have a personal stake in this. As a state, we should not pay to jail, prosecute and imprison a person who should be in federal custody. Overcrowding of court dockets and the cost of incarceration are common complaints in our criminal justice system. Why should Missouri taxpayers spend our dollars prosecuting someone who has already been convicted?

Our constitutional rights to freedom from double jeopardy should be protected. Committing a crime doesn't take away someone's constitutional protections. In fact, the protection from double jeopardy is specifically intended for those who have broken the law. If one person's constitutional rights can be stripped from them, so can the rest of ours.

Sensible justice is what we are working for, not the opening of the gates of prisons. We support punishment for crimes. No one in our effort thinks there should be a Get out of Jail Free Card. We must consider, what is a reasonable punishment for a first time offender of a fight? Shouldn't rehabilitation be the focus? If someone has rehabilitated, why continue to use prison bed space to incarcerate him if there are parole violators roaming our streets? Give parole boards the ability to determine readiness.

Our efforts to attain sensible justice are not limited to these two issues. In the future, we intend to work to make our state's system more fair and economical. It is in every citizen's best interest to make sure the process is as equitable and sensible as possible.

Chapter Thirty-Three

The Appeals

Keith

"There is in all a strong disposition to believe that anything lawful is also legitimate. This belief is so widespread that many persons have erroneously held that things are 'just' because the law makes them so." — Frederic Bastiat, 1850

I never contested the fact I committed twelve bank robberies. It was not until I realized the State of Missouri was pursuing a second conviction for seven of the robberies that I contested my state prosecution. Obviously, the robberies themselves are not at issue with my appeals. After all, I pled guilty to them in a federal court of law. My opposition is based on the constitutionality of the convictions and punishments handed down by Missouri. I couldn't believe an American could be convicted twice of the same crimes. Our Constitutional rights are vital to our way of life and mine were trampled.

Of course, I am outraged by the second convictions. Appealing them is something I am compelled to do. I will explain not only the mechanics, players and contents of my appeals, but also why every American citizen should be as outraged and perplexed as I am by those convictions. Whatever happened to our freedom from double jeopardy?

The majority of decisions handed down by courts are appealed by the losing party, whether the case is a criminal or civil proceeding. I did not appeal my federal conviction. I pled guilty to all twelve of the robberies and was willing to accept the responsibility attached to my guilty pleas in federal court. The second convictions at the hands of the St. Louis County Prosecutor, I will continue to appeal.

A common misconception in America is that the legal playing field is slanted in favor of the defendant. We grow up hearing defendants are innocent until proven guilty. My experience is the opposite. The prosecutors and judges are well aware of the advantages they have. The deck is stacked against anyone who is accused of a crime. Anyone arrested is immediately assumed guilty in the public eye. The media convicts the accused before a hearing ever occurs. The courts know this, making it much easier to convince a jury. Most minds are made up once an accusation of guilt is made.

Innocence until proven guilty and unalienable constitutional rights are all but gone in this land. They are a mere shell of what they once were and of what the framers of our Constitution intended. God forbid anyone is arrested and entered in this "justice" system. There is more truth to what I say than what citizens have been led to believe. It's the prosecution's sandbox. They control it and we as citizens are at their discretion.

My reasoning for appeal is simple: I was wronged. We as Americans were wronged in my case. When our government does any citizen wrong, we should not take it on the chin or sit and do nothing. Caroline and I are taking every legal step to right this wrong. Americans should consider if it can happen to me, it can happen to them. Constitutional rights apply to everyone, not only to those who have committed no crimes.

I am not an angry and bitter convict. I love this country and the state I grew up in. I love them enough to care when I see something wrong. All of us should. It's our country. Long before I was incarcerated, I questioned where our country was headed.

"It may not be perfect, but it's the best thing going." I heard this bumper sticker phrase often. As Americans, we should care and be actively concerned about how our country and respective states are governed and operated. We shouldn't be content to say it's good enough.

In many areas, America has left the path the founders and framers intended. The judicial and penal systems are two of these areas. The framers intended us to have an active say in how these (and all other parts of our government) operate. Our system is complicated and it isn't easy for the average citizen to be involved in the justice realm. Before becoming part of the system, I didn't know how it worked.

There are several steps in the appeals process in the state of Missouri. First, is the Notice of Appeal. Second is what is called the Direct Appeal. This covers all matters that are on the record pre-trial and during the actual trial. Third is what is called Post-Conviction Relief or the Missouri Rule 29.15 process. At this stage, the defendant claims the ineffectiveness of his or her trial counsel. The fourth step is taken up in the federal courts. It is a Federal Habeas Corpus ("free the body"). I am at this stage now. The fifth step would be a State Habeas Corpus. The last step in the appeals process is a plea for clemency or pardon from the governor.

The day after my sentencing in the circuit court, I filed a notice of appeal in the same court. Several weeks later, I was notified by the courts my right to appeal was granted. By this time, I had arrived at the South Central Correctional Center.

Being indigent, I applied to have a public defender to represent me in Direct Appeal. I was granted a public defender out of the Columbia, Missouri office at a cost of $800. The cost was to be paid later and I signed a promissory note.

I received a greeting letter from the attorney, Brittany Thomas, assigned to my case. Her letter said if I had questions, I could write her. She did not take telephone calls. I sent Ms. Thomas a letter asking her to let me play an active role in this and I listed claims valid and pertinent to the case for appeal. I also requested telephone contact with her. That never happened.

Before I knew it, my Direct Appeal was filed. Only one claim was made and that claim did not have a good chance historically in the courts. It wasn't even one of the twenty-one claims I suggested she try. The Direct Appeal failed, of course, in front of a panel of three judges from the Missouri Court of Appeals. Given the little investigation, time and effort put in by my appointed attorney, the outcome wasn't surprising.

During the Post-Conviction Relief phase, claims are presented solely on the basis of ineffective assistance of trial counsel, whether the claims are constitutional, procedural or an assertion of actual innocence. Oddly, these claims go in front of the same judge who presided over the case in the trial or circuit court. How many judges will rule a mistake was made in their own courtroom? This step, in its current form, is a waste of time and taxpayer dollars, since few judges will rule in favor of the convicted.

I had ninety days to file what is called a Form 40. On this form, the movant (convicted defendant) is asked to concisely state all claims of ineffective assistance of counsel. With my twenty-two claims, I did so and in a timely manner.

My motion was granted by Judge Perkins. Again, I was appointed a public defender via the same application process as on Direct Appeal. This time the promissory note was for $1,600. She was out of the St. Louis, Missouri office.

I received a greeting letter from Jenna McCalester several weeks later. She was reviewing my claims and would contact me after she did so. To my surprise, Ms. McCalester contacted me several times during the process by telephone at South Central. We discussed my claims in some depth. She said she would take no more than six of my claims and file an amended motion to the court. Only three were eventually amended. That was a disappointment. She did attach a copy of my Form 40 to her amended motion. McCalester was required to do because I asked her to. By doing so, all of my claims were preserved for further review in future appeal steps.

During our first conversation, she asked who my direct appellate attorney was. Jenna McCalester knew her and referred to her by a nickname. Obviously, they were acquainted with each other. She explained many of my claims should have been brought up on Direct Appeal. At that point, I suggested we claim the Direct Appeal attorney as ineffective as well. McCalester refused to do so. After all, they were friends or at the very least friendly colleagues, who worked for the same employer. She was not going to question the quality of a friend's work.

During the Post-Conviction Relief process, once the circuit judge receives the amended motion, he or she can rule to vacate or go against the sentence given. The judge can grant a hearing to get more facts in order to make an informed ruling. In this case, Judge Perkins chose to do none of the above. He denied all of the claims outright. His decision was appealed by Jenna McCalester and was denied by the court of appeals. McCalester refused to appeal their decision to the Missouri Supreme Court, even though she told me she would do so.

One noteworthy thing McCalester did occurred when I was in the hole during the final stages of her representation of me. She called me at the prison to check on my well-being after Caroline asked her to. She then let Caroline know I was okay. Her humanity and compassion are appreciated by both of us.

The public defender system in Missouri is riddled with problems and conflicts. Not without merit, the nickname for the system among Missouri inmates is "Public Pretender System." This system is supposedly in place to insure the rights of the poor or unrepresented needs repair. Rich or poor, guilty or innocent, Americans have the right to adequate counsel under the Constitution.

In the first two steps of my appeal, the claims were presented in the same cut-and-paste manner public defenders are famous for. The same precedent case law was used; the same presentation given. Public defenders were unwilling to try a new twist or to think outside the box. If the claim was a loser in last month's case, unless there has been a new ruling by a higher court, it will be a loser this month, too. Going through the motions, with no real strategy for success, is standard procedure for public defenders.

In turn, the Attorney General's Office uses the same method in their responses. They maintain each case is looked at by its circumstances and merit, but this is true only to the extent of applying existing case law to their advantage. The same old excuses are used to perpetuate mass incarceration.

When represented by a public defender in Missouri courts, either at trial, plea bargain or on appeal, it is not a question if the defendant will go to prison, but how long they go to prison. Many are guilty of crimes, a few are innocent and many defendants' rights are violated by legal process tantamount to an assembly line to conviction. Violations are streamlined through the system without recourse. Multiple cogs in the legal system allow this to happen. Legislators, judges and lawyers, including public defenders, play a part.

A good lawyer is crucial when accused of a crime. Some can afford a high-quality attorney, but many cannot. A class discrepancy in our justice system is created. Being poor makes it likely you will go to prison and for a long time. Not many rich people are sitting in prison.

Regardless of where we live, a laundry list of people (politicians, law enforcement, lawyers, celebrities, business tycoons and their families) who committed crimes but walked away either free or with a slap on the wrist can come to mind. I can think of many in Missouri right off the top of my head. None were represented by a public defender. If the common person, the unconnected or poor are accused, they are usually found guilty. In a state like Missouri with 85% mandatory minimum laws, the length of prison terms can be staggering.

Not every public defender is a bad lawyer with no conscience. In many respects, they are victims of the broken system themselves. Young and looking for experience, they want to move on to private practice or to the prosecutorial side, even want to play a noble part in our legal system. Many are well-educated, experienced attorneys I am sure, but others are there for a state paycheck and that's it.

When public defenders are employed by the same entity as the prosecutors and judges, a conflict exists. The same person signs all of their paychecks. In St. Louis County, the prosecutors and public defenders even share office space on the same floor of the Justice Center. The potential for corruption and back door deals is too tempting. People's lives are at stake in this game.

Public defenders have a supervisor in each office who may only let them go so far or spend so much time on each case. In other words, the defender's hands may be tied, making them unable to do the job they want to do.

Caseload is one of the best known issues with the public defender system; immense due to several factors. The obvious one is we commit too many crimes in this country. Another is the number of statutes or laws we have. It is absurd. One mistake can lead to multiple felony charges. Even conservative talk show host, Dr. Michael Savage, says, "We are all just one mistake away from going to prison in this country." We keep creating new laws. Behaviors that were not felonies before are now. These ingredients fuel the judicial system and tie up the courts. Combined, they create a massive caseload for the public defender system.

Like many states, Missouri has been cash-strapped for the better part of a decade. This puts strain on the public defender system while the prosecutors have seemingly unlimited resources. Much like a weather forecaster, prosecutors have no accountability if they are wrong. If years later a conviction is overturned because of their wrongdoing, prosecutors face no repercussions. They have more leeway in their approaches to trials. Public defenders have less money to work with and fewer resources to draw upon. It's easy to see the prosecution has an advantage. After all, every criminal case is called "The State of Missouri versus _____." Even economically struggling states do what they can to come out the winner in a trial.

Caseload is used by public defender offices to gain more funding. Of course, the prosecutors believe they deserve more money, too. The two sides battle with each other over funding more than they do in the courtroom. The bureaucracy grows and grows. Who suffers? The taxpayer and the defendants do.

A heavy caseload should not be an excuse for providing inadequate defense counsel. How many patients would give doctors the same professional pass? No one will say it's okay to let someone die because the doctor had too many patients. While most people are not sentenced to death in our legal system, that doesn't diminish the value of the years lost by someone inadequately defended. Just as we demand high-quality medical care, regardless of the caseload, people's rights deserve to be vigorously defended.

The Post-Conviction Relief stage in the appeals process is the last point where the appellant is provided state representation. For the next steps, I would be on my own to represent myself throughout the rest of the process. At least I thought so.

Filing a Habeas Corpus petition in the federal district court is a complicated matter. To present it properly, one must be very thorough. Many inmates try this themselves because they have no choice other than to give up. Many make mistakes in their appeals which eliminate their chances of success. Giving up was never an option for us, but we didn't want mistakes made either.

Caroline and I could have put together a presentable petition to the federal court, but neither of us are lawyers. It wouldn't have every chance possible to be successful. Caroline made a suggestion. She asked Jenna McCalester if she knew the names of any good federal appeals attorneys. She did and gave three to Caroline.

Caroline and I discussed the idea of hiring a real attorney for the appeal in the federal courts. At first, I was against the idea for financial reasons. I didn't want Caroline to go through the strain of paying for an attorney. I remember telling her, "That's the cost of a new car." She was persistent, and the more we talked, the more I was convinced.

Caroline reminded me she wasn't going to leave any stone unturned to help me. I was still a little hesitant, but it felt right to both of us. Caroline was between jobs and was working part time. She made a couple of moves before getting settled into a new teaching job. I was concerned about the financial burden.

Also, my trust in lawyers was at an all-time low. Rock bottom, in fact. After all I had been through in the legal system, it was difficult for me to trust one more attorney. Caroline did a great job of talking me through that fear.

This would be the last real chance to present my preserved claims to a court outside the state of Missouri. Caroline insisted it be done right. I finally agreed. She later told me that, regardless of what I thought, she was going to hire someone anyway. She wasn't going to let my last good shot at an appeal slip away unrepresented.

Caroline took the names McCalester sent her and made one call. That's all it took. In stepped Kevin Schriener. The lines of communication between Kevin, Caroline and I were immediately opened. I never had a lawyer who communicated with me before. Kevin returned Caroline's phone calls, contacted us on his own and was available on weekends to answer questions. He was friendly, professional and honest. Kevin became someone we consider a friend.

Caroline and Kevin discussed a suitable contract for his services. Caroline let him know how important this appeal was to us and how much I meant to her. She explained money was tight in the immediate, but she would gladly work out whatever payment plan Kevin thought was fair. Kevin is a not only a fine lawyer, he is a good human being. He worked with Caroline to come up with acceptable terms.

After reviewing the file on the case, Kevin called me. Before I met him, I was skeptical. We talked on the phone and a few weeks later I met him in person. My skepticism soon vanished. We only had a few months to get the petition filed in a timely manner, so we started right away.

While formulating the petition, Kevin listened to ideas Caroline and I had. I tried to express my ideas in this case since the beginning. Kevin added his own keen insight and legal expertise. Using the same old run-of-the-mill arguments would never yield a favorable result. Kevin agreed. Kevin let us be active participants in the case. I longed for this in an attorney from the beginning.

Kevin made no promises. He was up front and honest with us about the chances of a victory. Regardless of the merit of the claims, winning an appeal is difficult in any court of law in this country. A federal appeal is a steep hill to climb.

With results still pending in our appeal, I recommend Kevin Schriener as a skilled, honest, conscientious and hard-working lawyer. He is fair and has put his very best into this case. It definitely shows in his work.

Kevin helped with more than the appeal. He gave his time and talent drafting the legislation for House Bill 657. He testified before the Missouri House Committee when Caroline asked him to add his public support to the bill. Kevin is a good man and I am proud to have him represent me.

My claims cover legal injustice, procedural violations and constitutional violations. Without going into great technical detail, I will give a summary of what I am fighting for, though. The claims are public information and I invite anyone interested to study and view them for themselves.

Twenty-two claims in total, plus one on Direct Appeal are in my appeal. Kevin cleverly incorporated all of the claims into the six listed in the petition filed in federal district court.

This new, condensed claim questions the constitutionality and fairness of the Post-Conviction-Relief process by using the role of counsel as a platform. Success or failure, it is a fine piece of work.

One claim, of course, deals with the violation of my constitutional rights to be free from double jeopardy. We are given those freedoms under the 5th and 14th Amendments of the United States Constitution. Missouri's Constitution also states that citizens are free from double jeopardy. Another claim argues the violation of my constitutional right to a speedy trial. Citizens are given those rights under the 6th and 14th Amendments. Even though these two claims may not provide the greatest opportunity for relief in my case, if I am successful with these claims, they will provide dismissal of cause by law. It is a matter of principle and it is why I have fought these state prosecutions and convictions from their genesis. I believe our American rights are worth fighting for.

The violation of my right to a speedy trial is clear. Under federal law, a court has eight months to try a person accused of a crime. The government cannot hold a person excessively or delay their day in court in order to gain a tactical advantage. I was held for twenty-three months. I never asked for a continuance. Under any circumstance, twenty-three months is more than enough time to hold a trial. In our petition, we illustrate how the state delayed the trial until after I pled guilty in federal court so they could use my federal conviction as a tool against me. The federal government does not prosecute anyone for the exact same crimes twice. The State of Missouri knew this and let the feds go first so the state could pursue its second conviction of me.

A state trial never should have happened. The 5th Amendment of the United States Constitution is clear on the subject of multiple prosecutions for the same offense. It calls for no exceptions. Regardless, some states hide behind the shroud of the 10th Amendment which provides states' rights. Upon its adoption, President Lincoln said "The states should not use the 10th Amendment to do wrong." Well, some do. Missouri is one of those states.

The Dual Sovereignty Doctrine is used to justify state prosecutions after a federal conviction. It uses a clause in the 10th Amendment that says, "The states have the right to make and enforce their own laws." I don't disagree with that and some say the federal government should not be in the criminal law business at all. Whatever the case, one or the other should take jurisdiction, not both. Otherwise the rights given to us by the founding fathers are violated.

Dual Sovereignty is constitutionally uncomfortable in its entirety. It is a misuse of the doctrine adopted in the early 19th Century that continued to take shape in the mid-20th Century. Many states never apply the doctrine and others have laws against using certain provisions of it.

Law dictionaries define a sovereign as "a government that is not a member of a larger union." Are our states really separate sovereigns? What flag goes to the top of the pole first? Shouldn't the supreme governing law be the United States Constitution? As citizens, we should know more about the Constitution and our rights.

Starting in 1803, the U.S. Supreme Court began creating absolute power for itself. Using arbitrary decisions to create precedent case law diminished and polluted the Constitution. The framers did not have this in mind. No sitting Supreme Court has interpreted the actual meaning of the amendments to the Constitution. The framers of the Constitution created the judicial branch of government to do so. Rubberizing of the Constitution through the use of arbitrary case law precedent shouldn't happen. The Constitution has been bastardized and the result is a type of tyranny that we all live under. Our Constitution isn't a cafeteria plan. It isn't a pick-and-choose document to be used one way when it suits a prosecutor and another when it doesn't. Interpretation of the Constitution should be as simple as yes or no answers. Either something is expressed in the Constitution or it isn't.

For people who believe, since they are law-abiding, this has no bearing on them, consider this scenario: What if a law is passed that takes away free speech or the right to bear arms? What if the Supreme Court upholds it to be law? Having a law doesn't mean it is right. Slavery was legal. Segregation was legal. Prohibition was the law. This list goes on of laws that are no more because they were not right.

Having the Supreme Court dissolve or mold our Constitution doesn't make it right either. In reality, the power to decide what is legal is in the hands of a very few people who adapt it to their own liking. Why are Supreme Court nominations so important to political parties and presidents? Because Supreme Court decisions are swayed, liberal or conservative, by the makeup of the appointed judges on the panel. The Constitution shouldn't be politicized, but it is.

Does the Constitution specify which words or phrases you can or cannot write or say? No. Does it specify what type of arms you can bear? No. Does it mention anything about marriage or whom you can marry? No. Does the Constitution say citizens must purchase any product? No. Nine people have absolute power to decide these issues and countless others.

Constitutional rights of former inmates are trampled every day. How much time is enough to pay for one's crimes? Should going to prison be a life sentence, one that never leaves you or should you be able to have a life once again? Once someone serves his sentence in prison, he should be done. It should be a fresh start for him or her. There shouldn't be parole and there should be no public judgment. He paid his debt to society and should be left alone to live. As it stands now, the system won't let anyone off the chain of incarceration. It is a lifelong commitment for mistakes already paid for. Constitutional rights such as voting and bearing arms should not be banned for life once you have served your sentence. Travel abroad should be allowed as well. The Constitution does not bar anyone from these rights. Isn't it time we get back to what the Constitution allows?

The word "appeal" can be used in a different context than it is in the justice system. It is also a call to action. It is a request to bring about change. In our country, we are becoming more aware of the many problems facing us. Our problems are both social and economic. People of color and those of fewer means are more likely than their counterparts to go to prison. At the center of this issue are our broken justice and penal systems. Prosecutors tout the word "justice." Well, it is time for sensible justice. The issues are not conservative versus liberal, party versus party or rich versus poor. The current system of division keeps us diverted from the true source of our problems. The media and the government like us to think we are battling each other. All of us have allowed these problems to fester and it will take all of us to solve them. It's time to work together.

The saying "It takes a village..." applies here. It takes a country. My appeal to all Americans is to get involved. Use the process and vote. Hold elected officials' feet to the fire. Don't settle for bumper sticker answers to complex problems. Don't be swayed by flashy campaigns or empty promises.

Change starts with each of us. I am a convicted criminal and I know what the system is like. The first step is for us to stop committing crimes. I have been a part of the problem. As Americans, each citizen needs to do our part to fix things. Do the necessary things to get our country on the right track. Make sure our elected officials are doing their jobs. Educate ourselves on the issues. Become involved instead of acting as bystanders. Care about what is right.

Chapter Thirty-Four

What I've Learned

Keith

"Sometimes it's not what you know or who you know. It's what you know about who you know that matters." — Caroline

We can't count the number of times Caroline has heard the words, "You know, Keith isn't going to be the same person when he gets out of prison. He's going to change." Truthfully, this entire experience opened my eyes to many things, but I can't say it changed me; not the essence of who I am as a person. I have learned a great deal about people in my life before I went to prison and about those who entered our lives since my incarceration. I have learned a lot about the motivations of people and that we can't close our eyes to the fact that none of us are as free as we'd like to think we are.

I have learned too many times we are only as valuable as what we can provide someone else in the immediate. I have learned it's easy for people to beat you, kick you and ridicule you when you are down. When there is no way you can defend yourself, you see who really sticks by you. I've learned to value a relationship based on who has your back even when the situation looks like a losing venture.

I have learned blood isn't thicker than water. With the exception of a very few, family members rushed to abandon us. My family members might be expected to turn on me because of my crimes, but Caroline has been emotionally stabbed by family members when her only "fault" was loving me. We don't need to name who launched the most heinous attacks against us. They know who they are; the damage they have done. They also have made themselves a part of our past.

At the same time, we have friends who are better than family to us. Our list has been fairly short at times, but the ones who are on it mean more than either of us can ever express in words. People like Roger Pettinelli and Mary Shults are decades-long friends who have proven time and again their love and friendship is real. They have welcomed Caroline into their lives and home, and they have been adamantly in support of me. Roger and Mary have let us know we are always a part of their lives. Otherwise, my list of friends has grown depressingly short over the years. A few people have maintained correspondence with me, and I appreciate that.

I have learned that even in prison there are good people who can become great friends. Daniel Stewart has become family to both Caroline and me. Not everyone you meet in prison is trustworthy enough to call "friend," but Dan is one of those people. He has proven to be a loyal and trusted friend, and he will always be welcome at our house. There are more good people like Dan in prison than the public realizes.

Caroline receives an amazing amount of support from Mary Atwell, Laken Conaway-Brown, Christine Oakley, Norma Garrett and Justine Edwards. Each of them comes from a different part of her life, but they are as steadfast of friends as anyone could ever have.

Mary has been Caroline's friend since their first day of college at the University of Arizona. They were both seventeen at the time, and their friendship has endured every twist and turn that life has taken them on. Mary lives in Colorado, but rarely does a day go by that she and Caroline don't talk. That's not common to find in life given the span of time they have known each other.

Laken is a former student of Caroline's who is like family to us. She is caring, level-headed, and just enough of a rebel to keep life fun. Her steadfast loyalty to us is extraordinarily endearing.

Chris and Caroline's friendship began during Caroline's first year of teaching after college. Chris has faced struggles and heartbreak in life, but she has done so with love and grace that fills us with nothing but admiration for her. She is a wonderful mother, wife, and friend to those in her world.

Norma and Caroline met years ago while teaching on the Navajo Reservation in New Mexico. Norma's passions are teaching and social work, and she has a heart that is always willing to give. Her children and friends are blessed to have her enthusiastic support.

Justine joined our crew when she and Caroline met while working on reform of the mandatory minimums law. No one understands the struggles Caroline faces with my incarceration more than Justine. She is a giving and empathic soul. More than a valued team member in the fight for sensible justice, Justine is now family to us. When I can't be there physically for her, these wonderful women open their hearts to her, helping her through the difficult times.

Through the legislative lobbying, the Reverend Elston McCowan entered into our lives. Elston is an active leader of the state N.A.A.C.P. as well as an esteemed minister in the

St. Louis area. Elston is a good man with a good heart and strong convictions. We are honored to call him our friend.

Our intention is not to publicly skewer those who have wronged us, but to instead acknowledge and celebrate those who loved and supported us. It takes true character and strength of spirit to stand by people during adversity. Each of the people we named are our emotional heroes through this experience.

I have learned the public isn't as forgiving as I believed in the past. Once labeled, it's difficult for people to see past the stigma. People like things to be black and white. Far too many people believe once you make a mistake, you are tainted forever. Having "felon" stamped on your resume slams doors shut in people's minds. For those of us who have been to prison, we have done our time and paid the price the courts imposed on us. That should be the end of it. Instead, it's a mark against us some people will never forget.

I have learned people, by and large, are content to rely on the system without understanding how it operates. Too many people blindly trust in the legal system to do the right thing. After all, judges and lawyers are there to protect our rights. Too many mistakenly believe justice is blind or that whatever any given jury or judge decides is the right decision. Too many people stop questioning what goes on. That is, until their lives are affected, then sometimes it is too late at that point.

I have learned the justice system is a crap shoot. Plain and simple. I've seen child molesters get probation while kids who were in one fight are sentenced to twenty years. I witnessed my lawyers throw me under the bus for their own personal gain. I saw my rights to a speedy trial and freedom from double jeopardy trampled. I committed some serious crimes. I admit that, but I took responsibility for those crimes. My crimes don't erase my rights to what the Constitution guarantees. If my Constitutional rights mean nothing, just how much are yours worth? We should all worry about what happened to me. It could be anyone next.

I have learned most lawyers deserve the maligning the public gives them. Too many are interested in being a cog in the justice business; are more concerned about making partner than in representing a client. Jenna McCalester was one of the people who warned Caroline I would change. This woman didn't even know me. She didn't know who I was as a person. She didn't believe in me as a person or as a client. Her lackluster representation of me proved I was just another case on her overloaded desk. McCalester said she liked me, yet she felt compelled to tell Caroline she shouldn't count on having the same good man come home to her one day. Judges and lawyers are people; they're not gods nor perfect. They are human, and just like the rest of us humans, they can act out of their own biases and predispositions.

I have learned there are good attorneys out there, too. Kevin Schriener is the lawyer everyone wants on their side. He believes in us and fights for us. I seriously never thought I'd say I like a lawyer, but Kevin Schriener has earned my respect and admiration.

I have learned the public relies too much on the sensationalized media to help them learn the truth in this world. The media uses broad brushes when talking about right and wrong. This is true whether the station or newspaper you rely on for your news leans to the left or to the right. Misconceptions don't matter as long as the story sounds juicy enough. Truth is kept in the dark because reporters don't want to offend their law enforcement sources. Ratings and sensationalism get in the way of fairness and true investigative reporting. The average person may be intelligent, but as a public we tend to swallow whatever is fed to us by the media or by the system.

I have learned the prison system in Missouri is not about "corrections." It is not even necessarily designed to keep the public safer. It is an economic boost to small town Missouri that reduces the population's need for welfare. Missouri's prison system became a growth industry in the years between the 1980s and the present. It's sad a state resorts to employing citizens through the incarceration of others rather than attracting true business and industry.

So, in response to the people who thought I would change, I have to disagree. I have spent years in prison. This is true. Years spent anywhere will give a different perspective. Experiences, as I talked about in the first chapter, mold and shape the way we look at the world. People can change. I have seen people enter prison as first time offenders who become hardened and angry at the world. I have seen people choose to let the hatred bleed out of their lives so they can find peace. People change their behaviors to fit in and people can change when they lose hope. You have to choose to make those changes, though. We develop and evolve as people through time. For the most part, the very core of our personality doesn't change, but we do see the world through different lenses depending on what experiences we have.

Those who knew me before will find I am the same person I always was. I'm just wiser. I was always a private person, but I have put up more walls around my heart than I ever imagined possible. I've had to. What prison hasn't done to cause this, the painful losses of friends and family members have guaranteed. I only let a select few inside those walls now.

I'm no longer concerned with impressing others. I'm no longer concerned about trying to fit in. I haven't changed who I am as a person on the inside, though. I was always this person, but others couldn't see it. This experience didn't change who I am, but it has changed the way I view the world.

Last, but not least, I have learned with God and the love of the right woman, it doesn't matter what the rest of the world throws at me. I am still able to count all things joy.

Epilogue

My Dandelion in the Spring

Caroline

"In this world of glass houses, some people live in Crystal Cathedrals."
—Caroline

Keith and I are not the first or only couple to meet in a prison. The fact the Department of Corrections has a policy regarding overfamiliarity with offenders says it happens, and more often than the department would like to admit. Regulating emotions is a difficult thing to do. In the time since I left the prison system, I have gotten to know and learned of several other couples who met the same way we did. Would we have envisioned this was the way we met our loved ones? Of course not. Love finds us in strange places sometimes. In our case, it happened to be within the confines of a maximum security prison. Some may say it was a risky choice. For us, we don't feel like we had a choice.

Granted, some relationships formed in prison are not true relationships. There are game players and those who use authority as a weapon. We read headlines about relationships used for manipulation or as a means for escape. Those are not real relationships.

Keith and I have no power struggle in our relationship. Neither of us has any desire to trick or manipulate the other, and our feelings for one another are anything but a game to us. We are as real as we can be.

Low self-esteem is usually involved in manipulative relationships. This is true inside and outside of prison walls. Anyone who knows me will say self-esteem is not an issue for me. Being a confident, capable person does not mean I don't have a need for the right person to love and to be loved by. While we met under unusual circumstances, Keith is the right person for me. If others don't understand our feelings, we are okay with that. Not understanding something doesn't make it wrong.

We certainly have faced plenty of criticism for our relationship. Most of the people we confided in have supported us. We kept our relationship secret for several months before we told anyone outside of our children. My best friend from college, Mary Atwell, was the first person I told. Every time we confided in someone, we faced the possibility we would be given the cold shoulder or ridiculed. Some family members broke off all ties with me. The people who truly loved us wanted us to be happy.

Some people are skeptical and we understand that. Because Keith is in prison, people automatically assume he's trying to pull a scam. Keith knows only through time can he build trust with others. He appreciates those who feel protective of me and as he says, "In time they will see no one is more protective of you than I am."

It is a painful truth we will always have to deal with judgmental attitudes simply because we love each other while he is incarcerated, and even after. Some people will never be able to get past Keith's crimes to see the good man he is. Many will be able to change their opinions of him once they get to know him, others will not, whether they be strangers or family members.

Keith has sometimes said, "When will this ever end?" He agonizes over the idea the children and I will forever be measured by his past mistakes. My only answer for Keith is that it most likely will never end. There will be people who feel the need to judge. There will be people who need to find inferiority in others so they can make themselves feel better. There are others who have a keen sense of moral outrage. A lot of people live in those crystal cathedrals. We accept that not everyone is going to like us. Some people didn't like us before Keith's crimes and some won't like us in the future. It's the way life is.

That doesn't make it easy. Keith and I have found the companionship and happiness we wanted and needed our entire lives. Many people view the incarcerated as subhuman. Keith didn't stop being a human being with the full range of emotions and abilities God gave him once he went to prison. Inmates are often put on a shelf and forgotten about as if they are in suspended animation. The belief that inmates are without value causes people to then wonder what is wrong with the person who loves an inmate. We must not have as much worth or character because we love a felon.

I say those of us in this position have a great deal of character. It's easy to love someone when there are no obstacles. A test of one's commitment during hardship takes true devotion and character. Not just in my circumstance, but for the sake of all family members and loved ones who are suffering through a prison sentence, have a little compassion and recognize the strength it takes for us to get through the days. We don't need to be treated with disgust and we aren't looking for sympathy. We want to be viewed no differently than everyone else. Everyone has burdens to bear in life. Ours happen to include having an incarcerated loved one.

Our relationship made some of our dealings with the Department of Corrections more difficult than for other couples. We are met with resistance by some D.O.C. employees and by the system in general. When Keith transferred to the Southeast Correctional Center in February 2014, word spread of our relationship. We were big news. I didn't call the institution often, but when I called to inquire about him or had a question, conversations began friendly enough. With some employees, the conversations remained friendly. With others, once they connected the dots and realized I was a former D.O.C. employee romantically involved with an inmate, conversations came to an end. Icy venom came out. One administrator at S.E.C.C. made disdainful comments about me "dating" an inmate. She smirked that Keith was transferred to the boot heel of Missouri out of "convenience for the inmate," then laughed and said, "Oh yes, that's right. You live in Kansas City, don't you?" The prison was 397 miles from me.

Instead of asking questions, getting answers and being done with conversations, I was treated as a threat or as something inferior. We are not a threat to the prison system. We have what we have, regardless of how we met. If others can't understand that, then maybe they need to examine their own hearts.

We have all heard the saying, "Misery loves company." Misery is an easy thing to find in this world and prisons are by nature filled with misery. A lot of miserable people are in prison; some even work there. Such a negative atmosphere takes its toll on people and they internalize those feelings. Others were miserable before they ever worked at the prison; it may have been why they gravitated toward working there. It's hard to say if it was the chicken or the egg.

It would be easy for us and Keith in particular, to become negative and to begin to hate the world. Life isn't easy. Sometimes it makes more sense to give up and to become negative, too. It's easy to resent the good things others have when life isn't as fulfilling as you would like for it to be. We believe that misery isn't the only thing that loves company. Happiness loves company, too. Keith and I are happy and we enjoy seeing others experience happiness.

Keith is the most upbeat person I have ever met. He is able to find a silver lining in nearly every situation; not much gets him down or keeps him down for long. I have always been a positive person myself, but Keith's faith and optimism give me a solid foundation to rest upon and to turn to when things get rough. We certainly have our share of rough times and realize others are ahead. When the sound of someone's voice sweeps all fear, doubt and hesitation about the world away, it's incredibly special. Keith's voice does that for me.

Both Keith and I, as positive and outgoing as we are, felt alone most of our lives. Regardless of how many people we were surrounded by, each of us felt part of us was missing. We found that missing part in each other. Neither of us felt whole until we found each other. No rules, policies or social criticism will change that simple truth for us. Our love works for us.

Keith takes away the fear and pain of being alone in this world. When things seem too difficult, he is my reminder love will prevail. He is my constant source of reassurance that life will continue and that happiness exists. He refers to me as the flower of his life. That is so typical of this loving, kind man I am blessed to call mine. Keith provides the same beauty to my life. Keith is my dandelion in the spring. He gives me hope in this sometimes dark world that there is new life and joy.

Update

Caroline

Many people are wondering if Keith and I are able to visit each other yet. Sadly, the answer is "no." We appealed the ban all the way to the top of the Missouri Department of Corrections food chain, and it did no good. Even though Jim Marshall, the investigator who looked into us at the prison, contends to this day he found no reason for us to not visit, the D.O.C. won't budge. At every turn, a different excuse is used to deny us.

When we first appealed, Jim directed me to a man in Jefferson City, Mark Thompson, who is the keeper of all investigation reports. Jim suggested I ask Thompson for a copy of the report so we had a better idea of what the excuses were for the denial. When I spoke to him, Thompson was snide and rude. He said, "Oh, I remember this case. You told your supervisor that unless the inmate was put under your direct supervision you were going to quit. No, you aren't getting a copy of the report." I never said that to my supervisor or any other D.O.C. employee. It was a complete falsehood. Thompson went on to tell me that I couldn't have a copy of the report because I wasn't the one under investigation. Well, the denial letter said it was because I was under investigation, so that didn't add up. When I asked if Keith could have a copy then, he said he wasn't going to give an inmate an investigation report. So, basically, they are able to say whatever they want, treat people however they want, and change their stories however many times they want knowing the people they are screwing over have no access to the reports and accusations. It's an ugly circle they have created.

The shell game goes all the way up the chain of command. According to the Assistant Director of the Division of Adult Institutions, Keith and I admitted to having "avoidable contact." That is a flat-out lie. Neither of us ever said such a thing. Each classroom has two cameras going at all times. Jim Marshall reviewed all of the tapes. If there was any "avoidable" contact, he would have seen it. What happened to Marshall's original report that cleared us of wrongdoing? Obviously, it was changed to suit whatever challenge we made to the visiting ban. The stone walls were hit time and again, even though our attorney, Kevin, contacted both the Assistant Director and the Director through letters. Basically, the Missouri prison system believes it is untouchable. They can arbitrarily do whatever they want to people, knowing they are hidden under the misguided perception held by the public that they are the "good guys." The visiting ban is still in effect until October 24, 2018.

If rehabilitation and successful re-entry into society is the goal of the "Corrections" Department, then why do they insist on limiting positive contact with loved ones? It's a proven fact that one of the determining factors of success upon release is having a strong support network amongst family and friends. The Department of Corrections, at least here in Missouri, does everything it can to limit the connections inmates have with their loved ones. Keith needs to be able to see me. Nothing positive is gained by keeping us from having weekly visits. It's simply a power play by the Department of Corrections to show they hold all the cards. It's a destructive game they play with people's lives.

Keith and I are not the only ones this run-around happens to. Getting any information out of the Department of Corrections is like trying to scale Mt. Everest without a rope. Sometimes even life threatening events are held behind a curtain of secrecy. We know of one man who had a heart attack at the age of forty-seven, and he flat-lined three times on the way to the hospital. His family was never notified by the prison. His cellmate called his mother to give her the news the next morning. Every day for a week his mother called multiple times begging for information, and they told her nothing. All she knew was that her son was sent to the hospital. As his emergency contact, she should have been notified. She was told they only give out information in "serious" situations. A week later her son was told, "Here's the phone. Call your mother so she'll stop calling us." It wasn't until then that his family knew he had almost died three times. If that doesn't constitute a "serious" situation, what does? This scenario repeats itself time and again in a hundred different forms every day in the Missouri prison system.

The legislative reform effort gives me the opportunity to accomplish something positive that helps everyone involved. The state will benefit by reducing the costly expense of prison over-crowding, taxpayers will feel that relief and communities will have individuals returning who have rehabilitated and who are serious about staying on the right side of the law. Families will be reunited, and first time offenders will become contributors instead of a financial dead weight on our state.

I am proud to have Galen Higdon as the sponsor to the legislation the End 85% effort has worked to bring about. He has impressed me with his keen grasp of the intricacies of the proposal as well as an impressive ability to articulate his points. Galen isn't afraid to stand up for what is right. We are looking forward to success in this much-needed reform effort. As the inscription above the doors of the Missouri

House of Representatives chamber reads, "Progress is the Law of Life." Missouri needs to make that progress happen.

Feel free to notify Missouri legislators offering your support. Go to www.senate.mo.gov and www.house.mo.gov to follow the progress of the bill and to find out how to contact the lawmakers. If you are not from Missouri, consider beginning an effort in your own state to make sentencing and justice more sensible where you live.

I am a determined individual. If the D.O.C. thinks it will drive a wedge or lessen the intensity of our relationship by keeping us from visiting, they are sorely mistaken. I channel my energy into the legislative reform effort and into writing. It's important that change happens in a broad and systemic way in the Missouri prison system, and I believe it is important to make the public aware of the truth of how the department operates. *Bank Notes* is *not* going to be my only book. There's more to come.

Addendums

Addendum 1

The following are the pro-se motions Keith Giammanco filed on his own behalf when his attorneys refused to file them. In state court, his attorneys refused to argue these motions, and the judge refused to hear them, claiming he already had "adequate" counsel. Keith Giammanco did his best to retain his rights on his own, and these preserved claims are the basis of his on-going appeal at the federal level. Each lettered motion was filed separately by Keith Giammanco.

~~~~~~

A.

Comes now Defendant, pro per, and requesting removal of the above listed cause from the Circuit Court of St. Louis, County, State of Missouri, to the United States District Court, Eastern District of Missouri, Eastern Division. This pursuant to Rule 11, (28) (1446) jurisdiction and venue of the Federal Rules of Civil Procedure.

Defendant contends that he has been and is being prejudiced against on the following grounds:

1) The State is putting Defendant twice in jeopardy and conducting a Sham Prosecution in violation of defendant's Fifth and Fourteenth Amendment rights.

2) The State is using Selective Prosecution in the above listed cause in violation of defendant's Fifth and Fourteenth Amendment rights.

3) The State clearly is in violation of defendant's right to a speedy trial under the Sixth Amendment.

4) Defendant is being denied fair bail and pre-trial release into federal custody.

5) Defendant is being denied reason or good cause for denial of request, pleadings, and motions either in writing or in open court.

6) Defendant through ineffective counsel was not informed of this option (and others), hence the late filing of this request. The State Court has refused withdrawal of counsel after both counsel and Defendant gave reasons of conflict of interest and ethical violations by counsel.

Enclosed with this request are copies of process against the Defendant.

WHEREFORE, Defendant believes he has good cause for late filing of this request. Defendant requests that this honorable court investigate the above given reasons and rule to remove the above listed cause from state to federal court.

~~~~~

B.

Comes now the defendant, pro-per herein, pursuant to Supreme Court Rules 25.03 and 25.04, requests that state disclose to him the following:

1)   Request for audio taped statement given to XXXX XXXXXXX D.S.N. 3181, St. Louis County Police Department, by the defendant at about 10:30 P.M., the night of 09/18/08. Defendant requests this material be in the form of audio CD sent to his attorney for their review. The defendant also requests a transcribed type written, English version done by official court reporter for his review and file. The defendant is being held in the St. Louis County Jail were CDs are not permitted.

2)   Request all disclosure of discovery pertaining to cause no. 08SL-CR07124-01, pursuant to Brady v. Maryland, 373 U.S. 83, 83 S. Ct. 1194 (1963). Information or evidence that is favorable to a criminal defendant's case, and that the prosecution has a duty to disclose. The prosecution withholding of such information violates the defendant's due process rights.

WHEREFORE defendant respectfully requests that this court grant the motion.

~~~~~~~~

C.

Comes now Defendant, Donald K. Giammanco, pro-per and moves this Honorable Court to enter an order in limine prohibiting the state from making any reference in voir dire, opening statements, evidence or argument to any acts or offenses alleged to have been committed by Defendant other than the offense of with Defendant is on trial. Defendant requests this order include Defendant's prior convictions, arrests, uncharged crimes, and any other "prior history" as indicated in police reports. In support of his motion, Defendant states the following:

1)   Defendant has reason to believe the state will seek to introduce testimony regarding bad acts or uncharged crimes through the testimony of multiple state witnesses.
2)   Evidence of prior bad acts is inadmissible unless logically and legally relevant to the present charge. See State vs. Barton, 998, S.W.2d 19,28 (Mo. Banc 1999) cert. denied, 528 U.S. 1121 (2000). To be logically relevant, the evidence of prior misconduct must have legitimate tendency to establish directly the defendant's guilt of the charged crime. To be legally relevant, the probative value of the evidence must outweigh the prejudicial effect.

3)   Therefore, a court may admit evidence of prior bad acts/uncharged crimes only if the evidence has a legitimate tendency to establish motive or plan embracing the commission of two or more crimes so related to each other that the proof of one tends to establish the other, or identity, see State vs. Bernard, 849 S.W.2d 10,13 (Mo. Bac 1993). Evidence of uncharged crimes, wrongs, bad acts, or misconduct is inadmissible for showing Defendant's propensity to commit the charged crime.

4)   In this case, such evidence would not be logically relevant because it does not meet any of the five enumerated exceptions and is clearly used only for propensity purposes.

5)   The prejudicial effect of Defendant's prior convictions, arrests, uncharged crimes, or other "prior history" would substantially outweigh any possible probative value. Therefore it is not legally relevant.

6)   When properly related and logically relevant to the crime at issue, the introduction of other crime evidence violates the Defendant's right to be tried only for the offense for which he is charged. See State vs. Clover, 924 S.W.2d 853,855 (Mo. Banc 1996)

7)   An ordinary objection made during the course of trial, even if sustained and followed by a limiting instruction would be ineffective in removing the prejudice to Defendant that would be caused by placing such information before the jury. The only proper remedy would be to declare a mistrial.

8)   Placing such information before the jury would violate Defendant's right to due process of law, to be tried only for the offense charged, to present a defense to the charged offense, to a fair and impartial jury, and his right to reliable sentencing as guaranteed by the Sixth, Eighth, and Fourteenth Amendments to the United States Constitution and Article I, Section 10,14,17,18, and 18(a) of the Missouri Constitution.

WHEREFORE, the foregoing reasons, Defendant respectfully requests that this Honorable Court enter an order in limine prohibiting the state from making any reference in voir dire, opening statements, evidence or argument to any acts of offenses alleged to have been committed by Defendant other than the offense for which Defendant is on trial. Additionally, Defendant requests that this Honorable Court order the state to instruct each of the state's witnesses not to testify to any prior convictions or bad acts.

~~~~~

D.

Comes now Defendant, Donald K. Giammanco Pro-Per, respectfully requesting that the Honorable Court issue an order quashing the indictment in above cause and discharging the Defendant into the custody of the Federal Board of Prisons via the United States Marshal Service for reasons of double jeopardy. This motion is brought pursuant to the United States Constitution, Amendment Five, applicable to the states through Amendment Fourteen. The Defendant, through this motion will also challenge the states right to a subsequent prosecution following a federal conviction using the Tenth Amendment or "dual sovereignty" in the above cause. The Defendant will also show that the state is using in this subsequent prosecution the previous federal conviction as a tool to conduct wat is a "sham prosecution" in the above cause. This being a clear misuse of the dual sovereignty doctrine. Also, the Defendant believes that "dual sovereignty" is in direct conflict with Missouri's own statute V.A.M.S. 541.050. In this motion the Defendant will also be asking the Honorable Court to explore and consider if in fact the Great State of Missouri, or any of the fifty United States truly now, or ever been a stand alone "sovereign state," since the year of our Lord 1776 A.D. Four, July when the states united under one flag. Thus forming a larger union with common laws and citizens' rights to which each state must adhere.

1)   The framers of the United States Constitution (along with the Missouri Constitution, deemed to have the same meaning, State vs. Toombs 326 Mo. 981, 34 S.W. 2d 61, 63 1930) clearly state under the Fifth (5th) Amendment (Article One (1) Section Nineteen (19) respectfully) prosecution shall be barred for the defendant is being put twice in jeopardy for the same offense. This also being in violation of the defendant's right to have Due Process of the Law, to which the states are bound to adhere by the Fourteenth (14th) Amendment of the United States Constitution. This causing extreme undo stress, anguish, and anxiety to the Defendant, his family, and those who support them. In the above cause the Defendant has been convicted by plea in United States District Court and fully punished in all the counts as stated in the above listed cause. The Defendant is now being subject to being tired and punished a second time by the State of Missouri for the same offense, which is barred. Blockburger vs. United States 284 U.S. 299, 52S. Ct. 180, 76 L. Ed. 306 (1932), United States vs. Dixion 509 U.S. 688, 113 S. Ct. 2849, 125 L. Ed. 2d 556 (1993). The above listed are deeply rooted in English law, through the Dark Ages, Cannon Law, and the teachings of Christian writers, Bartkus vs. Illinois 359 U.S. 152, 79 S. Ct. 696 (dissenting opinions). The prosecution in the above listed cause being a fundamental breech of the Defendant's personal sovereignty.

2)   The States claim under the Tenth (10th) Amendment of the United States Constitution and the dual sovereignty doctrine, such gives them the right to a second prosecution of the same offense, after a prosecution by the federal government. The Tenth (10th) Amendment states the contrary, "powers not delegated to the United States by its Constitution." Clearly, since the financial institutions offended in the above listed cause are federally insured the power is delegated under the Tenth (10th) Amendment for a federal prosecu-

tion in this matter. Even though state law may also have been broken in this cause, the Tenth (10th) Amendment clearly states, "nor prohibited by it (U.S. Constitution) to the States." Therefore, the Fifth (5th) Amendment prohibits a second prosecution, conviction, and punishment in the above listed cause. The States must adhere to this per the Fourteenth (14th) Amendment of the United States Constitution under one's right to due process of law. In applying the dual sovereignty doctrine to the above listed cause, there is no prescient case law where that a defendant pleas guilty in one jurisdiction, is convicted, punished, and then brought to trial on the identical same charge (offense). Even when a defendant has been convicted a second time for the same offense, both by trial, under this doctrine, the court in which the second conviction took place refused to punish the defendant, ruling that one punishment is enough, State vs. Ivory 578 S.W. 2d 62 Mo. (1978).

3)   The evidence shows that after the state's indictment on October Twenty-Second (22nd), 2008, the state deliberately caused delay in its proceedings in the above listed cause in order to conduct a "sham prosecution." Some ten (10) weeks after the state indictment was handed down the defendant was indicted in the United States District Court, Eastern District of Missouri on December Thirty-first (31st), 2007 for the exact same charges as the state indictment (same identical crimes). At that point the state halted its proceedings "pending outcome of federal case" (see: court docket for the above listed cause). The state then continued its proceedings on August Fourteenth (14th), 2009, one day after the conviction and sentencing of the Defendant in federal court. During this entire period the state had custody of the Defendant (seven and one-half months) other than a mere five (5) days to complete the federal proceedings against him. The dual sovereignty doctrine clearly states that it makes no difference which jurisdiction proceeds with its prosecution first. The evidence clearly shows that the state deliberately delayed its proceedings in order to use the federal conviction of the de-

fendant as a "tool" in building their case against him. This delay also has given the state a clear tactical advantage by their having the federal conviction (for the exact same crime) to use as evidence against him in a subsequent trial at the state level, creating a clear violation of right to due process. The above stated "sham prosecution" being conducted by the state is a gross misuse of the dual sovereignty doctrine in the above listed causes against the defendant.

4)   The prosecution in the above listed cause is in direct conflict with Missouri's own statute V.A.M.S. 541.050 which states that a person cannot be convicted of stealing or robbery of the same item(s) if already convicted of the same crime in another state or county.

5)   Black's Law Dictionary defines a sovereign state as: "A state that possesses an independent existence, being complete in itself, without being merely a part of a larger whole to whose government it is subject." This raising the question, is Missouri or any of the fifty (50) United States really an in truth stand alone independent sovereign state? This since all fifty (50) states receive aid, grants of monies, and depend on the United States central government for military protection. It is also the law of the land that all the United States must adhere to the Constitution of the larger whole which acts as supreme law and trumps all other law.

WHEREFORE Defendant prays and requests with honor and respect that this court quash the indictment for reasons of double jeopardy, a fundamental breach of our Constitution(s). Thus granting this motion.

~~~~~

E.

Now comes Defendant, Pro-Per, who remains in jeopardy of prosecution for the crime of robbery after a previous conviction and punishment for the identical charges and events in United States District Court. Defendant seeks to show that the State of Missouri is treating the defendant "unequal and oppressive in their practical denial of equal protection of the law" in the above listed cause (United States vs. Armstrong, 517 U.S. 456,116 S. Ct. 1480, 134 L. Ed. 2d 687 (1996), quoting Yick Wo vs. Hopkins, 118 U.S. 356, 6 S. Ct. 1064, 30 L. Ed. 220 (1886)). Specifically, police and prosecutors may not base the decision to arrest a person for, or charge a person with a criminal offense based on "an unjustifiable standard such as race, religion, or other arbitrary classification" (United States vs. Armstrong, quoting Oyler vs. Boles, 368 U.S. 448, 82 S. Ct. 501, 7 L. Ed. 2d 446 (1962)).

Defendant readily concedes that in more routine cases, "so long as the prosecutor has probable cause to believe that the accused committed an offense defined by statue, the decision whether or not to prosecute, and what charge to file or bring before a grand jury, generally rest entirely in his discretion" (Bordenkircher vs. Hayes 434, U.S. 357, 364 (1978)).

On the other hand, a prosecutor's discretion is "subject to constitutional constraints," (United States vs. Batchelder, 442 U.S. 114, 125 (1979)). The equal protection component of the due process clause of the Fifth Amendment imposes such a constraint to the extent that the decision whether to prosecute or not, may not be based on "an unjustifiable standard such as race, religion, or other arbitrary classification," (Oyler vs. Boles, 368 U.s. 448, 456 (1962), also see Yick Wo vs. Hopkins, 118 U.S. 356, 373, (1886)).

Defendant believes he has been of special selection to continue prosecution for robbery of a federal institution (bank, post office, etc.) that is insured by the Federal Deposit Insurance Corporation (F.D.I.C.), even after the federal government has convicted and punished him for the exact same robberies, using the same stated charge. Defendant claims and is seeking to prove that the State is prosecuting him in an arbitrary manner and is motivated by discriminatory purpose, (Oyler, Supra at 456). This could include, but not be limited to, race, national origin, religion, and/or gender of the defendant, location of the crime(s) (state, county, city, township), number of counts charged in the indictment, and punishment/sentence recommended and/or received by the defendant. Defendant believes he can show that similarly situated individuals were not prosecuted, (Ah Sin vs. Wittman, 198 U.S. 500 (1905)). Defendant believes that the discovery requested below will show that throughout the history of the State such dual prosecutions are selective and very rare. This discovery will also show that the vast majority of bank or post office robberies that result in a federal conviction, the State never seeks and indictment (refers). And in the cases where the State has already indicted the subject (as in the above listed cause), and the federal government proceeds to indict, convict, and punish the subject, the States will normally dismiss their charges against the subject with prejudice. Ah Sin, the rule, has since been applied to federal prosecutions and the United States Executive Branch as well, (United States vs. Armstrong, 517 U.S. 456 (1996)). The States must adhere to the same rules and laws under the due process clause of the Fourteenth Amendment of the United States Constitution. Armstrong, like Ah Sin, places a requirement on the defendant to demonstrate a showing of failure to prosecute similarly situated individuals.

Insofar as granting discovery, Armstrong holds:

The vast majority of the Courts of Appeals require the defendant to produce some evidence that similarly situated defendants or other races could have been prosecuted, but were not, and this requirement is consistent with our equal protection case law...As the three-judge panel explained, "(s)elective prosecution implies that a selection has taken place." 21 F. 3d, at 1436.

Defendant acknowledges he has a heavy burden to carry to establish a due process and equal protection violation. Therefore, defendant respectfully requests the following list of additional discovery on this issue, along with suggestions in support.

1) All internal memorandums, letters, emails, and other documents between the St. Louis County Prosecution Attorney's Office and the United States Attorney, or the State Attorney General's Office concerning the request and subsequent authorization to proceed with prosecution in the above listed cause.

2) All similar documents listed in paragraph one (1), if any exist, with respect to all robberies of federally insured institutions (banks, savings and loans, post offices, etc.), or any other crimes where both the federal government and the State of Missouri prosecuted a defendant for the same exact crime, using the same exact charge (offense).

3) Any internal Missouri Attorney General's Office policy memorandum, letters, or manual authored by that office that sets forth criteria and standards to be applied by the Attorney General, District Prosecuting Attorneys or their subordinates in making the apparent subjective determination of which "dual" prosecutions similar to the above listed cause in which to proceed with.

4) All Missouri Department of Justice statistical data as to how many robberies (or any other crimes charged exactly the same by both the federal and state authorities) of federal institutions (F.D.I.C. insured as aforementioned) that have taken place in the State. Of such robberies (crimes) which were prosecuted by both the federal government and the State. Which were prosecuted by the federal government only. Which were prosecuted by the State only. Which were at first prosecuted by both federal and state, and the State dropped its charges after the federal prosecution resulted in a conviction and punishment of the defendant. Which did the State continue with its prosecution after the completed feder-

al prosecution ended with either an acquittal or conviction. Defendant requests this statistical information include, but not be limited to, the type of crime, number of counts in the indictment, location of the crime(s) (city, county, etc.), the age, race, national origin, religion, gender, criminal history, and place of residence (city, county, state, country) of all the defendants. Also if there was extensive media coverage of the crime(s), and was the defendant given a "nickname" by law enforcement (hence "The Gentleman Bandit, Grandfather Bandit, Pony Tail Bandit, etc.), and the number of defendants prosecuted in the crime(s). Defendant also requests this discovery include any defendant found to be prosecuted to prevent their exercise of constitutional rights.

Supporting Case Law:

United States vs. Kelley, 152 F. 3d 881 C.A.8 (Mo.) 1998

United States vs. Cammisano, 413 F. Supp. 886, Vacated 546, F. 2d 238, on remand 433 F. Supp. 964 (W.D. Mo.) 1976

State vs. Camillo, 610 S.W. 2d 116 (Mo. App. W.D.) 1980

Defendant contends that not all similarly situated individuals are prosecuted (or continued to be prosecuted) by the State of Missouri, following a federal conviction of the same robbery and/or)) of a federally insured institution(s). Therefore, Defendant submits that he is entitled to this limited discovery based on his right to demonstrate clearly different standards applied in this county, state, and likely nationwide.

WHEREFORE, Defendant moves the court for an order directing the State of Missouri to produce the discovery requested herein, or dismiss the indictment on the grounds of selective prosecution.

~~~~~

F.

Comes now Defendant, Donald K. Giammanco, Pro-Per requesting reduction of set bond and to be released into the custody of the Federal Board of Prisons via the United States Marshal Service. The Defendant also requests to move the honorable court to a prompt evidentiary hearing in exploration of the facts stated henceforth.

The Defendant will show that his presence at any and all court dates and his not being a danger to the community will be guaranteed by the fact of his being held in the midst of serving a seventy-six month federal sentence for the exact same offense as charged in the above listed cause.

Also, by granting this motion the honorable court will give relief to the good people of St. Louis County and the Great State of Missouri from the continued needless burden of shouldering the cost of housing, feeding, and providing medical care for the Defendant. The people have been doing so since Nineteen December, 2008, with no movement in the above cause.

The Defendant now hereby asks through prayer, respect, and honor that the honorable court grant this motion, and that he be released on his own recognizance into federal custody.

~~~~~

Addendum 2

The following are the claims Keith Giammanco made on his Form 40 to appeal his state conviction. These claims are preserved and are used as the basis for his current appeal in federal court. The form specifies that points should be "concise," so the explanations have not been included.

a)   Request to vacate judgment for violation of Right to a Speedy Trial.

b)   Failure to disclose evidence in a timely manner.

c)   Request to vacate judgment for violation of Double Jeopardy and Double Jeopardy via Sham Prosecution (amended, with request for additional discovery).

d)   Request to vacate judgment for Selective Prosecution (with request for additional discovery).

e)   Change of Venue.

f)   Bond Pending Appeal.

g)   Request to dismiss and change defendant/movant's trial counsel.

h)   Ineffective assistance of trial counsel.

i)   Ineffective assistance of appellate counsel.

j)   Abandonment of cause by trial counsel.

k)   Prejudice of Circuit Court towards defendant/movant (pre-trial and sentencing)

l)   Failure of Trial Court to follow proper rules and procedure with instructions.

m)   Jurisdiction (additional discovery required).

n)   Sleeping jurors during trial.

o)   Defendant/movant had no opportunity to review and choose from sets of jury instructions.

p)   Improper courtroom seating and furniture arrangement.

q)   Defendant/movant denied by Trial Court to wear wardrobe of his choice during trial.

r)   Improper sentencing by Trial Court regarding aggravated circumstances.

s)   Improper and unethical conduct by St. Louis County Prosecutor and lead trial Prosecutor (misconduct).

t)   Malicious Prosecution (with request for additional discovery).

u)   Unethical and gross misconduct of trial counsel.

v)   Sentence and percentage of sentence to be served by movant vs. women convicted of the same crime(s) is in violation of the equal protection clause of the 14th Amendment of the United States Constitution.

About the Author

Caroline Giammanco

Caroline Giammanco grew up on a farm in the Ozark Mountains of southern Missouri. After high school, she attended the University of Arizona in Tucson, earning a Bachelor of Arts in political science. She later completed the post-baccalaureate education program at the University of Arizona. She has taught English in public schools for over twenty years in Arizona, New Mexico and now Missouri.

She is the English Department Chairperson at her current high school. She is the mother of two sons, Rick and Kevin, and is active in the lives of Keith's children, Marissa and Elise. Caroline and Keith plan on living on a small farm in rural Missouri upon his release.

Keith Giammanco

CPSIA information can be obtained
at www.ICGtesting.com
Printed in the USA
BVOW06s1927010217

475089BV00009B/302/P